1.95

77 - 280

P9-CFH-764

77-280

Katherine Anne Porter & the Art of Rejection

By William L. Nance

THE UNIVERSITY OF NORTH CAROLINA PRESS · CHAPEL HILL

To

Father William Hegge, O.S.C.

Father Thomas Loughrey

Mr. Albert Lum

Preface

The original purpose of this study was to define the central thematic pattern which unifies the fiction of Katherine Anne Porter and to examine its embodiment in each of her short stories and novelettes and in the novel *Ship of Fools*. That is still its principal purpose, though my pursuit of Miss Porter's central theme has led me ultimately into every important department of her work and even some distance into the much more problematic field of her life. I hope my inquiry has been characterized by respect both for the artist and for her art.

The career of Katherine Anne Porter presents an extreme instance of the inseparability of the writer's life and work. In her case life and work combine into a pattern so unusual that one cannot help seeking an explanation for it. In spite of the fact that she has been often in the literary limelight, an air of romantic mystery for many years surrounded Miss Porter's early life. Now, however, at least its main outlines are generally known. The new biographical details which I have accumulated during the course of this study, while I may say that in general they seem to corroborate my conclusions, have nevertheless come from sources of such varied dependability that for this reason, if for no other, I have not included them here. I have confined myself to pointing out, in the appropriate places, the most important correspondences between Miss Porter's life and her fiction.

Among several unusual characteristics of Miss Porter's work are its extremely high quality and its remarkably small quantity; during most of her long life of devotion to writing, her very high reputation has been based on three slim volumes of short fiction. Equally striking is the pattern presented by Porter criticism. Since the publication of her first story in 1922, she has probably received more unqualified praise than any other American writer; yet, aside from avowals of her excellence, critics have found little to say about her. Although this highly respected writer belongs to the generation of Hemingway and Faulkner, there is, in 1964, not yet one book-length study of her work. A considerable number of critical essays and brief mentions have accumulated but few attempt general surveys of her work, and of these only about ten are, in my opinion, of real significance. Among Miss Porter's most capable critics are Robert Penn Warren, Lodwick Hartley, Vernon A. Young, Edward Schwartz, Harry J. Mooney, Ray B. West, Glenway Wescott, and James W. Johnson. Warren's brief early study came close to the heart of her meaning in defining her central intuition as an ironic skepticism. Ray B. West has justly emphasized her dependence on memory and the consequent highly personal nature of her work. James W. Johnson recently undertook the long-overdue task of formulating her artistic philosophy of life. One of the purposes I have had in the present study is to bring together some of the insights of these critics, for although none of them has fully treated the subject of Miss Porter's artistic vision of life, collectively they have gone far toward doing so.

In my discussion of the stories the order followed has usually been that of the publication of the volumes and of the arrangement of the stories in them. The only important exception to this has been the grouping together of all the Miranda stories. In the discussions themselves, while directing my attention principally to the thematic pattern, I have tried to examine each story comprehensively enough to place the thematic elements in the proper perspective, to give due recognition to each work's unique characteristics, and to provide the reader who does not have the stories immediately at hand with a reasonably coherent impression of each. I have attempted in this way to avoid the extremes of a too narrow focus and a view so broad as to obscure my principal purpose.

Those who have helped me in this work, either directly or indirectly, are too numerous to name here. In particular I wish to express my gratitude to Professors John Edward Hardy; Seymour Gross; Alvan S. Ryan; Paul E. Beichner, C.S.C.; John T. Frederick; and Ernest E. Sandeen; along with other members of the Department of English of the University of Notre Dame, for their sound and inspiring teaching, and in particular for the encouragement, generosity, and friendship which I never failed to find among them. I am grateful in a very special way to Miss Porter for her generous permission to quote from her works and for the extreme graciousness she has shown me during a brief and transatlantic correspondence. I also wish to thank Mr. Glenway Wescott for his permission to quote from *Images of Truth*. To the director and staff of The University of North Carolina Press I owe a large debt of gratitude for their patience, constant encouragement, and constructive criticism. For various kinds of critical and secretarial assistance I wish to thank especially Mrs. Judy Miller; Mr. and Mrs. Allan Schwartzman; Mr. Joseph Ching; Mrs. William R. Porretto; Miss Connie Nance; Brother Edwin Johnson, S.M.; Mr. Sam Shamoon; Mr. John Herrera; Mr. Paul A. Lister; and Mr. Donald A. Miller. Most of all I am grateful to the Society of Mary and to my parents.

I wish to thank the following for permission to quote from the works indicated:

Harcourt, Brace & World, Inc.: *Flowering Judas and Other Stories,* copyright 1930, 1934, 1935 by Katherine Anne Porter; *Pale Horse, Pale Rider: Three Short Novels,* copyright 1936, 1937, 1939 by Katherine Anne Porter; *The Leaning Tower and Other Stories,* copyright 1934, 1935, 1936, 1939, 1940, 1941, 1944 by Katherine Anne Porter.

W. L. N.

Contents

Katherine
Anne
Porter
& the
Art of
Rejection

1

The Rejection Theme

From "María Concepción" to *Ship of Fools,* one central impulse unites the fiction of Katherine Anne Porter. This impulse has its most explicit formulation in the short story "Theft": "She remembered how she had never locked a door in her life, on some principle of rejection in her that made her uncomfortable in the ownership of things. . . . a certain fixed, otherwise baseless and general faith which ordered the movements of her life without regard to her will in the matter."[1] At the heart of Katherine Anne Porter's literary achievement lies a principle of rejection. While the term "rejection" is negative and rather pejorative in tone, its full meaning in Miss Porter's work is complex and will have to be revealed gradually in the course of this study. It is obvious even at the start that this

1. *Flowering Judas and Other Stories* (New York: The Modern Library, 1940), p. 89. All citations from Miss Porter's volumes of fiction are from this edition and the following: *Pale Horse, Pale Rider: Three Short Novels* (New York: The Modern Library, [n.d.]); *The Leaning Tower and Other Stories* (New York: Delta Books, 1962); *Ship of Fools* (Boston: Little, Brown and Company, 1962).

rejection is ambiguous. In "Theft" it is equated with a "general faith which ordered" the heroine's life, and it will be found to contain in its total meaning large proportions of courage and nobility. But for the sake of brevity a single term must be used, and this one is selected with reason.

The principle of rejection is the dynamic core of a clearly defined pattern of behavior with accompanying motifs. Again for the sake of brevity, this pattern will be termed the rejection theme. The term "theme" is used here only for want of a better one, and since it may lead to confusion, some clarification is necessary at the start. "Theme" usually implies, if not the pre-determined "moral" of a story, at least its conscious "meaning." But the meaning or meanings of a work of literature may not be consciously recognized by the artist during or even after the creative act. The rejection theme is a pattern of emotional thrusts comparable to invisible magnetic lines of force which form a visible design only when sensitive material is placed within their field. Because of Miss Porter's strict adherence to a secret, inner way of writing, it seems that the rejection theme asserts itself strongly through selection and orientation of the elements of the story before the design nears that level of consciousness and final complexity at which it is ready to be written down. This hypothesis is suggested by the fact that elements of the rejection theme, while they appear in every story, sometimes lie below the surface and may even assert themselves in opposition to surface elements. The rejection theme makes itself known by its pervasiveness and by the evident strength with which its elements are reflected, as if the author worked with greatest zest when moving parallel to these strong impulses within herself, and when at cross purposes with them, tended unconsciously to defeat her own aims in various ways. The classic example of this debilitating process is the portrayal of Adam in "Pale Horse, Pale Rider." The rejection theme then, although in a few instances it does not coincide with the apparently intended theme, does reveal the truest meanings of the stories, individually and collectively, in terms of the author's fundamental artistic drives. Consequently, an understanding of this theme helps one to understand the virtues of the stories but perhaps even more their faults, for the principle of rejection is so strong that it sometimes does violence to structural or dramatic order. Furthermore, as will be seen, the rejection principle is discernible not only in thematic content but in every facet of Miss Porter's art. The most remarkable fact about her fiction is not its rich variety of form and subject but the fundamental unity within this variety.

Preparatory to a detailed description of the rejection theme pattern, attention must be drawn to an important fact about the stories—a fact partially observed by several critics but never formulated with sufficient clarity. This fact is that Miss Porter's stories are sharply divided into two groups, with only two or three borderline cases requiring special classification. The criterion for this division is the presence or absence of the semi-autobiographical or subjective protagonist embodied most fully in Miranda, who is identifiable with the author even in many of the biographical details of her life. There are a few secondary distinctions to be made, but the basic division is as follows: stories containing the semi-autobiographical protagonist are, in order of publication, "Theft," "The Jilting of Granny Weatherall," "Flowering Judas," "Hacienda," "Old Mortality," "Pale Horse, Pale Rider," the seven sketches,[2] and "The Leaning Tower." This body of Miss Porter's work will here be called the alpha group;[3] the beta group contains the remaining stories: "María Concepción," "Magic," "Rope," "He," "That Tree," "The Cracked Looking-Glass," "Noon Wine," "The Downward Path to Wisdom," and "A Day's Work." Within the alpha group the following subdivisions should be noted: The Miranda stories (the sketches, "Old Mortality," "Pale Horse, Pale Rider"); implicit Miranda stories ("Theft," "Flowering Judas," "Hacienda," "The Leaning Tower"); and Grandmother stories ("The

2. "The Source," "The Witness," "The Circus," "The Old Order," "The Last Leaf," "The Grave," and "The Fig Tree." The first six appeared in *The Leaning Tower and Other Stories;* "The Fig Tree" was written in 1934 but lost for several years, and it was finally published in *Harper's Magazine* for June, 1960, pp. 55-59. The sketches are classified here as a single unit.

3. I have adopted these nonliterary designations only after an unsuccessful search for more descriptive terms of equal convenience and precision.

Jilting of Granny Weatherall," the sketches). "Hacienda" may be called an implicit Miranda story because its narrator, while identifiable with Miranda, does not play an important dramatic part in the story. The presence of "The Leaning Tower" in the alpha group may surprise the reader, but its protagonist, Charles Upton, is essentially an implicit Miranda. In a very real sense, in fact, there are only two protagonists in Miss Porter's short fiction—at least in the alpha stories, her most characteristic work. These protagonists are Miranda and the Grandmother. The latter is biographically distinct from Miranda but in a deeper sense identifiable with her, and therefore her stories are included in the alpha group. The principal Grandmother stories are the sketches, which are also Miranda stories. Granny Weatherall is an implicit Grandmother. Generalizations about the alpha protagonist apply most fully to Miranda.

The initial division of the stories into two groups is quite easy, for all stories which do not contain the alpha protagonist are peopled by characters distinctly inferior to or remote from that protagonist in terms of intelligence, sensibility, self-aware-ness, courage, independence, desire for truth, "spirit." The alpha protagonist is, in terms of these characteristics, almost identical with the author. Beta characters are distinctly removed from the author by: portrayal as inferior in the aforementioned qualities, obvious remoteness in race or social class, and/or ironic criticism of their vices and defects. Characters in alpha stories other than the central protagonist may be more closely comparable to her in some of these respects. Quantitatively the alpha group contains the greater part of Miss Porter's short fiction, comprising three of the eleven short works and five of the six longer ones.

Three stories in the beta group—"María Concepción," "That Tree," and "The Downward Path to Wisdom"—require special mention. "María Concepción," the first of Miss Porter's pub-lished works, foreshadows the later subjective stories in that it centers around a strong, self-sufficient, admirable heroine. "That Tree" is in a certain respect unique among the stories. Its two main characters, the narrator and his estranged wife, are removed both biographically and ironically from the author, yet both share certain qualities and interests with her. They may be viewed as a composite character embodying opposing forces within the author. This composite character is, then, an implicit Miranda, and in this sense the story belongs to the alpha group. "The Downward Path to Wisdom" occupies a separate and highly important position in relation to the alpha-beta distinction. Its protagonist, a young boy, is removed by his youth and biographical circumstances from the author, but in a more essential way he may be identified as an alpha protagonist. His story sums up in miniature and, as it were, in its genesis the characteristic life-sequence of the rejection theme, and the title of his story is a perfect description of it.

Ship of Fools, a work which differs from the earlier fiction not only in length but in several other respects and which, by the author's testimony, sums up all she has to say about life, combines among its semi-isolated individuals and groups both alpha and beta characters. Consequently, it embodies the rejection theme in a new and complex manner.

Since rejection implies something to be rejected, there is always an initial sense of oppression. Oppression-rejection appears in every phase of Miss Porter's work—language, imagery, dramatic situations both important and incidental, symbolic objects and acts—but it operates primarily on the level of human relations and has its fullest embodiment in the alpha protagonist. This protagonist is always portrayed as threatened by an oppressive relationship with other persons. Since it is the principle of rejection which defines relationships as oppressive, the prime characteristic of the alpha protagonist is the possession of a principle of rejection so strong that it defines *every* relationship as oppressive. It is at this initial stage of the sequence that the alpha-beta distinction comes into play. The alpha protagonist has sufficient power of rejection to escape the oppressive union but beta characters do not. For them, consequently, the usual setting is an unhappy or even mutually destructive marriage, while the natural state of the alpha heroine is the ambivalent one of independence-isolation. These general observations may easily be confirmed by a glance at the stories. Every beta story has as its dramatic center an enforced relationship between two individuals. Beta characters in the alpha stories are also usually enmeshed in oppressive unions and thus contrast with the heroine. The pure alpha protagonist (Miranda or implicit Miranda) is, on the contrary, always essentially alone. By progressive rejections of the unions into which life unavoidably brings her she advances along her "downward path to wisdom." The wisdom toward which such a path leads is a complete rejection of life. Miranda never realizes fully the ultimate meaning of this negativistic tendency in herself, and there is an opposing life-urge in her which prevents her from pursuing the downward path to its logical conclusion; yet her every step along this path is approved and justified by the author, though at some stages, especially in "Pale Horse, Pale Rider," the approval is disguised—apparently even from the author herself. The rejections of implicit Mirandas are less fully approved, but even they are at bottom inevitable.

The rejection theme, described here in the abstract, is the heart of Katherine Anne Porter's artistic vision. In terms of her fictional world, it is a tragic vision. It presents an ideal of conduct by which most individuals are found wanting. The lives of the weak and the gross are full of pain and so is Miranda's—but her pain is more intense than theirs precisely because she is more aware of reality. Because she does not try to evade the awareness, hers is a nobler and more fully human response to an essentially painful world. The rejection theme is embodied in the rich concreteness of the life of Miranda and, through her, in the particular world in which she lives. While the portrayal of this heroine shares in the freedom and objectivity of fictionality, Miss Porter has made no secret of the fact that Miranda is autobiographical both in the general outline of her life and in many of its specific details. The close correspondence between the biography and the fiction has, as will be shown, a multiple relevance to this study. Meanwhile, something more needs to be said about Miranda's embodiment of the rejection theme and her relation to four characters who also reflect its pattern to some extent—the Grandmother, Aunt Amy, Cousin Eva, and Old Nannie.

The three crucial rejections in Miranda's life are her escape from her family and the society which shaped it, her escape from marriage, and her almost complete rejection of life itself after the experiences of her illness. The first of these rejections, the one which sets the pattern of her life, is fully portrayed at the end of "Old Mortality"; the second is only mentioned; and the third is the subject of "Pale Horse, Pale Rider," the story which presents, in the visions of Miranda's illness, the key to her entire life of rejection. The first rejection is prepared for throughout her childhood, as "Old Mortality" illustrates most graphically. The spirit which will impel her all through life is present from the start. Her name, while it designates her as the admirable heroine, more appropriately suggests that all her surroundings are to her *Miranda*—wonder-full. She is the wonderer, the seer, the truth-seeker, the artist. It is her hunger to see and to know combined with the ideal vision of life generated by her appetite for happiness that forces her along an endless path of disillusion. Fleeing the oppressions which smother life, she finds herself in an ambivalent state of independence-isolation, a state imperative but painful, and this ambiguity dogs her path to the end. For in seeking life she is rejecting it: her vision of life lies at the brink of death, as "Pale Horse, Pale Rider" reveals in a splendid epiphany.

Miranda's disillusion, in its early stages, is initiation. In "The Grave" she kneels with her brother over the freshly killed rabbit, murmuring, "Oh, I want to *see*," and what she sees is a vision of birth and death, a foreshortened view of her own future that marks her indelibly. Throughout life she is characterized by a certain detached, objective view of her surroundings and a concentration on their aesthetic aspects. The South of the "Old Order" is stifling to her, and the new freedom and mobility possessed by women in the new century enable her to escape it completely. But her earlier counterparts were not so fortunate. In the generations immediately preceding hers there is a cluster of women, related to her by blood and kindred spirit, who pay a greater price for the limited independence they achieve. Superficially they differ in many respects but deep down they are all sisters. This concentration of spirited women explains Edmund Wilson's detection in Miss Porter's stories of a "natural human spirit in terms of their bearing on which all the other forces of society are appraised," a spirit "peculiar to Louisianians in Texas" and identifiable with "the special personality of a woman."[4]

The most important of these women is the Grandmother. She is the fixed center of Miranda's childhood and sums up in herself the familial, social, and moral system of the old order. Miranda's eventual rejection of that order does not conflict at the deepest level with her respect for her Grandmother, for in her Miranda respects not the society she represents but the triumph over it she has achieved while yet remaining a part of it. Since the time and circumstances of her life make literal flight impossible, the Grandmother partially escapes from the oppressions of her society by dominating it. On the spiritual level she remains largely a captive of the old order's strict orthodoxy and narrow morality, and in this capacity she is not exempt from the ironic criticism directed at that order. On the social level, however, her supremacy is virtually complete. She and women like her achieve mastery by acting upon a profound scorn for men.[5] Forced by society into marriages with men whom they usually scorned from the start, they immediately begin the process of rejecting them, aided by the irresponsibility, departure, or even death of the spouse. They then reject even their own "feminine" weakness and dependence and eventually establish that "matriarchal tyranny" which men resent bitterly but suffer nonetheless. Unaided, they perform the sacred duty of raising children and then grandchildren in the same stern, sentimental, futile way they themselves were raised.

4. "Katherine Anne Porter," *The New Yorker,* XX (September 30, 1944), 65.

5. Disdain for men, more or less bitter and usually in the form of regarding them as spoiled children, is one of the principal motifs of the rejection theme. The ultimate expressions of this motif and the motif of the mutually destructive marriage will be found, fittingly enough, in *Ship of Fools.*

Evidence of the relative impossibility for women to escape from the old order is furnished by the careers of two of Miranda's counterparts, Aunt Amy and Cousin Eva. Amy, whose mysterious, magnetic charm fills the first part of "Old Mortality," is surrounded by a romantic aura precisely because she has asserted her independence at the cost of death. Cousin Eva's escape is in strong contrast to Amy's, a fact emphasized by her dominance of the last section of "Old Mortality," yet it is not without nobility. Though Miranda clearly sees her cousin's defects, she says honestly, "I loved your courage" (*PH,* 69).[6] Even Old Nannie, whose life would seem to have been one of complete subjection, imitates the independence of her mistress. "The Last Leaf" is the story of her disdain for her peripatetic husband Uncle Jimbilly and her rejection even of the Grandmother's children. The admiration accorded her by the author is whimsical but sincere.

This, then, is the rejection theme, a pattern of forces which may or may not coincide with the explicit thematic intention of a given story, yet always governs its dominant emotional effect. In her introduction to the 1940 edition of *Flowering Judas,* Miss Porter says of the stories it contains, "Looking at them again, it is possible still to say that I do not repent of them; if they were not yet written, I should have to write them still." So uncompromising has she been in her determination to give true testimony to the truth that is in her, so deeply faithful an expression has each of her stories been of her central intuition of life, that she can no more deny the least of them than a mother could deny her child, who is the image of herself.

6. The rejection theme highlights a balance in "Old Mortality" which has not, to my knowledge, been previously noted: the first section is devoted to Amy's escape; the third, to Eva's. Miranda's own escape, confirmed by her disillusion with the Amy story in the middle section, is emphasized by her subjection to the myth in the first part and her superiority to it in the third.

2

The Emerging Pattern

Katherine Anne Porter's first published story, "María Concepción," appeared in 1922, and several others followed during the next few years. A limited edition of *Flowering Judas and Other Stories* came in 1930, containing that first story and, ‘ in order of their original publication, "Magic," "Rope," "He," "The Jilting of Granny Weatherall," and "Flowering Judas." The 1935 edition included also "Theft," "That Tree," "The Cracked Looking-Glass," and ‘ "Hacienda." The stories in *Flowering Judas* are marked by a wide diversity of setting, material, style, and structure, but also by a fundamental similarity in technique and thematic content. The earliest of them possess an impersonal objectivity which will gradually yield to the increased subjectivity of the later work. Only one of these stories, "The Jilting of Granny Weatherall," takes place in the social and geographical world which will become Miss Porter's most characteristic setting, the matriarchal South of the old order. Two other stories, however, "Theft" and "Flowering Judas," have as center the subjective heroine who will carry the thematic weight of the later works. All of the stories, as critics have agreed unanimously, display a technical mastery achieved through years of lonely artistic discipline. More important still, and less clearly seen by the critics, they possess an underlying thematic unity which indicates that all without exception were refined and oriented at some spiritual center deep within the author and written with fundamental truthfulness to the intuition found there. This central intuition is the rejection theme, which may be seen gradually taking form in the stories of *Flowering Judas*.

Although Katherine Anne Porter's first story, "María Concepción," clearly belongs to the beta class by virtue of its semi-primitive characters, its heroine possesses the proud self-reliance that will appear later in the autobiographical heroine Miranda. María Concepción is the only character in the stories, if one excepts some of the women of the old order, who is portrayed at length and with evident admiration and yet is not at all identifiable with Miranda. Miss Porter has considerable respect for the simple, passionate, elemental life of the Mexican peasant, and as in her portrayals of the South, she sees the best qualities of a society embodied in its women. Juan Villegas, like the vast majority of her Southern men, is an overgrown child. María has only a narrow field in which to exercise her strength of character. Her instincts, corroborated by society and her strong Catholic faith, demand that she preserve her family by any means. Like the grandmothers of the Old South, she finds herself in a predominantly painful marriage, and like them she asserts her integrity and independence not by escaping from the social framework but by dominating it. During the months while her husband is away at war, accompanied by María Rosa, María Concepción lives an isolated life of prayer and hard work, rejecting every offer of sympathy and help from the women of the village: "Keep your prayers to yourself, Lupe, or offer them for others who need them. I will ask God for what I want in this world" (*FJ*, 14). She is not pining for an absent lover; she is, by a long and painful asceticism, purging herself of all dependence and developing the strength she will need to restore by violent and decisive action the family of which she is guardian. In her this process is instinctive, inarticulate, and obscured by a superstitious piety which gives an air of near madness to her behavior; yet the emphasis on her self-sufficiency is unmistakable. She is the first of a long line of strong, proud, independent heroines, and in her these qualities receive the approval of instinct, of society, and, as the story's closing lines suggest, of all nature.

As its title indicates, the story is primarily a portrayal of María, background and plot serving mainly to reveal her nature. The austere, apparently simple style is so perfectly adapted to her serene, elemental wisdom that it is sometimes impossible to say whether a given sentence, such as the last one in this passage, is a description of her or a recording of her own thoughts: "She walked with the free, natural, guarded ease of the primitive woman carrying an unborn child. The shape of her body was easy, the swelling life was not a distortion, but the right inevitable proportions of a woman. She was entirely contented. Her husband was at work and she was on her way to market to sell her fowls" (*FJ,* 4). María clearly dominates the marriage. It was she who bought the license and insisted on a wedding in the church. Though Juan has a job, he is delinquent during the entire period covered by the story; it is María who earns and saves. "It was commonly known that if she wished to buy a new rebozo for herself or a shirt for Juan, she could bring out a sack of hard silver coins for the purpose" (*FJ,* 5). The hut in which they live is referred to as her house. During the emergency of the murder investigation, Juan assumes with courage and resourcefulness the position of family leadership required by society, but he is only acting out another facet of his romantic idea of himself, and his short time in the role exhausts him completely. The end of the story finds him returned to his former narrow selfishness, sprawled in sleep while María sits holding the child of his love for another, which she has in a sense conceived and borne without his help by her act of murder. Juan, however, has learned something; he has new respect for his wife, enough of which will probably endure to preserve their marriage from this time on: "He could not fathom her, nor himself, nor the mysterious fortunes of life grown so instantly confused where all had seemed so gay and simple. He felt too that she had become invaluable, a woman without equal among a million women, and he could not tell why" (*FJ,* 25).

In this first of her published stories Katherine Anne Porter confronts the mysterious forces of nature through the transparency of primitive society and finds that these forces act most strongly through a woman. In obeying them this woman attains a dignity which sets her apart from others. No act of hers, not even murder, rings false to nature. Her brief, violent disturbance after the deed lasts only long enough to free her from the imputation of inhumanity, and soon gives way to a calm which is not broken even by the sight of the dead girl's face. The women who had criticized her for standing alone now approve of her conduct. Even wise old Soledad (whose name means "solitude") comments, "When I saw María Concepción in the market today, I said, 'Good luck to you, María Concepción, this is a happy day for you,' " and bestows upon her "the smile of a born wise-woman" (*FJ,* 32). Miss Porter obviously smiles upon her too.

The second story in *Flowering Judas* seems at first glance to be the work of another author, so different is it from "María Concepción." "Magic" is unique among Miss Porter's stories in its brevity, its fiercely ironic monologue technique, and the sordidness of its subject matter, yet it is not as remote from the mainstream of her work as this suggests.[1] The extreme example of her early experimental and highly objective approach, it is a minor technical masterpiece. In terms of the rejection theme it is one of the purest examples of the destructively oppressive union. Ninette, a flat beta character who contrasts with María Concepción in almost every respect except participation in a bitterly oppressive union, is pathetically impotent to free herself. Since the reader knows her only as victim, however, the emphasis

1. Robert Penn Warren, in his important study of Miss Porter's work—"Katherine Anne Porter (Irony with a Center)," *Kenyon Review,* IV (Winter, 1942), 42—finds it necessary, in proposing *ironical balance* as the common denominator of her stories, to set aside "Magic" and "Hacienda" as apparently "outside the general body of Miss Porter's work."

of the story is not on sympathy with her but rather on the horror of her situation. Everything contributes to this effect—the detachment of the glib, callous narration; the doubly callous curiosity of the listener; the irony of the greeting, "Welcome home, Ninette," when she returns; the understatement of the last line, "And after that she lived there quietly." The failure of her attempted escape re-emphasizes her enslavement, and the ambiguity of her return—whether by magic or merely through the determinism of her situation—is a master stroke of further emphasis. This ambiguity arouses the reader's curiosity and holds it suspended, not quite free to rest in certainty of the answer, which is also the theme: Ninette's imprisonment is no mere matter of locked doors and barred windows, but an enslavement of the spirit. Meanwhile, the preparation of the spell has added symbolic resonance to the young prostitute's degradation:

They took the chamber pot of this girl from under her bed, and in it they mixed with water and milk all the relics of her they found there: the hair from her brush, and the face powder from the puff, and even little bits of her nails they found about the edges of the carpet where she sat by habit to cut her finger- and toe-nails; and they dipped the sheets with her blood into the water, and all the time the cook said something over it in a low voice; I could not hear all, but at last she said to the madam, Now spit in it: and the madam spat, and the cook said, When she comes back she will be dirt under your feet.

(FJ, 42-43)

The loathsomeness with which Ninette's subjection is portrayed is exactly the commentary one would expect from Miss Porter on this utter frustration, typical of the beta character's plight, of the basic element of the rejection theme: the urge to escape from oppression. This urge is no less present, though much more ambiguous, in the story which follows.

The contrast between "Magic" and "Rope" makes particularly striking their underlying thematic similarity. The bitter tie that binds is symbolized in the first story by the black magic of spiritual subjugation and in the second by rope, which binds, lashes, and strangles. There is, of course, an ambivalence in the second story lacking in the first, which concerns a bond evil in its very nature. A quarrel between a harried young husband and wife need signify nothing more than the instability of human emotions; yet the deep antagonism uncovered by this gratuitous argument, with its traded taunts of barrenness and infidelity, casts a baleful light on this marriage.

"Rope" is a tour de force, a delicately graphed record of a verbal duel between a generic "he" and "she." There is a masterful manipulation of elements—setting, accident, masculine and feminine mentality. The distinctive technical instrument employed is a kind of dialogue which hovers between direct and indirect, reproducing speech almost exactly but without the usual dialogue signals. It has subtle and powerful effects, the most obvious of which is the speed and smoothness resulting from the absence of retarding punctuation and the seamless blending of dialogue with narrative. This acceleration gives the story a sort of hectic intensity. A more important effect of the dialogue technique is the impression that the author is constantly present, governing tone and unobtrusively commenting with quiet irony; or better, providing a steady line of reference by which each evil and irrational word of the characters judges itself. Never do the characters appear in the complete freedom of direct speech:

The whole trouble with her was she needed something weaker than she was to heckle and tyrannize over. He wished to God now they had a couple of children she could take it out on. Maybe he'd get some rest.

Her face changed at this, she reminded him he had forgot the coffee and had bought a worthless piece of rope. And when she thought of all the things they actually needed to make the place even decently fit to live in, well, she could cry, that was all. She looked so forlorn, so lost and despairing he couldn't believe it was only a piece of rope that was causing all the racket. What *was* the matter, for God's sake?

(*FJ*, 51)

The disproportion between effect and apparent cause draws attention to the major thematic impact of the story: awareness of the free-floating hatred in marriage. It may be argued that the cessation of hostilities at the end is meant to show that quarrels are only passing storms on the calm sea of matrimony, but even superficially the evidence points the other way. The readiness with which the opponents use their deadliest weapons and the familiarity of many of their grievances argue that the enmity that fills most of the story is more natural to them than the brief, timid geniality of the conclusion. The wounds inflicted and reopened are too deep to be healed by an evening's reconciliation over steak and coffee. Even if the provoking causes be taken as adequate explanation of the quarrel, the emotional weight of the story remains undeniably on the bitterness of the union. And it is precisely in the fundamental emotional pattern of the stories that the rejection theme inheres.

The sense of oppression is built up by emphasis on the stifling heat of the day and the clutter in the house. The husband sums up this feeling as he leaves the second time for the store, after the violent separation which was needed to end the conflict: "Things accumulated, things were mountainous, you couldn't move them or sort them out or get rid of them. They just lay and rotted around" (*FJ,* 57). His escape is only temporary, and indications are that both he and she continue to stagnate in this destructive marriage. But then, neither of the two is a fully developed character, nor does either have the intelligent self-awareness and intensity of spirit with which Miranda will confront the deep mysteries and painful complexities of life. With "María Concepción," "Rope" may be classed as a fine but relatively conventional short story, carefully designed, self-contained, stylistically brilliant. But its characters do not belong to the alpha group. They are among those which Miss Porter regards from a distance and from above.

One of the most popular and frequently anthologized of Katherine Anne Porter's stories, "He" is a masterpiece of finely balanced satire and pathos. It is also, like the other stories examined so far, a work in which the author expresses her attitude not through the instrumentality of a highly subjective character but through the all-judging ironic narrator. Even less than in "Rope" is there any person here with whom author or reader is inclined to identify sympathetically. The single character who suffers undeservedly is the one who is least human. The question of just how human he is, is the crux of the story. Before the concluding scene, in which the revelation of his humanity strikes a note of ambiguity that vibrates back through the story, the retarded boy functions simply as a reference point by which the reader measures a growing distaste for Mrs. Whipple, the real center of emotional interest.

Though obscured by the enigmatic presence of the boy, a familiar pattern is nevertheless acting strongly in the story. The Whipple family is an oppressive union, bleak and enervating, made oppressive in this case not primarily by the incompatibility of the spouses but by their common burden. This burden is made doubly heavy by their lack of vitality and love and the mother's totally inadequate response to reality. The story's emphasis on the folly of Mrs. Whipple is the first strong manifestation of an important motif of the rejection theme: the folly of self-delusion. Willful blindness is one of the distinguishing qualities of the beta character, contrasting as it does with the alpha heroine's thirst for truth. One of the major hazards of life, it threatens even that heroine. As a natural part of her youthful idealism it is criticized gently by the author, particularly in the last line of "Old Mortality." When traces of it appear in the mature heroine—when there is a slight implication that she has deceived herself into erroneous conduct, as in "Flowering Judas" and especially "Theft"—it will be noted that she is not explicitly identified with Miranda.

The meaning of the story is concentrated in its title. The failure of the boy's parents to recognize his personality, symbolized by their failure to give him a name, is the root of their error and suffering. Mrs. Whipple's refusal to face reality has become true blindness, yet retains that degree of willfulness which makes it a vice and exposes her to the irony with which Miss Porter diligently dissects her. The clearest sign of her self-delusion is a habitual hypocrisy which leads her to base virtually every judgment on "what the neighbors will say." This motif and several others of importance are initiated in the effective opening paragraph:

Life was very hard for the Whipples. It was hard to feed all the hungry mouths, it was hard to keep the children in flannels during the winter, short as it was: "God knows what would become of us if we lived north," they would say: keeping them decently clean was hard. "It looks like our luck won't never let up on us," said Mr. Whipple, but Mrs. Whipple was all for taking what was sent and calling it good, anyhow when the neighbors were in earshot. "Don't ever let a soul hear us complain," she kept saying to her husband. She couldn't stand to be pitied. "No, not if it comes to it that we have to live in a wagon and pick cotton around the country," she said, "nobody's going to get a chance to look down on us."

(*FJ*, 61)

Aside from fixing the setting and socially classifying the family, this introduction begins immediately to crystallize the attitude to be taken toward them. The opening observations, with their repetition of the word "hard," seem sympathetic toward these poor country people until the self-pity in the following lines reveals them to be subtle echoes of the Whipples' own sing-song complaints. Mrs. Whipple's "love" for her simple-minded son is quickly exposed as selfish sentimentality: "Mrs. Whipple loved her second son, the simple-minded one, better than she loved the other two children put together. She was forever saying so, and when she talked with certain of her neighbors, she would even throw in her husband and her mother for good measure" (*FJ*, 61). Knowing her as we do, we feel that the claim could well be true. Here and elsewhere words carry strong dramatic irony because of their unintended truth. When the doctor suggests sending the boy to the County Home, Mrs. Whipple protests, "I won't have it said I sent my sick child off among strangers," and when he replies, "I know how you feel. You can't tell me anything about that, Mrs. Whipple. I've got a boy of my own" (*FJ*, 75), the words are truer than either of them knows.

The second half of the story, like the first, begins on the constant note of complaint which keeps the oppressiveness of the Whipples' lives always in the foreground. Though their poverty is caused primarily by their own laziness and ineptitude, not even Mr. Whipple will admit this, in spite of the fact that his main function in the story is to furnish a welcome contrast to his wife by acting as the laconic voice of plain truth. When, after her relatives' visit, she rhapsodizes over their "refined" avoidance of uncomfortable comments about Him, Mr. Whipple observes, "Yes, we're out three hundred pounds of pork, that's all. It's easy to be polite when you come to eat. Who knows what they had in their minds all along?" (*FJ,* 69). The doctor is another gauge of Mrs. Whipple's insincerity. When he says near the end of the story, "It's no use, I think you'd better put him in the County Home. . . . He'll have good care there and be off your hands" (*FJ,* 74-75), his frankness stands out sharply against the surrounding haze of her evasions.

Mrs. Whipple gradually agrees to sending the boy away, disguising her relief with false optimism in spite of her husband's relentless frankness: "The doctor has told you and told you time and again He can't ever get better, and you might as well stop talking" (*FJ,* 76). All the lines in the story converge and climax in the closing scene, in which Mrs. Whipple and her son ride in a neighbor's wagon toward the County Home. When He suddenly begins to cry she tries to fight back the dawning of truth. " 'Oh, honey, you don't feel so bad, do you? You don't feel so bad, do you?' for He seemed to be accusing her of something" (*FJ,* 77). Seeing her past treatment of him in a harsh new light, she too begins to cry, violently. Holding him tightly, she tells herself she has "loved Him as much as she possibly could"; that "There was nothing she could do to make up to Him for His life. Oh, what a mortal pity He was ever born" (*FJ,* 77-78). The ambiguity in the scene and in all these thoughts, especially the last, leaves the reader suspended between condemnation and sympathy for this weak woman in her hard fate. It is a good example of that "delicate balancing of rival considerations" proposed by Warren as the core of Miss Porter's work.[2] Meanwhile, the accumulated bitterness, unable to flow off in either direction, enforces the real impact of the story: the sense of the

2. *Ibid.*

tedious oppressiveness of hypocrisy, of family life, of existence itself.

In the four stories so far examined, the most striking similarity beneath numerous differences is the presence in each of them of some facet of the following composite pattern: an oppressive union, usually a marriage, from which an intelligent and spirited individual—if such a one were present—would escape, but in which the vicious and the weak seem content, or helpless. Only in "María Concepción" is emphasis deflected from this theme to the character of the heroine, a strong, self-sufficient woman and the only really admirable person so far encountered. With the partial exception of María, there has not yet appeared a character whose stature approaches that of the author herself. Such a character appears in the next story.

With "Flowering Judas" a new sense of immediacy enters the fiction of Katherine Anne Porter. For the first time the extreme distance between the fictional mind through which the thread of the story runs and the ironic mind of the author diminishes considerably—though a distinct ironic partition does remain. In other words, it is the first of the alpha stories. Two characteristics of these stories, the first of which becomes more pronounced as the series continues, are their formal idiosyncrasy and interdependence and their thematic immediacy and complexity. In them one confronts with great personal intensity the deepest and most painful mysteries of life—birth, death, suffering, the nature of man. "Flowering Judas" introduces this new subjectivity only partially. Technically it is more objective than the later alpha stories will be, particularly in its style and in the characterization of its heroine. The vibrant, semi-poetic language, especially in the final scene, calls attention to itself more than does the transparent style of most of the later stories and imparts an iconic remoteness. The heroine is given her own name and set apart somewhat from author and reader by concrete description and objective comment. Like the young Miranda of the last part of "Old Mortality" she is still naïve in her idealism and sees into herself only imperfectly; her fullest revelation comes under the symbolism of a dream. In a commentary on the story for Whit Burnett's anthology, *This Is My Best,* Miss Porter casts light on both the objectivity of the characterization and the naïveté of Laura: "All the characters and episodes are based on real persons and events, but naturally, as my memory worked upon them and time passed, all assumed different shapes and colors, formed gradually around a central idea, that of self-delusion, the order and meaning of the episodes changed, and became in a word fiction."[3] Miss Porter's method of working from memory has received considerable critical comment; she herself has revealed real-life sources for at least three works, not to mention the Miranda stories.[4] But, in the present case as in every other, the remembered details are so thoroughly transmuted in her deep artistic center that the emerging stories bear a remarkable resemblance to each other.

In Laura the principle of rejection is exposed as having over-extended itself. Through its operation she has become, for all her youth and femininity, a strong, detached, self-sufficient woman; but she has also become almost completely isolated from humanity. The important distinction between her case and that of Miranda is this: fundamentally both are governed completely by the rejection principle, which involves constant flight from human contacts and hence a permanent state of independence-isolation; but while Miranda's rejections are either justified or disguised by the plot and her isolation is portrayed as nobly inevitable, Laura's isolation is revealed in a less flattering and truer light, as possibly caused by the heroine's own mistakes. This is why she is not identified with Miranda. Furthermore, as in "María Concepción," so also here it is necessary to distinguish carefully between the superficial plot and theme and the real thematic implications of the story as revealed in its concretely

3. New York, 1942, p. 539.

4. The subject of Miss Porter's artistic dependence on memory has been treated most fully by Ray B. West in his essay, "Katherine Anne Porter and 'Historic Memory,' " included in the anthology, *South: Modern Southern Literature in Its Cultural Setting,* ed. Louis D. Rubin and Robert D. Jacobs (Garden City, 1961), pp. 301-13.

realized emotional forces. The principal plot element employed to expose the bitterness of Laura's isolationism is her imputed love for Eugenio; the principal means of revealing the presence of the rejection theme in the story will be the demonstration of the essential unreality of that love. As a preliminary to this, some attention must be given to other aspects of the story.

The chief technical innovation in "Flowering Judas" is the use of the present tense instead of the conventional past. The present tense gives a sense of generalization in which time is blurred—desirable because much of the story deals with monotonous daily events—and a hallucinatory immediacy, to which detailed descriptions also contribute. Laura's rejection of life is finely symbolized by the nun-like severity of her clothing with its numerous restraints: ". . . she is tired of her hairpins and the feel of her long tight sleeves" (*FJ*, 139). Braggioni's clothing also fits him tightly, but whereas Laura's seems to succeed in confining her flesh, his only emphasizes his sensual corpulence: "He bulges marvelously in his expensive garments. Over his lavender collar, crushed upon a purple necktie, held by a diamond hoop: over his ammunition belt of tooled leather worked in silver, buckled cruelly around his gasping middle: over the tops of his glossy yellow shoes Braggioni swells with ominous ripeness, his mauve silk hose stretched taut, his ankles bound with the stout leather thongs of his shoes" (*FJ*, 143). Braggioni typifies the warm-blooded people among whom Laura seems so out of place.

Although the ostensible justification of Laura's austerity is her dedication to the remote cause of the revolution—"She wears the uniform of an idea, and has renounced vanities" (*FJ*, 142)—it is clearly much more radical than that:

She is not at home in the world. Every day she teaches children who remain strangers to her, though she loves their tender round hands and their charming opportunist savagery. She knocks at unfamiliar doors not knowing whether a friend or a stranger shall answer, and even if a known face emerges from the sour gloom of that unknown interior, still it is the face of a stranger. No matter what this stranger says to her, nor what her message to him, the very cells of her flesh reject knowledge and kinship in one monotonous word. No. No. No. She draws her strength from this one holy talismanic word which does not suffer her to be led into evil. Denying everything, she may walk anywhere in safety, she looks at everything without amazement.

(*FJ,* 151)

The only human relationship in her life is the stillborn one with Eugenio. Even her interest in the children is only another phase of that detached, aesthetic curiosity with which she "haunts the markets listening to the ballad singers" (*FJ,* 140) and otherwise absorbs the local color. Braggioni, the only other important character, is also isolated; his immense love is only for himself. The shadowy Eugenio rejects life completely.

Laura's life has been a series of disillusions. Barren though her present situation seems, "there is no pleasure in remembering her life before she came here" (*FJ,* 145). In revolutionary zeal she has "promised herself to this place" (*FJ,* 145), and though the ideal is still remote enough to remain sacred, the concrete reality has been a severe disappointment: "The gluttonous bulk of Braggioni has become a symbol of her many disillusions, for a revolutionist should be lean, animated by heroic faith, a vessel of abstract virtues. This is nonsense, she knows it now and is ashamed of it. Revolution must have leaders, and leadership is a career for energetic men. She is, her comrades tell her, full of romantic error, for what she defines as cynicism in them is merely 'a developed sense of reality' " (*FJ,* 141). Intelligent and frank, she examines her own motives, but can find no assurance. Yet she will stay, for she can think of no alternative. With a dawning suspicion of the futility and even, perhaps, selfishness of all her self-discipline comes a new feeling of loss. Has this ambiguous austerity cheated her of other possible sources of happiness? If so, what is left? " 'It may be true I am as corrupt, in another way, as Braggioni,' she thinks in spite of herself, 'as callous, as incomplete,' and if this is so, any kind of death seems preferable" (*FJ,* 145). Full of the sense of loss, she thinks of its possible applications. She wonders if it were wise to spur her horse and escape from the young captain who tried to embrace her. At the same time she seeks comfort in the thought that "her negation of all external events as they occur is a sign that she is gradually perfecting herself in the stoicism she strives to cultivate against that disaster she fears, though she cannot name it" (*FJ*, 150). Thus the root of all her fears of loss is seen to be the fear of death. All her cold asceticism has only brought her closer to that last oppression. Listening to her ominous guest she feels "a slow chill, a purely physical sense of danger, a warning in her blood that violence, mutilation, a shocking death, wait for her with lessening patience" (*FJ*, 144). She is not now fated to die, however, but to taste the full bitterness of self-inflicted isolation.

The reader learns only near the end of the story of the existence of Eugenio and of Laura's feeling for him. The superficial story is that she loves him, and that her failure to reveal her love to him and thus give him something to live for robs her of happiness with him and leaves her that much more alone. The reader will, however, notice factors which militate against the reality of this man and this love, safeguarding the heroine, according to the rejection theme pattern, from violating her lonely integrity by entering a real human relationship. Eugenio is presumably the lean, ideal revolutionist, whereas the only revolutionist who actually appears in the story is the disappointing Braggioni, and there is abundant evidence that the others are as un-ideal as he. At any rate, Eugenio is already dead when first mentioned, and Laura has communicated with him only to give him the means of his death. He has no more concrete reality than the revolutionary ideal which faded before her eyes, and her love for him is hardly more human than her love for that ideal. He is employed in the story to increase the anguish of the heroine's final isolation, just as are the unreal lovers in "Theft" and "Pale Horse, Pale Rider," but the sense of loss proves strong enough in all three stories without the help of convincing reality in their heroes. This is, of course, what one would expect of one of the principal motifs of the rejection theme. In terms of the plot, however, there is considerable dramatic power in the delayed revelation of Eugenio's existence. The first reference to him is sufficient only to surprise the reader and excite his curiosity: "Laura has just come from a visit to the prison, and she is waiting for tomorrow with a bitter anxiety as if tomorrow may not come, but time may be caught immovably in this hour, with herself transfixed, Braggioni singing on forever, and Eugenio's body not yet discovered by the guard" (*FJ*, 155). Nothing more is said of him for two pages, but when Braggioni, shortly before leaving, asks Laura if love for a man is behind her revolutionary zeal, her "No" takes on a heavy weight of ambiguity. It is the only answer she can give in the circumstances, yet it is, with or without her awareness, quite possibly true. But the reader now suspects why she has doubted the purity of her revolutionary motives. Her love for Eugenio completes her disillusion with revolutionary ideals even in herself, just at the moment when her spurious zeal and reticent love have robbed her of him, and with him, her only other means of fulfillment.

Then, with the reality of her love still uncertain, the air around her suddenly becomes heavy with a blend of revolution, sex, corruption and death. Braggioni has asked her to oil and load his pistols, unbuckling his ammunition belt and spreading it "laden across her knees" (*FJ*, 156). As she does so he degrades the term "love" by telling her that no woman, not even "the legless beggar woman in the Alameda," need be without a lover. Laura, faintly disturbed, cleans his pistol while he "curves his swollen fingers around the throat of the guitar and softly smothers the music out of it" (*FJ*, 156). He speaks urgently of the coming revolution, the disruption of all that has "rotted for centuries," and the elect who will "procreate" a new world. He "strokes the pistol lying in her hands" and speaks of how the city has fallen before him "like an overripe pear" (*FJ*, 157). As Laura sits "with the shells slipping through the cleaning cloth dipped in oil," he repeats that he cannot understand "why she works so hard for the revolutionary idea unless she loves some man who is in it" (*FJ*, 156). Then, made restless by his own words, he stands, and she holds out the belt, saying softly, "Put that on, and go kill somebody in Morelia, and you will be happier" (*FJ*, 157). Finally, "the presence of death in the room" makes her bold to speak of the concern which has her "bogged in a nightmare": "Today, I found Eugenio going into a stupor. He refused to allow me to call the prison doctor. He had taken all the tablets I brought him yesterday. He said he took them because he was bored. . . . I told him if he had waited only a little while longer, you would have got him set free. . . . He said he did not want to wait" (*FJ*, 157). "He is a fool, and his death is his own business," answers Braggioni, and then he leaves, his series of visits ended.

Laura dons a white linen nightgown symbolic of the sterility of her life and falls asleep trying vainly to impose order on her rebellious emotions: "1-2-3-4-5—it is monstrous to confuse love with revolution, night with day, life with death—ah, Eugenio" (*FJ*, 159). In the beautiful impressionistic dream which follows, recorded in the more naturally smooth past tense and cast in the symbolism of Christ's betrayal by Judas and of the Judas Tree myth, she sees Eugenio, who calls her, poor prisoner, to elope with him to "a new country." Wondering but fearless, she refuses to follow unless he takes her hand: only in a dream can she express freely her need for him, and his involvement with her revolutionary hopes. Her "No" is still a refusal, this time of the ultimate mystery which has hidden behind all her other fears, though in demanding Eugenio's hand it now also means "Yes." But it is too late. He eludes her and calls her "Murderer," yet she is helplessly drawn after him. When he tells her it is to death they are going she again refuses his hand. He offers her the warm bleeding Judas flowers with the Eucharistic bidding, "Take and eat." Only after she has eaten them greedily, satisfying hunger and thirst, does he say, "Murderer! . . . and Cannibal! This is my body and my blood" (*FJ*, 160). At this Laura cries "No!" and wakes at the sound of her own voice, afraid to sleep again. She has seen Eugenio as the savior who can lead her out of futility and isolation into the new country of their shared revolutionary dream, but finds that because her ambiguous gift of sleep has killed him, he can lead her only to death. The Judas tree which sets her on the earth reminds her that by "confusing love with revolution" she has betrayed not only Eugenio but also the cause which both he and she have served. Still compelled to follow him out across the waste land to death, but also still afraid to take his hand, she eats the sacrificial offering he gives her, the Judas flowers which have symbolized love but which are now warm with blood. She is nourished by them as she had begun to feel nourished by her love for Eugenio, but learns with horror that, by hesitating too long to take his hand, by compromising between love and fear, she has consumed his body and blood. The denial with which she wakes to her empty life now has a complexity of meanings. In the dream it is a terrified denial that she has killed her beloved; as she wakes it becomes a flight from the entire dream vision and the realizations it has forced upon her. For the dream has crystallized the doubts and fears which she has so carefully repressed. It has shown her that her romantic and too timid love has killed her lover and left her doubly alone. Earlier she had been disillusioned by the destruction of her revolutionary ideals; now she suffers the ultimate disillusions—with love and with self. "After such knowledge, what forgiveness?" she can ask with Gerontion.

The crucial fact about Laura's love for Eugenio is that no matter how convincing it at first seems, and even if it is really intended to be taken as genuine (on *some* of the internal evidence), it is not given fictional reality as anything more than a romantic dream. It is not a real opening of self to another with the sacrifices which such commitment entails; the only suffering involved is the sense of loss which, if embedded in the soul, really needs no immediate external cause. In terms, moreover, of the possibility of future love for Laura, the conclusion of the story is felt as a dead end. From here she can only go on to become the heroine of "Theft," even more wary of the false paradise of love, though never free of the haunting sense of loss which its vanishing has left in her. For her there remains only pain. She will ask no more of life than the strength to bear it and will value nothing but the pride of her strength.

"Theft" carries farther the subjectivity and formal complexity introduced into Miss Porter's work by "Flowering Judas." For the first time the heroine might, both in character and in the concrete details of her life, be completely identified with the author. This is highly significant in spite of the fact that Miss Porter is clearly critical of this heroine—because "Theft" contains the clearest expression of the author's characteristic rejection theme. The heroine is an implicit Miranda, and the story is related closely to "Flowering Judas" in that it is concerned primarily with the over-rejection of the heroine, who could be Laura about twenty years later. A formal irregularity new to Miss Porter's stories is most evident in the fact that "Theft" does not follow the normal time order. Subjectivity and formal complexity are intimately related in the handling of time in "Theft." "Flowering Judas" was written in a generalized present tense and contained some passages of generalized recollection in the past tense, some of them briefly dramatized by composition of scene and dialogue. The present story employs the flashback more extensively. For example, it opens on the morning when the heroine, just come from her bath, first misses her purse. Immediately her thoughts jump back, with the purse as connecting link, to the moment on the previous evening when she looked to see if she had train fare to get home from a date with Camilo. From there the scene continues almost uninterrupted through two meetings with men friends, until she reaches her apartment. This transition and others, made with Miss Porter's usual smooth economy, give the impression that the story is taking place in the heroine's mind, with its temporal fluidity, and this is precisely the desired effect. The important action of the story does take place in the heroine's mind. The external plot is extremely simple: by chance, she rides home with one man from a date with another; pays a short visit to a third; reaches her apartment, reads a letter from a former lover, and goes to bed; misses her purse the next morning, finds that the janitress has stolen it, and after a brief quarrel with the thief, gets it back. This action has two purposes: to typify and to symbolize the pattern of her life. There is virtually no evidence of the presence of the ironic narrator; the heroine, seemingly of equal intelligence and insight with the author, judges herself.

There is a new atmosphere in this story, only partially foreshadowed by "Flowering Judas." For the first time the setting is that of modern urban life, a setting in which the mature author has lived, and she seems to be confronting, with all her intelligence and personal involvement, one of the urgent and painful mysteries of life. Her fictional narrator no longer occupies a secure artistic world in which she can manipulate relatively simple characters and look down on them with ironic superiority. She is, rather, at the very frontiers of her own world, where knowledge shades off into fear and darkness. The reader is introduced into the heroine's mind informally, to share her preoccupied groping for the flaw in her life. She is not formally introduced, as was María Concepción, but defined gradually by casual references to her surroundings and especially by the analogical and symbolic revelation of her deepest motivation. Never once is the reader separated from the heroine by detailed visual description of her.

All the elements in the story point clearly toward rejection. It opens just as the heroine becomes aware of the loss of her purse, which is representative of all her possessions, a symbolic extension of her personality. A birthday gift from her former lover, it signifies love and the new life that love seemed to bring, but it also marks the unlovely approach of middle age, which is a painful preoccupation of the alpha heroine. Between the initial sense of material loss and the profound anguish of spiritual loss with which the story ends, there are three distinct movements, each climaxed by a rejection. The long first scene culminates in the heroine's relinquishment of fifty dollars which she sorely needs and which rightfully belong to her. After a one-line shift to the present which serves to separate these two movements, there is a short continuation of the remembered scene, in which she rereads the letter, then tears it carefully into narrow strips and burns it, in a ritual rejection of the lover. Night passes, and after a quick narrative which brings the action up to the moment at which the story began, there is the long final scene in which the heroine rejects the purse by trying to give it to the janitress. The first of these three rejections typifies her willingness to give up valuable possessions in everyday life. The second is the crucial rejection of love—the most important of her life, perhaps.

The third rejection, that of the purse, while the concrete value involved is by far the smallest, is dramatically the most important. It comes immediately after the rejection of love which has left the heroine profoundly disturbed and sensitive to loss. The element in this third loss which was lacking in the two earlier ones is the presence of a thief, or scapegoat, who can be blamed. Just as the heroine decides to "let it go," thus reminding herself of the link between this loss and all the earlier ones, there rises up in her blood "a deep almost murderous anger" (*FJ*, 88). Suddenly projecting the resentment and guilt of all the losses of her life on to the thief, she sees her as a figure of fantastic evil, and finds her in the infernal regions of the building, facing her "with hot flickering eyes, a red light from the furnace reflected in them" (*FJ*, 89). She makes the accusation, but at the first denial of guilt the instinct of rejection reasserts itself and she says bitterly, "Oh, well then, keep it." The form of the woman's denial—"Before God I never laid eyes on your purse, and that's the holy truth"—gives an ironic note of solemnity to the revelation which her accuser suffers at this instant. Suddenly she realizes that this disproportionate anger, the resentment of hundreds of losses, should be directed at herself:

> She remembered how she had never locked a door in her life, on some principle of rejection in her that made her uncomfortable in the ownership of things, and her paradoxical boast before the warnings of her friends, that she had never lost a penny by theft; and she had been pleased with the bleak humility of this concrete example designed to illustrate and justify a certain fixed, otherwise baseless and general faith which ordered the movements of her life without regard to her will in the matter.

> (*FJ*, 89)

In realizing the extent of her own guilt for the present loss she has taken the first step toward an intuition of her deeper guilt for more serious ones. Meanwhile, the mountain of remembered losses, not yet fully related to the previous thought, rushes down upon her:

> In this moment she felt that she had been robbed of an enormous number of valuable things, whether material or intangible: things lost

or broken by her own fault, things she had forgotten and left in houses when she moved: books borrowed from her and not returned, journeys she had planned and had not made, words she had waited to hear spoken to her and had not heard, and the words she had meant to answer with; bitter alternatives and intolerable substitutes worse than nothing, and yet inescapable: the long patient suffering of dying friendships and the dark inexplicable death of love—all that she had had, and all that she had missed, were lost together, and were twice lost in this landslide of remembered losses.

(*FJ*, 89-90)

The janitress follows her up the stairs to return the purse, and reminds her of the extent to which she has, with seeming indifference, left her belongings exposed to theft. The heroine's anger has cooled somewhat at the realization of her own complicity, but the woman revives it by touching on a particularly painful aspect of loss—the decline of youth and beauty—and by unwittingly reminding her of the loss of her lover by saying that he will buy her another purse if she needs it. Bitterly, the heroine thrusts the purse upon her, rejecting with it both the sufferings and the values it represents. By now the woman has twisted things around to the extent of calling the heroine a thief: "It's not from me, it's from her you're stealing it" (*FJ*, 91).

Back in her own room, over cold coffee, she feels the lesson sink in. Once more she has seen herself instinctively reject her own possessions, this time in a parody of generosity which has left her even more alienated than before. She is now painfully conscious of the extent of her self-impoverishment, though how far she sees into its causes remains uncertain. Leonard Prager gives an indication of them: "The protagonist's childishly dimmed proprietary sense is a function of a more generalized flight from feeling. To own is to be responsible for, to be concerned with, to expend effort on. Her irrational certainty that the world will not take from her is but the negative of the infantile wish to be cared for regardless of what she does or does not do. The form of the wish betrays a fear of feeling and commitment."[5] Surely she realizes at least in a dim way that it is her fear of contact and commitment that motivates the principle of rejection which

5. "Getting and Spending: Porter's 'Theft,' " *Perspective*, XI (1960), 234.

robs her of life. Further analysis of the meaning of her rejection may be reserved to a later chapter; the essential point here is to observe the form it takes. Because of the aforementioned closeness of the reader to the heroine in this story, his final attitude toward her is approximately the same as her own toward herself, as expressed in the last line—"I was right not to be afraid of any thief but myself, who will end by leaving me nothing" (*FJ*, 91). She has been sympathetically presented, but one is inclined to blame her over-rejection for a large part of her suffering, just as in the case of Laura in "Flowering Judas."

This is not to say that the reader feels a closeness of affection to the heroine. There is a pronounced coldness about her and her story which has undoubtedly contributed to its lack of general popularity—an observation which may be extended to almost all of Miss Porter's work. As was said above, everything in the story points toward rejection. The general orientation is in fact too explicit, just as is the moralistic statement of the theme at the end. Yet some of the pointers are subtle enough to merit brief comment.

The motif of fastidious restraint in relations with others fills the story. There is no indication of unquestioning acceptance or donation on the part of any important character. The heroine is inwardly distant and superior toward Camilo, and even with Roger there is a delicate equilibrium, in spite of swerving taxi and foggy mind.[6] When she asks about his play he states firmly that he will not compromise for success, and she comments ad-

6. Relevant here is the clearly deliberate use of men's hats as symbols of male sexuality. The heroine notes that Camilo is wearing "a new hat of a pretty biscuit shade, for it never occurred to him to buy anything of a practical color; he had put it on for the first time and the rain was spoiling it" (*FJ*, 81-82). She pities this boyish gesture of masculinity and later feels guilty when she sees Camilo secretly remove the hat and hide it under his overcoat. She thinks in contrast of Eddie, whose hats "always seemed to be precisely seven years old and as if they had been quite purposely left out in the rain, and yet . . . sat with a careless and incidental rightness on Eddie" (*FJ*, 82). She feels a certain respect for this man, though he may well be the lover she has turned away. It is only with Roger, who has frankly abandoned the aggressive role and buttoned his hat under his coat, and casually tells her so, that she relaxes, leaning against the bulge which the crushed hat forms over his breast.

miringly, "It's absolutely a matter of holding out, isn't it?" (*FJ*, 85) Here the pattern of rejection is placed in a definitely admirable light, artistically and even morally. Even here, however, the question mark hints that the heroine is thinking of her own life and beginning to question the value of the firm line of rejection. Calculated self-protection in human relations appears in two conversations overheard by the heroine and Roger while their cab is waiting for a light. Three drunken boys pass and one says, "When I get married it won't be jus' for getting married, I'm gonna marry for *love*, see?" (*FJ*, 84) His advocacy of love has the effect of degrading it, and his romanticism is roundly ridiculed first by his companions, then by the more sophisticated Roger, whose comment on the scene is, "Nuts, pure nuts." Next two girls pass and one contributes her voice to the general chorus of cynicism: "Yes, I know all about *that*. But what about me? You're always so sorry for *him* . . ." (*FJ*, 84). These scenes present vulgar parallels to the heroine and her former lover (of whom the reader learns only later), whose romantic faith in love is revealed in the few words quoted from his letter. The heroine's meditation on these choric utterances should remind her of the self-interest in her own position. It is immediately after this that we learn of Roger's coldly calculated marriage and the heroine's own abortive love affair: ". . . after a while Roger said: 'I had a letter from Stella today, and she'll be home on the twenty-sixth, so I suppose she's made up her mind and it's all settled.' 'I had a sort of letter today too,' she said, 'making up my mind for me. I think it is time for you and Stella to do something definite' " (*FJ*, 84-85). The heroine sees selfishness in Camilo's "series of compromises," mentioned at the beginning of the story, by which he makes "a fairly complete set of smaller courtesies" do for the "larger and more troublesome ones" (*FJ*, 81). During her visit with Bill he is calculating whether he should send alimony to his estranged wife. The casual first-name familiarity with which these people associate is a pathetic contrast with the profound isolation which separates them. Of the five marriages or love affairs referred to, not one is happy or successful.

The heroine of "Theft" is another of the strong, self-sufficient women who begin to appear in the stories. She is seen only in perfect spiritual isolation. Although the apparent suggestion of the plot, evident for example in her disturbance over the letter, is that she loved this man before finally breaking off with him, the impression of real love is entirely absent from the story. The pain she feels, like Laura's, is the anguish of loss—an entirely different thing. There is, moreover, not the least evidence that she will or can love in the future. Her bitterness over the path not taken does not suggest that she might turn back, or even, really, that she has made an avoidable mistake. One of the many evidences of the permanence of her isolation is her generous share of the alpha heroine's scorn for men. It is expressed principally in the rejection of her lover, her patronizing attitude toward Camilo, and her refusal to press Bill for the money he owes her, combined with the unflattering characterization of him.

The extremely strong polarization of this story by the rejection theme is the basic cause of the obscurities and structural weaknesses which have attracted to it in recent years more critical attention, including some pedantic symbol-hunting, than has been devoted to most of the other stories. There is little need for reference to this criticism, for failure to see the general pattern of Miss Porter's work below its surface has led most of it wide of the mark. The powerful drive of rejection pulls everything with it; and its correlative, the powerful sense of loss, is responsible for the long meditations and the explicit conclusion which strike many readers as excessive. They *are* excessive, insufficiently dramatized, and sentimental—but an awareness of the rejection theme makes them at least understandable. It also makes understandable the undeniable power with which the story portrays the common human experiences of isolation and loss.

"Theft," and to a smaller extent "Flowering Judas," seem to have served the author as spells with which to exorcise the most obviously negative and destructive aspects of the rejection theme before embodying that theme in her autobiographic heroine, Miranda. The exorcism is, however, only superficial. It cannot be too strongly emphasized that all these alpha heroines follow the same pattern, and it should be by now quite evident that this pattern is strongly negative. The difference between these two stories and Miranda's is that in the latter the plot is arranged so as to conceal or justify rejection and emphasize its inevitability for the noble individual, while in the former it is left more fully exposed in its negative aspects. Constantly showing in all these stories, on the surface or just below it, is the same thematic pattern—and all these heroines are Miranda.

The two remaining stories in *Flowering Judas* which are closely related to the alpha heroine are "That Tree" and "The Jilting of Granny Weatherall," the first because its two main characters form a sort of composite Miranda, and the second because of its heroine's implicit kinship with the Grandmother of "The Old Order." "That Tree" is an almost uninterrupted monologue in which a successful American journalist in Mexico, agitated by a letter from his estranged first wife asking him to take her back—and by his decision to do so—tells the story of their marriage and divorce to a guest with whom he is drinking in a cafe. Part of the interest of the story is its description of life in Mexico City, especially among the arty set. The heart of the story, however, is a close examination of the deep conflict between romanticism and realism in life and of some of its implications for psychology and marriage. In one respect this examination takes the form of a study of the American temperament as seen against the background of the Mexican.

The protagonist's monologue is recorded in a third person form reminiscent of "Rope" in that it permits the ironic narrator to be constantly present, judging the speaker by his own words. One of the strongest signs of his degradation is the very fact that, in his drunken loquacity, he tells this story of the sordidness of his life. It is impossible to distinguish sharply between his own statements and the observations of the ironic narrator (which may be viewed as the stream of his thoughts flowing beneath his speech), but it seems certain that, no matter how deep his shamelessness, he does not actually tell all the humiliating details recorded in the story. On the first page there is this observation: "Long after he had become quite an important journalist, . . . he confessed to any friends and acquaintances who would listen to him—he enjoyed this confession, it gave him a chance to talk about the thing he believed he loved best, the idle free romantic life of a poet—that the day Miriam kicked him out was the luckiest day of his life" (*FJ*, 95). This deep bit of introspection is almost certainly inserted by the narrator— yet one is never quite sure, and the effect is that even such condemnatory lines as these add to the atmosphere of maudlin self-revelation.

To begin with, the marriage described in this story may be classified as a particularly destructive union. One is certain that even its forthcoming renewal will be stable only to the extent that the wife has succeeded in killing the husband's spirit—a considerable extent indeed. The separation has been a sort of escape for both of them, but their reunion after such a long estrangement only emphasizes their enslavement. This particular unhappy marriage has special interest because it is a sort of allegory of the conflict within the protagonist's own mind. His wife is an embodiment of repressed traits in himself, as the following passage points out:

Miriam had become an avenging fury, yet he could not condemn her. Hate her, yes, that was almost too simple. His old-fashioned respectable middle-class hard-working American ancestry and training rose up in him and fought on Miriam's side. He felt he had broken about every bone in him to get away from them and live them down, and here he had been overtaken at last and beaten into resignation that had nothing to do with his mind or heart. It was as if his blood stream had betrayed him.

(*FJ*, 113-14)

"That Tree" is another exorcism of some of the weakest traits in the alpha protagonist. True, both characters are in the beta class by virtue of their lack of spirit, their inability to escape from an oppressive union. This is made clear by the abundant irony with which the author removes the protagonist from herself.

Yet, more than most beta characters, this would-be poet possesses qualities similar to Miranda's—intelligence, considerable talent, desire for a free life of dedication to artistic truth. Like her he has escaped to Mexico, and like her he has been disillusioned; but he has been fatally slow in his recognition of the truth. It has required a gradual and painful reassertion of the practical, common-sense part of him in the person of his wife. This side of his nature has, however, finally forced his idealistic side into submission. It is here that he parts company with Miranda. Fundamentally, they have both been impelled by the same urge. In both, because of their basically artistic natures (though his is less genuine), the desire for escape to truth has taken the form of a flight to an ideal artistic life. Inevitably, the reality proves too human, there is disillusion, and the alpha protagonist makes a second escape. But here the present protagonist fails to pass the test, and it is his own nature, represented by his wife, that drags him down. His wife's departure is an incipient escape—a characteristically passive one—for him. After his first shock his thoughts are remarkably close to Miranda's. As she confirms her first major escape at the end of "Old Mortality," she feels a sudden liberation at daring to break out of her childhood belief in the sacredness of love: "But what was good, and what was evil? I hate love, she thought, as if this were the answer, I hate loving and being loved, I hate it. And her disturbed and seething mind received a shock of comfort from this sudden collapse of an old painful structure of distorted images and misconceptions" (*PH*, 87-88). In "That Tree" we read, "So she went, and she did him a great favor without knowing it. He had fallen into the cowardly habit of thinking their marriage was permanent, no matter how evil it might be, that they loved each other, and so it did not matter what cruelties they committed against each other" (*FJ*, 115). The instinct in both is exactly the same but in Miranda's case it is justified, while in the present case it is only a pseudo-escape from cowardice. Foolishly, this protagonist falls again into his original idealistic error about his arty companions. He will emerge from it this time only into the abject and sodden defeat vividly portrayed at the end of the story.

The author scorns this protagonist as a masculine weak sister, a traitor to the rejection instinct, and so he becomes another addition to her gallery of immature, despicable males. His defeat is bitter because he had represented some very real values. In him, however, the escapist aspect dominated over the desire for truth and beauty. This is the weakness which gave Miriam her deathlike grip on him. It is, furthermore, this respect in which he serves as a scapegoat for Miranda. For his conflict is a very real one. There is an element of escape and irresponsibility in the rejection urge which sends Americans to foreign artists' colonies, and their puritan-utilitarian background places a strong emphasis on it. Even in her superficial school-teacher romanticism, Miriam is the embodiment of this background, and as such she has real power: "No doubt about it, Miriam had force. She could make her personality, which no one need really respect, felt in a bitter, sinister way. She had a background, and solid earth under her feet, and a point of view and a strong spine: even when she danced with him he could feel her tense controlled hips and her locked knees, which gave her dancing a most attractive strength and lightness without any yielding at all" (*FJ*, 111). This hero's idealism has been a perfect echo of Laura's (political and artistic idealism being here interchangeable) and so is his disillusion. Miriam has seen through it all "with half an eye": "The trouble was that Miriam was right, damn her. I am not a poet, my poetry is filthy, and I had notions about artists that I must have got out of books" (*FJ*, 113). Miriam shares the author's scornful estimate of him as an overgrown child, as she reveals to him in the particularly cutting way she says, without any special emphasis, "Ah your mother" (*FJ*, 111). She herself has from the start been a domineering mother to him, not a wife. Her American middle-class frigidity, which is a root cause of the destructiveness of this marriage on the social plane, is the highly organic symbol of her coldness to all his aspirations. It is an ironic commentary on his blindness to his own desires that subconsciously he too sees Miriam as his mother

—the oppressive embodiment of reason, authority, even punishment. This explains, on one level, his compulsion to take her back. They have really never been apart. During their separation each is preoccupied with the other. She reads all his articles, and his newly-adopted vocation is testimony to her power over him. His two intervening marriages are superficial, and at least one of them is broken up by his resentment of the new wife's criticism of Miriam, his hateful but inescapable other self. Like every other apparent love affair in Miss Porter's work, the present one is unconvincing. There is necessarily a pretext of love for the marriage in the first place, but the emphasis is overwhelmingly on hatred. In speaking of his love for Miriam the protagonist is at a loss for words. He can only refer to a "special kind of beauty," as usual predominantly aesthetic, which gives him a "clutch in the pit of the stomach" (*FJ,* 97-98). But he can go on for hours on her faults, and he admits that, after all, she isn't really beautiful. They achieve no communion through sex. Upon Miriam's first arrival in Mexico there is not the slightest indication of love on her part as she views the nuptial chamber strewn with flowers. She shifts immediately into the role of disapproving mother.

Individually the protagonist of "That Tree" is an abortive Miranda. In the composite he forms with his wife, who forces him to bitter self-knowledge, he possesses an insight not too inferior to hers. He, too, is disillusioned by the human embodiment of his romantic ideal, but, because of the warring of elements within, he does not have the power to escape from it. Each party sees the values of the other depreciatively, and in their union each betrays, to some extent, his own. The composite individual they form sacrifices the important values to the smaller, safer ones, and is fated to permanent bitterness at the knowledge of what it has done—to an overwhelming sense of lost possibilities. The title of the story emphasizes this sense of loss. The tree under which the would-be poet wanted to sit is the symbol of the ambiguous ideal of independence-isolation—in his case muted to irresponsibility-degradation—which he will never reach. This protagonist is unique in Miss Porter's short fiction, representing as he does the potential alpha character, significantly a man, who quits trying and sinks into the beta class. The single parallel to the composite character he forms with his wife is the Jenny-David polarity in *Ship of Fools*.

"Theft" and "Flowering Judas" have brought Katherine Anne Porter close to her fictional heartland. The story which follows approaches it from a new direction. The account of Granny Weatherall's disappointments is the first of the stories to be set in the atmosphere of the Old South, and she herself is the first portrayal of the Grandmother, whose position on the rejection scale is second only to Miranda's. The center of interest is the dying lady's mind, and the consequent similarity of her story to "Pale Horse, Pale Rider," as also her experience of an evanescent love affair, gives her similarities with Miranda which the later Grandmother does not possess. There is also a charm about Granny Weatherall which is lacking in the later Grandmother, and the principal cause of it seems to be the gentle humor with which she is portrayed. She has the author's genuine respect and sympathy, but the respect does not become tiresome and sentimental, as it sometimes does in such stories as "The Source" and "The Old Order." The humor of the present story, rather unusual in Miss Porter's work and not at all characteristic of her central rejection theme, is one of its strongest artistic assets. Greater and more familiar assets are the vibrant poetic texture and the dream-like interweaving of present and past which cause the story to radiate some of the mystery of life and death, and of death in life.

Granny is one of those women who are respected exactly in proportion as they have escaped from the spiritual limitations of their surroundings by dominating them. Paradoxically, in her case and in similar ones, a major source of strength is, on the level of plot, one of these spiritual limitations: the puritanical fear of sex instilled into her by her religious and moral tradition. Among the women of the old order (as among the more recent ones in a subtler manner—for example, Miriam in "That Tree") this fear was an impediment to satisfying spiritual intimacy with their husbands. This in turn gave the men many of the faults which led the women to scorn them, in an unconscious defense reaction, and to stand alone with hardened hearts. Granny is essentially true to this pattern, though in her some of its elements are disguised. As is true of the heroines of "Flowering Judas" and "Theft," her first apparent love has been simply a romantic dream, never in any danger of becoming real. The jilting provides a perfect "escape" from the marriage and an ideal excuse for hating men—and for refusing to let her eventual marriage affect her intimately. The whole point of the story is her lifelong sense of loss, but the very real poignancy of that loss has nothing to do with love. In spite of the genuine beauty of its portrayal and the very real courage it evokes in her, Granny's sense of loss is clearly symptomatic of a juvenile fixation on romance which is in turn nourished by that basic characteristic of the alpha heroine—rejection of men.

Artistically speaking, "The Jilting" is beautifully balanced— much more perfectly self-contained than "Pale Horse, Pale Rider," which resembles it in its poetic stream-of-consciousness treatment of the mind at the approach of death. Even before the perfect immediacy of her final visions pulls the reader into Granny's mind, he has begun to feel an intellectual sympathy with her. The route to this sympathy is opened by the humor which softens the hard shell of her self-sufficiency, and it is founded primarily on the obvious appeal of some of her judgments. For example: "It was like Cornelia to whisper around doors. She always kept things secret in such a public way. She was always being tactful and kind. Cornelia was dutiful; that was the trouble with her. Dutiful and good: 'So good and dutiful,' said Granny, 'that I'd like to spank her' " (*FJ*, 122-23). This passage is, incidentally, an illustration of a fact which has been mentioned before and which holds true for all Miss Porter's work: even in relationships which are obviously intended as loving, irritations and antagonisms are always portrayed much more strongly and convincingly than love.

The reader is brought completely into the heroine's mind by means of powerful, dream-like descriptions of her thoughts and by the author's brilliant technique of making him share her sensory confusions and progressive clarifications, as in the following lines: "Her eyes closed of themselves, it was like a dark curtain drawn around the bed. The pillow rose and floated under her, pleasant as a hammock in a light wind. She listened to the leaves rustling outside the window. No, somebody was swishing newspapers: no, Cornelia and Doctor Harry were whispering together. She leaped broad awake, thinking they whispered in her ear" (*FJ,* 122). The story refutes deathbed sentimentality by showing the ironic discrepancy between the thoughts of the dying person and those of the mourners. In this respect "The Jilting" resembles Flannery O'Connor's story, "A Late Encounter with the Enemy."

This story about death is also about life, or time. It studies the meaning of time by investigating the way in which the individual mind preserves, blends, and reshapes experience. A good example of this is the heroine's confusion of death with childbirth, a parallel which, while valid enough, casts a bit more light on her basic attitude toward sex and marriage: "Yes, John, get the Doctor now, no more talk, my time has come. When this one was born it would be the last" (*FJ,* 131). The entire story turns upon the fact that, at the moment of her death, the scene which Granny recalls in all its pain and detail is that of her jilting, an event which for sixty years she has "prayed against remembering" because the hatred it arouses is "hell" (*FJ,* 128). It is part of the meaning of the story's title that these two crucial events become one for her. At the very instant of death her mind is on the day of her first bitter disappointment, for even in her last seconds God refuses to give the sign she has expected, and the emptiness of the last day blends with that of the first: "For the second time there was no sign. Again no bridegroom and the priest in the house" (*FJ,* 136). The Divine Bridegroom, like the earthly one, proves to have been a romantic dream, but Granny's courage will do her no good after this disillusion. Since her first great disappointment she has always hated surprises, but when death finally comes it is "by surprise." She has desired order, time to "spread out the plan of life and tuck in the edges orderly" (*FJ*, 123), but death catches her with loose ends still to be tied up. Her last thoughts reflect a life of heroic and compulsive effort to build a rampart of order against the radical disorder of her frustrated heart: "It was good to be strong enough for everything, even if all you made melted and changed and slipped under your hands, so that by the time you finished you almost forgot what you were working for" (*FJ*, 127). Only after a mental survey of a long life of achievement does her memory return to the fateful day, making the jump by means of a weather link: "Such a fresh breeze blowing and such a green day with no threats in it. But he had not come, just the same" (*FJ*, 128). Throughout the story her mind follows the law of association, as when her pain recalls childbirth, and the presence of a priest again recalls the jilting. Light-dark symbolism is employed several times, most effectively at her death, which is strikingly similar to Miranda's death vision in "Pale Horse, Pale Rider," a scene which constitutes in several respects an ultimate in Miss Porter's fiction. Granny scorns Cornelia's frilly blue lamps, but the light from one of them becomes, in a masterful blend of realism and symbol, the image of her dwindling life: "The blue light from Cornelia's lampshade drew into a tiny point in the center of her brain, it flickered and winked like an eye, quietly it fluttered and dwindled. Granny lay curled down within herself, amazed and watchful, staring at the point of light that was herself; her body was now only a deeper mass of shadow in an endless darkness and this darkness would curl around the light and swallow it up" (*FJ*, 136). Her thoughts return to the jilting, and she retires from life as she retired to bed after that bitter day: "Oh, no, there's nothing more cruel than this—I'll never forgive it. She stretched herself with a deep breath and blew out the light" (*FJ*, 136).

The emphasis in Granny's characterization is upon her strength—the positive structure she has built up on a negative basis. This and the moderate degree of human warmth she reveals, mainly in her humor, make her an attractive character and hers a successful story. The final revelation of her hidden emptiness only emphasizes her achievement, and she keeps her hard-earned domination to the end, when she blows out her own light.

A few reflections of the motifs of scorn for men and the sense of loss remain to be pointed out. Granny's marriage to John and the raising of her children she regards primarily as a job done, and the image she keeps of her husband is that of a boy, looking younger now than her children, for he deserted her by an early death, leaving her to dig post holes and do the other work that "changed a woman." Neither the doctor nor the priest receives much respect from her, and while she can boast to John that her children seem to have turned out well and have done all right for themselves, except for "that worthless husband" of Lydia's, it is her youngest daughter, Hapsy, that she really wants. The origin of her sense of loss is clear, but it is interesting to note its manifestations, such as the following: "I want you to pick all the fruit this year and see that nothing is wasted. There's always someone who can use it. Don't let good things rot for want of using. You waste life when you waste good food. Don't let things get lost. It's bitter to lose things" (*FJ*, 128). In her delirium, Granny asks Cornelia to find George and "tell him I was given back everything he took away and more. Oh, no, oh, God, no, there was something else besides the house and the man and the children. Oh, surely they were not all? What was it? Something not given back" (*FJ*, 131).

The *Flowering Judas* volume concludes with two long stories, "The Cracked Looking-Glass" and "Hacienda," which appeared only in the second edition, "Hacienda" having been published separately in 1934 in Paris. It is the shorter of the two, and both are slightly shorter than the novelettes. "Looking-Glass," while clearly related to the rejection theme and illustrative of several of its motifs, stands apart from the main body of Katherine Anne Porter's fiction in virtue of the gentle humor which fills it. The marriage in this story and that of the Thompsons in "Noon Wine" provide the closest approaches in Miss Porter's work to a portrayal of human love, though in the former it is not normal married love and in the latter the love is hardly emphasized; significantly, only beta characters are involved.

"Looking-Glass" is a loose and leisurely short story which seems to delight in long Irish monologues. Its most noteworthy stylistic quality is its excellent imitation of Irish speech-rhythms, both in and out of the dialogue. This quality, which it shares with "A Day's Work," is evidence of Miss Porter's careful listening. Indeed, each of her stories is pervaded by the diction and speech-rhythms of the characters it portrays. The dialect in "Looking-Glass" is an integral part of its warm humor, most of which derives from the loquacity and the prejudices of Rosaleen. Humor, in addition to adding its own values, plays an integral part in the characterizations. Even the long comic story Rosaleen tells about the time she and her sister gossiped beside the bed of their dying great-grandfather, who expired cursing them for their inattention, touches upon the important youth-age theme. So also does the very telling of the story, another instance of Rosaleen's compulsive speech and Dennis' sleepy patience. Both characters are partly comic, and the humor, though it may touch tragedy, is never bitter and always leads to greater sympathy.

"The man today was selling pipes," she said, "and I bought the finest he had." It was an imitation meerschaum pipe carved with a crested lion glaring out of a jungle and it was as big as a man's fist.

Dennis said, "You must have paid a pretty penny for that."

"It doesn't concern ye," said Rosaleen. "I wanted to give ye a pipe." Dennis said, "It's grand carving, I wonder if it'll draw at all." He filled it and lit it and said there wasn't much taste on a new one, for he was tired holding it up.

"It is such a pipe as my father had once," Rosaleen said to encourage him. "And in no time it was fit to knock ye off your feet, he said. So it will be a fine pipe some day."

"And some day I'll be in my tomb," thought Dennis, bitterly, "and she'll find a man can keep her quiet."

(*FJ*, 180)

A more fundamental method employed to gain the reader's sympathy is alternating the point of view between the major characters. This achieves a balance found in none of the other stories and is a major cause of this story's air of difference. Such a balance is notably absent, for example, in that other tale of an Irish marriage, "A Day's Work."

"The Cracked Looking-Glass" embodies several aspects of the rejection theme, though the warm tone of the story gives unfamiliar emphases to some of them. Her marriage is for Rosaleen an unsatisfactory union and her trip to Boston is a flight from its oppression. The marriage is rather unpleasant for Dennis too, aware as he is of Rosaleen's discontent—and his first was even worse: "He was not unhappy over his first wife's death a few years after they left England, because they had never really liked each other, and it seemed to him now that even before she was dead he had made up his mind, if she did die, never to marry again" (*FJ*, 169). Rosaleen is not fully aware of the motives of her flight, and this lack of insight is an important factor separating her from the alpha heroine. It is also the heart of the story, uniting in itself the explicit theme, appearance-reality, and the rejection theme. The central problem is the heroine's failure to distinguish between appearance and reality, especially in herself, and the dominant reality within her is the desire to make an impossible escape from her marriage. The cracked looking-glass, one of the few explicit object-symbols in the stories, represents her dream-distorted view of herself and the world. James W. Johnson sums up its meaning as follows: "Rosaleen is constantly distressed about the cracked mirror, which blurs her face so unrecognizably; but her imperfect and unsatisfactory marriage as mirrored in her 'cracked' imagination cannot be replaced, and so the cracked looking glass remains hanging in the kitchen, after Rosaleen has fully pondered the consequences of its doing so."[7] Rosaleen escapes unconsciously through her dreams and tall tales, her innocent friendships with young men, and finally her dream-inspired trip to Boston. False vision leads to her error about the young man she meets there, which leads in turn to her disillusion and return to reality. She receives a strong lesson in the harmful effects of crediting ap-

7. "Another Look at Katherine Anne Porter," The *Virginia Quarterly Review*, XXXVI (Autumn, 1960), 607.

pearances when she learns that her own moral character has been seriously misjudged by her neighbors, just as it was by the young man. It is her meditation on this shocking discovery that leads her to the comforting conclusion that "life is a dream" (*FJ*, 215). She begins to suspect that all appearances, even her dreams, may be deceiving, and that it is the plain certainties of the heart in which we must trust: "She knew in her heart what she was, and Dennis knew, and that was enough" (*FJ*, 215).

Rosaleen's return is inevitable, but she returns to dominate. Here the tone of the story gives a new meaning to the familiar theme. Because the oppressiveness of this marriage results only from the disparity in age, her dominance will take the form not of destructive nagging but of gentle mothering. She returns to Dennis not as to a lover but as to a child: "She sat up and felt his sleeves carefully. 'I want you to wrap up warm this bitter weather, Dennis,' she told him. 'With two pairs of socks and the chest protector, for if anything happened to you, whatever would become of me in this world?' " (*FJ*, 218-19) Her disillusion is not without pain, however, or her acceptance without suffering, and in this she reflects the familiar theme of loss. Her "wondering what had become of her life" (*FJ*, 218) recalls another character's musing on that tree he never found, and the regret of many others over their lost dreams.

There could hardly be a greater apparent contrast than that between "The Cracked Looking-Glass" and the strange work which follows it. "Hacienda" has caused the critics some difficulty. Warren feels forced to separate it, with "Magic," from the main body of Miss Porter's work, whereas Johnson sees in it an amalgam of all her themes.[8] The latter view is the more nearly correct. Certainly "Hacienda" is unique among the stories, if it may even be classed among them. One may, with Glenway Wescott, call it a "nouvelle in memoir form." Wescott gives some interesting background material on this strange work by his friend: "It is," he says, "a rarity in her lifework in that it is

8. *Ibid.*, p. 606.

all à clef; mainly a portrait of the great Russian film maker, Eisenstein, with others of note, helpers and hinderers of his work in Mexico, clustered around."[9] The work is loosely organized and employs several varieties of style, most of which have been seen in earlier works. Its only principle of unity, aside from the perceptive, ironic narrator, is the brief visit of a small group to a pulque hacienda which is a distillation of the spirit of Mexico. "Hacienda" is a piece of local color, a study in atmosphere; the effect desired, and attained, is one of monotony, unreality, futility. It is the only one of Miss Porter's stories told in the first person, and the narrator is certainly Miranda or even the author herself.

Although the nature of this work did not permit the long inner refinement which went into most of the stories, and although the alpha protagonist who narrates it plays only a passive role in what can hardly be described as a unified dramatic plot, "Hacienda" nevertheless is permeated by the rejection theme. The one overwhelming quality of the hacienda is its oppressiveness. It is a place of corruption and death and hence calls attention to the last and greatest oppression. The life of the Mexican peasants is one of suffering, boredom, and defeat, made bearable only by the soothing "corpse-white liquor," pulque. The death-wish seems to hang in the air of Mexico, familiar to and respected by natives but terrifying to others. It is Kennerly, with his superficial awe at the "reality" of death, who is shown to have no true sense of its meaning. When assured that there is no danger of a lawsuit resulting from a young man's jealous murder of his sister, he comments, "Oh, I see. . . . If he wasn't on the set, it doesn't matter" (*FJ*, 246). Kennerly himself initiates the death theme at the beginning by his compulsive chatter about the poisons surrounding him in this primitive country. The narrator is particularly sensitive to the atmosphere of the place and describes it graphically: "The smell had not been out of my nostrils since I came, but here it rose in a thick vapor

9. *Images of Truth: Remembrances and Criticism* (New York, 1962), p. 32. The movie being made was "Thunder Over Mexico."

through the heavy drone of flies, sour, stale, like rotting milk and blood" (*FJ*, 269).

The material decay which pervades the hacienda symbolizes and is subtly related to the moral corruption among the people there. This corruption has an air of mystery which makes it particularly oppressive to the visitor. Sexual perversion is almost nonexistent in Miss Porter's short fiction, but here there are suspicions of incest as the motive for the murder and suggestions of aberration in the unwholesome affection between Don Genaro's foolish child-wife and his mistress, Lolita, who reveals male tones in her "deep throaty voice" and on one occasion forgets her usual "role" and "swings her leg over the saddle in a gesture unknown to ladies of 1898" (the era of the costume she wears) (*FJ*, 240). Political corruption permits murderers to go free, yet coexists with moral formalism. Various characters embody animalism, decayed gentility, and diabolical malice.

The theme of appearance-reality seen in "The Cracked Looking-Glass" is also strong in "Hacienda," which was published in the same year. It is inherent in the very situation—the filming of a movie version of Mexican reality, falsified by the efforts of the government, represented by Betancourt, to exclude the harsh truths of peasant life. Betancourt himself personifies unreality with his hybrid background, his belief in fanciful mystiques, and his falsification of the life of Carlos Montaña. The murder parallels a scene shot earlier for the movie, and there is a conspiracy to make the real crime seem as untrue as the acted one. Lolita's acting seems to extend into real life, and Doña Julia, with her exotic costumes and doll-like painted face, seems an unreal wife to Don Genaro. The theme works both ways, further blurring the shape of reality: Doña Julia's fur piece is a live dog; the judge offers Don Genaro live prisoners to be shot in the movie; Kennerly regrets that the real murder was not filmed. The last line of the story evokes the theme with subtle power. As the narrator leaves the hacienda her Indian driver says, "If you should come back in about ten days, you would see a different place. It is very sad here now. But then the green corn will be ready, and ah, there will be enough to eat again!" (*FJ*, 285) But she has already seen "a different place"—an oasis of unreality in a desert of hunger and pain.

In this world of illusion, the most desirable of human qualities, in the scale of values by which the narrator judges all characters, are those of the true artist—insight, sensitivity, courage, humility. She gives her highest praise to the poet-musician, Carlos Montaña: "He was full of humanity and good humor" (*FJ*, 266). As his name suggests, he has the nobility and earthy solidity of a mountain. At the bottom of the scale are Betancourt and Kennerly, and it is difficult to say which is greater, the author's revulsion for the cosmopolitan devil or her scorn for the American fool. With respect to the motif of scorn for men, it is interesting to note that the two characters admired by the author are admired not as men but as fellow artists. The thoroughness with which Kennerly is flayed, while justified in terms of plot, is another indication of the power with which she works when following her thematic lines of force.

One aspect of artistic virtue is respect for the native culture and the elemental, often violent peasant life.[10] A quality evident here—as in Miss Porter's first work, "María Concepción," and her last, *Ship of Fools*—is the tendency to romanticize the peon. Scorn is heaped on Kennerly for his blindness to the values in the native life. This attitude of sensitive knowledgeability regarding the native scene—which might be called the Hemingway stance —is often justified to a great extent but always a bit annoying in an author who is himself an American. Miss Porter's peasants are, moreover, usually seen at a distance and aesthetically, as in photograph albums and moving pictures. Related to the leisurely Mexican folkways is the hacienda's air of timelessness. The production of pulque is invested with primeval sacredness through the legend of its discovery recorded in a faded fresco on the

10. Miss Porter has shown a great interest in the native cultures of some of the countries in which she has lived, especially Mexico, by her efforts to publicize their arts. She was instrumental in bringing the first exhibition of Mexican-Indian folk art to the United States in 1922, and among her publications are an *Outline of Mexican Popular Arts and Crafts* (Los Angeles, 1922), a translation, with introduction, of Lizardi's *The Itching Parrot* (Garden City, 1942), *Katherine Anne Porter's French Song-Book* (Paris, 1933), and several articles on Mexican popular art.

walls of the vat room. An anecdote is told of an old man who revisited the hacienda after an absence of fifty years and went about "looking at everything with delight. 'Nothing has changed,' he said, 'nothing at all!' " (*FJ,* 236). This apparent timelessness, though romantic, is unnatural, and part of the atmosphere of monotony and corruption.

It is significant that "Hacienda," apparently so factual and "uncreated," conforms faithfully to Miss Porter's central theme of rejection. This would suggest that the elements of the theme must be intensely present in a situation before it is able to stimulate her to the writing of fiction. (The enforced intimacy of the voyage that inspired *Ship of Fools* is further evidence of this.) Since, in this story of stagnation, no one progresses or develops—even the scenes shot must be repeated—and since Miranda is present but static, as it were, at one point on her thematic path, the rejection theme appears not in a central protagonist, but in numerous small reflections and in the setting itself. The marriage of Don Genaro and Doña Julia is a bizarre variation on the oppressive union. The host seems hardly aware of his wife's existence and is constantly escaping by infidelity and by frequent departures at ever-increasing speeds. The Betancourt-Montaña relationship is a destructive one from which Carlos does not seem to have the energy to escape. The movie makers only tolerate their association with Kennerly as a necessary evil. Even the escaping murderer is captured by a "friend" and taken to jail, a development which everyone, including the same friend, seems later to consider unfortunate. Nowhere is there a strong, normal bond of love or friendship. The two unions which seem strongest reek of incest and homosexuality. The oppressiveness of the gathering, with its stifling tangle of antipathy, confusion, opposed purposes, unwholesome loves, boredom, futility, and murder, all permeated by the sickening odor of the deathly narcotic, steadily increases toward a climax: "A silence like a light trance fell over the whole room in which all these chance-gathered people who had nothing to say to each other were for the moment imprisoned. Action was their defense against the predicament they were in, all together, and for the moment nothing was happening. The suspense in the air seemed ready to explode when Kennerly came in almost on tiptoe, like a man entering church. Everybody turned toward him as if he were in himself a whole rescue party" (*FJ*, 283). When these people turn to Kennerly for rescue, their situation must be grave indeed. As usual, there is no comfort in being in the predicament "all together"; being together is precisely the problem. Almost at once there begins "a gradual drift back to town, by train, by automobile" (*FJ*, 284). Invitations to stay until the next day when "they are going to do some of the best scenes over again" (*FJ*, 284) only reinforce the sense of stagnation and futility. When the narrator escapes she does not even seem to be with her friend and host, Andreyev, but alone.

As an artistic pilgrimage, the visit to the hacienda ends in disillusion. It seems in a general way symbolic of Miranda's whole experience in Mexico, one of the stages in her pattern of escape, disillusion, escape. "Hacienda," which at first glance seems to conclude *Flowering Judas* on an alien note, is in reality firmly bound to the stories which precede it by its reflection of some of its author's favorite thematic motifs, especially by its powerful statement of the central impulse of the rejection theme —the urge to escape.

3

Theme and Variations

It was in *Pale Horse, Pale Rider: Three Short Novels* (1939) that Katherine Anne Porter reached the center of her fictional world with the introduction of the semi-auto-biographical heroine Miranda. The latest episodes in this heroine's life were recorded first, and it remained for *The Leaning Tower and Other Stories* (1944) to portray her childhood and even her ancestors. This delayed start and reversed chronology are characteristic of memory, which seems to return progressively to earlier and yet earlier recollections; readers who hoped for later stories carrying Miranda beyond the age of twenty-four were to be disappointed. *Pale Horse, Pale Rider* contains three novelettes—"Old Mortality," which introduces Miranda at the age of eight and leaves her at eighteen; "Noon Wine"; and the title story, which records her illness at twenty-four. All the Miranda stories will be treated in the next chapter; the present one will treat, in the order of their appearance, the remaining stories from the two volumes, *Pale Horse, Pale Rider* and *The Leaning Tower.*

Miss Porter has several times described the manner in which she wrote the three stories included in *Pale Horse, Pale Rider*. The best description with regard to "Noon Wine" is in the essay, " 'Noon Wine': The Sources":

When the moment came to write this story, I knew it; and I had to make quite a number of practical arrangements to get the time free for it, without fear of interruptions. I wrote it as it stands except for a few pen corrections, in just seven days of trance-like absorption in a small room in an inn in rural Pennsylvania, from the early evening of November 7 to November 14, 1936. Yet I had written the central part, the scene between Mr. Hatch and Mr. Thompson, which leads up to the murder, in Basel, Switzerland, in the summer of 1932.[1]

Elsewhere she adds that the three stories were written almost consecutively, each taking approximately a week. "Noon Wine" contrasts remarkably with its two companion pieces. It is one of Miss Porter's most objective works, whereas "Pale Horse, Pale Rider" is by far her most subjective. All three stories are excellent, but in widely varying ways. Though many critics rank "Noon Wine" as the best of the author's stories, these three novelettes furnish proof of the difficulty of attempting to rank works of art. It does seem that in "Noon Wine" Katherine Anne Porter transcended in some respects the limitations of the central thematic pattern which governs most of her work. In it there is little evidence of the familiar ironic narrator. There is gentle humor, seen in the stories only rarely, and the single convincing portrayal in all the works of normal love between husband and wife. It is the story of Miss Porter's which most nearly approaches tragedy. A brilliant work, it belongs unquestionably to its author; yet it certainly is not among her most characteristic. Unlike most of her fiction, it stands apart in its own bright world, reminding the reader, at least in its plot, of similar stories such as Hamlin Garland's "Under the Lion's Paw" and Flannery O'Connor's "The Displaced Person." It also contains some of the author's finest writing, beautifully adapted to character and setting. Interest centers in the mind of Mr. Thompson, where conflicting motives are delicately probed; his wife

1. *Yale Review*, XLVI (September, 1956), 24-25.

is portrayed less directly, though her mind is entered in a few passages with the result that she also becomes real. Some of the finest descriptive lines are devoted to her. Here is the earliest in which she is described in detail—her first confrontation with Helton: "She was a little frail woman with long thick brown hair in a braid, a suffering patient mouth and diseased eyes which cried easily. She wove her fingers into an eyeshade, thumbs on temples, and, winking her tearful lids, said with a polite little manner, 'Howdy do, sir. I'm Miz Thompson, and I wanted to tell you I think you did real well in the milk house. It's always been a hard place to keep' " (*PH*, 102-3). Convincing description of the setting and of ordinary life provides a solid and contrasting background for the murder. That action itself is described with quick economy, in a suggestive understatement which lets the violence strike the reader directly.

As usual the title points toward the central meaning of the story. It refers most directly to the words of the song which Helton plays constantly on his harmonicas—as Hatch says, "that part about getting so gay you jus' go ahead and drink up all the likker you got on hand before noon. It seems like up in them Swede countries a man carries a bottle of wine around with him as a matter of course, at least that's the way I understood it. Those fellers will tell you anything, though" (*PH*, 146). Hence the words symbolize all the slightly twisted information which Hatch brings to Thompson. It is this new and shocking information, apparently so unrelated to the present Mr. Helton, which revives the first murder and leads to the second. All of this calls attention to the strong parallel between the two murders. Both are unpremeditated and committed with tools. Helton is declared to have been "crazy with the heat" (*PH*, 144), and the deliberately emphasized heat of the day surely helps to induce Thompson's violent state of mind. The apparently casual statement that "The idea of drinking any kind of liquor in this heat made Mr. Thompson dizzy" (*PH*, 146) suggests that Helton might have been dizzy with his noon wine when he killed his brother—a possibility that increases immensely the bitter injustice of the treatment he receives. A combination of small things causes Thompson's resentment to mount rapidly; the following words of Hatch seem almost deliberately directed at him as well as Helton. "Now you know he musta been crazy to get all worked up over a little thing like that" (*PH*, 145). Hatch has subtly suggested this before by twisting a remark of Thompson's:

"You took the words right out of my mouth. There ain't every man in a straightjacket that ought to be there. Ha, ha, you're right all right all right. You got the idea."

Mr. Thompson sat silent and chewed steadily and stared at a spot on the ground about six feet away and felt a slow muffled resentment climbing from somewhere deep down in him, climbing and spreading all through him. What was this fellow driving at? What was he trying to say? It wasn't so much his words, but his looks and his way of talking: that droopy look in the eye, that tone of voice, as if he was trying to mortify Mr. Thompson about something.

(*PH*, 142-43)

The two murders are parallel in their consequences. Each leads to other murders; Thompson's guilt obsession is a milder version of Helton's insanity. Particularly in view of Helton's death, the title of the story has ironic reference to his happy youthful life. It also suggests the sight of Hatch's blood, "running away in a greasy-looking puddle" (*PH*, 153) in the midday sun.

"Noon Wine" is the minor tragedy of the destruction of a goodhearted but weak man, brought on him by circumstances and some mysterious defect in himself. He has good luck, not entirely deserved, in Helton's coming, but pays a great price for it. His "tragic flaw," carefully emphasized from the beginning of the story, is his excessive concern for his standing in the eyes of others; he is a small man, but proud.[2] The wily Hatch plays on this sensitive point. He tells him that harboring an escaped lunatic "won't look very good" to his neighbors, and "Mr. Thompson knew almost before he heard the words that it would look funny. It would put him in a mighty awkward position" (*PH*, 151). After the murder, while a man less concerned with

2. In her essay on the story (*ibid.*, p. 28) Miss Porter shows that she considers Thompson's pride rather typical of his social milieu. He is a man who married slightly above himself and is intensely aware of social status.

status-seeking would have kept his guilt obsession on a more personal basis, Thompson's takes the form of a compulsive need to explain. Like Mrs. Whipple, he has become so accustomed to judging himself through the eyes of others that his self-justification must follow the same path. It is not his social sense which is condemned but its excess. This is only one aspect of the torturing ambiguity of his situation. He has enough honesty and self-awareness to recognize his mixed motives but lacks the strength of character to escape from his moral impasse by accepting it. He is also deeply disturbed, as his suicide note reveals, by the fact that he has lied and caused his wife to lie in the trial which exonerated him.

Mrs. Thompson's dilemma is hardly less painful than her husband's. She is formed on the pattern of blind adherence to a strict moral code. Her sense of duty leads her to lie in public but it can never lead her to accept the lie or extend it further, even by repeating it to her husband. This, in Thompson's eyes, is his strongest condemnation. He begins his suicide note on the familiar pattern of self-justification, but when he reaches the point of calling on his wife's testimony he stops after writing "My wife—" (*PH*, 175). After thinking for a moment he marks out these words and sits a while "blacking out the words until he had made a neat oblong patch where they had been"—a patch which resembles a coffin enclosing the wife whom he has brought to spiritual, and soon perhaps physical, death. Then he writes a second brief message, expressing as well as he can his true feelings: "It was Mr. Homer T. Hatch who came to do wrong to a harmless man. He caused all this trouble and he deserved to die but I am sorry it was me who had to kill him" (*PH*, 175). Then he kills himself. Fate would seem to have been, if not positively against him, at least indifferent.

The excellence of "Noon Wine" is owing in large part to the fact that in achieving its great objectivity Miss Porter did not weaken correspondingly her understanding of her characters or sympathy with them. Why this should be the case is one of the mysteries of art, but the almost life-long rumination on elements of the story which the author reveals in her essay on it gives a clue to the answer. Although the Thompsons are beta characters and do not resemble the author in many respects, they are of a type well known to her childhood. She looks down on them in terms of social and cultural level, intellect, and degree of self-awareness; but she grants them full human stature in the essentials—personal moral character and consideration, even love, for others. By now it should not be necessary to emphasize that this is rare in her stories.

The central elements of the rejection theme are present in "Noon Wine," but in an unusual pattern. For example, while the oppressive union is usually oppressive because of the vices of its members, that is not exactly the case in this story. The Thompson family is composed of good people. They love each other and have that prime essential, the ability to communicate. Thompson feels that his wife's delicate health has been a major obstacle to his success with the farm, but still she is "his dear wife, Ellie, who was not strong" (*PH,* 114). She wishes she could count on him more confidently and scolds him occasionally, but never with bitterness. Yet their situation is one of the most destructive in all of Miss Porter's fiction. Here it is necessary to emphasize again an important fact. The rejection theme functions not necessarily on the superficial plot level, but among the underlying emotional forces in a story. It stipulates that existence in any human relationship be oppressive for the individual but does not, at least at its deepest level, prescribe the reasons. The Thompsons are oppressed by the ironic good fortune of the presence of Helton—first by his taciturnity, next by his harsh treatment of the boys, and finally by the flood of evil he brings upon them. The oppression motif is, in fact, carried further in this story than in any other by the actual portrayal of the final destruction wrought by the union. Yet, and herein lies the tragic significance, the union is destroyed not because of, but in spite of, the fundamental moral character of its members.

"Noon Wine" contains another important embodiment of the oppression motif in Helton's legal subjection to society, a subjection which remains remotely in effect in spite of his escape and finally takes the more immediate and evil form of his subjection to Hatch. Since Helton, like the retarded boy who oppresses another family in "He," is seen more as victim than as person (though his harmonica-playing indicates an ambivalence in this regard), his subjugation is unwitting, and its emotional force is transmitted to the reader directly and through the effects it has on the Thompsons. There are numerous incidental reflections of the theme. At two points in his conversation with Hatch Mr. Thompson adverts to the intolerability of such restraint as Helton has suffered. Learning that he had been in an asylum and worn a straightjacket, Thompson tells about his Aunt Ida who died in the state asylum: "She got vi'lent, and they put her in one of these jackets with long sleeves and tied her to an iron ring in the wall, and Aunt Ida got so wild she broke a blood vessel and when they went to look after her she was dead. I'd think one of them things was dangerous" (*PH*, 137). Thompson's resentment at Hatch's handcuffs sets his head buzzing and is one of the proximate incitements to the murder. Helton succeeds in his first escape and his second is effected by the ambiguous murder, but leads ultimately to his death. The evil in Hatch is based on his function as captor, and the power with which he is portrayed, as well as the fact that his scene was the first to crystalize in the author's mind, suggests that a strong basic thematic note has been struck. The escape impulse lies, though somewhat obliquely, behind the explicit theme of the story: Thompson's excessive deference to public opinion makes a prison of society and stern judges of all his neighbors.

Sometimes the air around him was so thick with their blame he fought and pushed with his fists, and the sweat broke out all over him, he shouted his story in a dust-choked voice, he would fairly bellow at last: "My wife, here, you know her, she was there, she saw and heard it all, if you don't believe me, ask her, she won't lie!" and Mrs. Thompson, with her hands knotted together, aching, her chin trembling, would never fail to say: "Yes, that's right, that's the truth—"

(*PH*, 165)

The ambivalent escape of the alpha protagonist consists of a progressive descent toward death; Thompson's tragic fate seems to thrust him into this austere fellowship. Finally rejected even by his wife and sons, he is to compress his escape into a single action, a liberation of the bitterest kind. Having experienced the ultimate disillusion, he seems already claimed by death:

Now lying on his bed, Mr. Thompson knew the end had come. . . . there as he was with his whiskers already sprouting since his shave that morning; with his fingers feeling his bony chin, Mr. Thompson felt he was a dead man. He was dead to his other life, he had got to the end of something without knowing why, and he had to make a fresh start, he did not know how. Something different was going to begin, he didn't know what. It was in some way not his business. He didn't feel he was going to have much to do with it.

(*PH,* 168)

The sense of oppression is familiar, but Thompson's is cosmic and complete. Though they speak different languages, his feeling is similar to Miranda's when she comes close to the mystery of death.

From "Noon Wine" one must go on to *The Leaning Tower* (1944) for the next non-Miranda story—"The Downward Path to Wisdom." This account of the sufferings and initiations of a little boy seems to occupy a different world from the rest of Katherine Anne Porter's fiction. It gives new evidence of her wide scope in subject and style, adopting brilliantly the point of view of its child protagonist. It is not new thematically, however, but occupies a unique position at the center of Miss Porter's artistic vision. It is a microcosm of the rejection theme pattern and an examination of its genesis in the heart of the alpha protagonist. Superficially, the disparity between Stephen and Miranda places the story clearly in the beta class, yet its young hero is portrayed with remarkably little condescension. The author is much closer to him, for example, than to Rosaleen of "The Cracked Looking-Glass" or the young wife in "Rope." At the end of his story, Stephen is a true alpha protagonist, old in the wisdom of suffering and firm in resisting it.

Technically the story is one of Miss Porter's best. Its strong sympathy for the protagonist is combined with artistic objectivity of a different kind from that of "Noon Wine." Like "Rope" and "Magic," it seems to be more pattern than portrait. Stephen is quite convincing as learner and sufferer, but the other characters, while adequately developed and sometimes described in fine detail, are all subservient to the intricately compressed pattern of initiation. While a limitation in one way, this is not a fault in the story. One of its greatest virtues is its strict adherence to Stephen's viewpoint, from which all other characters are seen in large, impressionistic outline. This viewpoint is evident from the opening sentence, with its careful use of simple and concretely descriptive words: "In the square bedroom with the big window Mama and Papa were lolling back on their pillows handing each other things from the wide black tray on the small table with crossed legs" (*LT*, 81). This could be—particularly as Miss Porter reads it on the Caedmon record—a nursery story.

"The Downward Path to Wisdom" enacts several of the crucial steps in a child's initiation into social life. On the level of plot it is a tragedy of pathos, for the inadequacy of Stephen's family leads him to a complete rejection, not maturely willed as in Miranda's case but instinctive and inevitable, and calculated almost certainly to warp him into abnormality. The pattern of rejection is so clear that little commentary should be necessary. Stephen's initial oppressive union is, like Miranda's, the family. Mother, father, grandmother, and uncle are immature and almost completely selfish. Stephen receives no wholesome love from them or from the bullying nurses who care for him most of the time; he is positively harmed by the nurse who teaches him a guilty fear of sex. His school relations are normal; the teacher is kind and the children are fickle as children are. But his life within the home taints his life outside it, and at the end he includes everyone in a blanket rejection. This rejection is his only possible escape and brings at least momentary relief: "Stephen began suddenly to sing to himself, a quiet, inside song so Mama would not hear. He sang his new secret; it was a comfortable, sleepy song: 'I hate Papa, I hate Mama, I hate Grandma, I hate Uncle David, I hate Old Janet, I hate Marjory, I hate Papa, I hate Mama . . .'" (*LT*, 111). The sad irony of his precocious hatred is emphasized by the fact that during this song "his head bobbed, leaned, came to rest on Mama's knee, eyes closed."

The cold clarity of the rejection theme and her usual objectivity of surface vision safeguard Miss Porter from the crude sentimentality which threatens in this story more than elsewhere. The following passage suggests the risk and the author's considerable success in avoiding it:

> The little boy had to pass his father on the way to the door. He shrank into himself when he saw the big hand raised above him. "Yes, get out of here and stay out," said Papa, giving him a little shove toward the door. It was not a hard shove, but it hurt the little boy. He slunk out, and trotted down the hall trying not to look back. He was afraid something was coming after him, he could not imagine what. Something hurt him all over, he did not know why.
>
> (*LT*, 83)

(The verbal similarity between Stephen's thoughts and Mr. Thompson's just before his death is a reminder of their kinship in subjection to overwhelming oppression.) Objectivity in description prevents excess of another kind when the sight of his parents quarreling causes Stephen to vomit—an indication of his emotional disturbance and, some psychologists would add, a symbolic rejection. "He stood still, doubled over, and all his body seemed to dissolve, sickly, from the pit of his stomach" (*LT*, 85).

The point of the story, the malformation of a child, is subtly contained in physical descriptions at beginning and end, in which bodily plasticity symbolizes the malleability of the soul. When his father lifts him into bed in the first scene he goes "limp as a rag for Papa to take him under the arms and swing him up over a broad, tough chest" (*LT*, 81). The description of him lying between his parents like "a bear cub in a warm litter" recalls the ancient superstition that bears licked their young into shape; a few moments later when his mother hugs him, his neck and shoulders are "quite boneless in her firm embrace" (*LT*, 82). In the course of the story Stephen moves from passivity to activity, and at the end the greater solidification of his nature is again reflected in physical description. (His lack of success in clay sculpture on his first day at school, when he tries to make a cat but ends up with a horse, echoes this malformation motif.) As they leave Grandmother's house Stephen's mother tells him that his father is waiting to see him. "He raised his head and put out his chin a little" and replied that he did not want to go home or see his father (*LT*, 110). As she drives home with angry speed he is almost flung out of the seat. "He sat braced then with all his might, hands digging into the cushions" (*LT*, 110). In this tense position he sings his song of rejection. Only after falling asleep does he relax and lean against his mother. With pathetic speed he has completed his trip along the downward path to wisdom.

Little need be said here about Miss Porter's next story, her second and last treatment of Irish family life. "A Day's Work" contains more unrelieved bitterness than any other story she has written. It is the example par excellence of the destructive union and of the degraded type of character who is doomed to remain in it. As in several other stories, the basic flaw in the marriage is a failure of communication rooted in the wife's religion-sanctioned frigidity. Like the husbands in "That Tree" and "Noon Wine," Halloran blames his wife for his failure to achieve success, ignoring his own laziness and incompetence. Like Rosaleen, another Irish dreamer, he refuses to face reality. With the help of the author's brilliant Irish dialogue—a ready vehicle for the story's heavy dramatic irony, filled as it is with comfortable stock phrases—he builds a dream world to compensate for his failure and thus confirms himself in it. The opening scene and his long meditation on the way to Billy's Place furnish numerous examples: McCorkery has "gone straight on up the ladder with Rosie," while he himself has gone "downward with Lacey Mahaffy" (*LT*, 121-22). He might have "cashed in on the numbers game with the best of them, . . . good quiet profit and none the wiser" (*LT*, 129-30). He still thinks that Mc-Corkery won't "forget an old friend," for "never did man deserve more of the world" than Halloran (*LT*, 130). McCorkery will give him a job with "nothing to it at all" for a man of his talents: he will "toss it off with one hand tied, and good money in it" (*LT*, 130-31). And so he keeps himself hypnotized with the mystic formulas of politics and the numbers racket. Lacey too has her language of self-justification, drawn from her Catholic training and shrunken to pharisaic righteousness by the complete evaporation of charity. She uses her piety to fight her husband and pass on bitterness to her daughter. Her telephone conversation with the latter, an evil link between the generations, provides a study in Miss Porter's frequent theme of the transmission of family corruption. She tells her daughter, as Halloran listens, "So now all you've got to do is stand by your married vows and make the best of it. . . . The woman has to do right first, and then if the man won't do right in turn it's no fault of hers" (*LT*, 120). She reports later to her husband, "I told her to bear with the trouble God sends as her mother did before her" (*LT*, 124).

Lacey is another in a long line of women who have derived from narrow religious training a fear of sex which foredooms their marriages and colors their entire outlook on life. She is also, like the wives in "That Tree" and "Noon Wine," a woman whose early-fading beauty constitutes one of the disillusions of marriage for her husband. Halloran refers to this in his imaginary talk with McCorkery:

Yes, but McCorkery, you forget that Lacey Mahaffy had legs and hair and eyes and a complexion fit for a chorus girl. But would she do anything with them? Never. Would you believe there was a woman wouldn't take off all her clothes at once even to bathe herself? What a hateful thing she was with her evil mind thinking everything was a sin, and never giving a man a chance to show himself a man in any way. But she's faded away now, her mean soul shows out all over her, she's ugly as sin itself now, McCorkery.

(*LT*, 131-32)

Lacey's comforting assurance of "doing right" enables her to judge and condemn others. Years before, after her husband had introduced her to McCorkery's wife Rosie, she had "turned upon him a face ugly as an angry cat's and said, 'She's a loose, low woman, and 'twas an insult to introduce her to me' " (*LT,* 119). Miss Porter's use of symbolism coupled with appropriateness in the naming of characters has been pointed out by James W. Johnson.[3] "Lacey," while perfectly suited to the setting, is a triumph of suggestiveness. Lace might have suited the early delicate beauty mourned by her husband, but it is hardly appropriate for the "scrawny strange woman" (*LT,* 116) she has become, except as it may refer to frayed edges or a sagging slip. It suggests the fancy feminine apparel she irons to support the family, such as the "salmon-colored chiffon nightgown with cream-colored lace and broad ribbons" over which she exclaims, "God's mercy, look at that indecent thing" (*LT,* 115), and perhaps even the altar lace related to her formalistic piety. At the climax of the story the real nature of Lacey's resentment exposes itself. When Halloran comes home drunk from his unsuccessful meeting with McCorkery and taunts her with soullessness, she cries, "Surely I have a soul and I'll save it yet in spite of you . . ." (*LT,* 140). He throws the iron and hits her, raising on her forehead a "great lumpy clout of flesh, . . . all colors" (*LT,* 142), then collapses on the bed. Methodically she wets a towel, ties knots in the end of it, and begins beating him in the face, repaying each of her grudges against him with a stroke, and finally coming to the deepest. " 'For your sock feet,' Mrs. Halloran told him, whack, 'and all your laziness, and this is for missing Mass and'—here she swung half a dozen times— 'that is for your daughter and your part in her' " (*LT,* 143). She has never forgiven her husband for violating her virginity. Finishing the job, she ties the wet towel around her head, "the knotted end hanging over her shoulder"—like a bridal veil.

Lacey's position is morally complex. She probably has kept her husband from a life of petty crime, and even he has admitted to himself that McCorkery's helpful wife Rosie is a low woman. It is precisely in this ostensible goodness that the irony of Lacey's viciousness lies. The damage she has done easily outweighs the good. This blend of outward goodness and inward destructiveness is brilliantly illuminated when the young policeman, scold-

3. "Another Look," p. 607.

ing the drunken Halloran, praises Lacey in one of his own stock phrases: " 'I knew her from old when I used to run errands for St. Veronica's Altar Society,' said the cop, 'and she was a great one, even then. Nothing good enough.' 'It's the same today,' said Mr. Halloran, almost sober for a moment" (*LT,* 139).

There are other instances of powerful irony. Halloran thinks admiringly, on the way to Billy's Place, that McCorkery, a "born judge of human nature," could "look a man over, size him up, and there was an end to it" (*LT,* 118), just before this great talent is turned against him. The central irony, emphasized by the story's title, is Lacey's belief at the end that Halloran, in spite of his drunkenness, at least has a job. There is irony also in the impressionistic descriptions of the onset of drunkenness from the point of view of Halloran, the victim—"Mr. Halloran reached for the bottle but it skipped sideways, rolled out of reach like a creature, and exploded at his feet. When he stood up the chair fell backward from under him. He leaned on the table and it folded up under his hands like cardboard" (*LT,* 136)—and of Lacey's transformation into a death figure as he enters the room drunk—"She was standing there before him in a kind of faded gingham winding sheet, with her dead hands upraised, her dead eyes blind but fixed upon him, her voice coming up hollow from the deep tomb, her throat thick with grave damp" (*LT,* 140).

The terrible power of this story results from the fact that its explicit theme corresponds exactly, at least in its central emotional force, to one of the fundamental motifs of the rejection theme. Subordinate themes of the story such as the destructive nature of narrow morality and the transmission of evil through the generations frequently accompany the rejection theme. Escape is impossible for this couple but Halloran asserts his desire for it vicariously by advising that his daughter escape from her unhappy marriage. Lacey, of course, favors perpetuation of the destructive union, and the story closes on a note of despair. And despair, though quite different in kind and scope, characterizes the story which follows.

The novelette which concludes and gives its name to Miss Porter's last book of short fiction, while it introduces new elements into her work, is close to the heart of her artistic vision and important in the study of the rejection theme. Its protagonist, although not a woman, is closely related to Miranda and is Miss Porter's fullest presentation of the protagonist as artist. The story covers a short period in the life of Charles Upton, a young artist from Texas visiting in the Berlin of 1931 in which Hitler is beginning his rise to power. It concentrates upon the atmosphere of the city and the character of the German people as seen by the young man. Its simple plot records a suicide attempt by a young German boarder in the house where Charles is staying, several conversations in the rooming house, and a long discussion of Germany, Europe, and America at a New Year's party in a newly-opened cabaret.

The story has several defects. Dramatically it is loose, with several barren stretches of discussion, and it contains suggestions of the travelogue. During the discussions of world affairs the language sometimes becomes formalized at the expense of verisimilitude and dramatic force, and the entire story suffers from a lack of humor. The Berliners are repeatedly portrayed as pig-like, malicious, and sentimental. Charles sketches many of them, emphasizing their unpleasant features; his suspicion that he is a caricaturist may be applied to the author as well. Her efforts to convey the impression of repulsiveness and evil portent cost too much in terms of realism. The leaning tower symbol is another defect; it is insufficiently integrated with its surroundings to represent them effectively, and excessive discussion and explanation of it dim the aura of mystery and suggestiveness which a symbol should possess. The meaning of the symbol is explored most thoroughly in the short closing scene in which Charles returns to his room drunk and sees it, repaired, in the corner cabinet, now protected from him by glass. The fragile tower is intended to represent the precarious German culture, once nearly destroyed by a crude America. Rather gratuitously it takes on for Charles obscure and frightening meanings:

Leaning, suspended, perpetually ready to fall but never falling quite, the venturesome little object—a mistake in the first place, a whimsical pain in the neck, really, towers shouldn't lean in the first place; a curiosity, like those cupids falling off the roof—yet had some kind of meaning in Charles' mind. Well, what? . . . What had the silly little thing reminded him of before? There was an answer if he could think what it was, but this was not the time. But just the same, there was something terribly urgent at work, in him or around him, he could not tell which. There was something perishable but threatening, uneasy, hanging over his head or stirring angrily, dangerously, at his back.

(LT, 245)

Reading this story, one cannot help but recall that it was published late in the Second World War, when anti-German feeling was high.[4] "The Leaning Tower" attempts to present a theme of world-wide scope in terms of personal relationships extended symbolically and explicitly. The extension is unsuccessful, for the author's power lies only in the portrayal of the individual and his immediate relationships. The closing section's solemn threats seem overblown as well as over-explicit.

"The Leaning Tower" belongs to that large American genre, the initiation story, and, more specifically, reflects in its broadest outlines the international theme treated by such diverse writers as James, Howells, and Hemingway. Charles is young and on his first trip away from home. His early actions and thoughts emphasize his naïveté: "He felt young, ignorant, awkward, he had so much to learn he hardly knew where to begin" (*LT,* 186). Tadeusz Mey, the urbane, cosmopolitan Pole, is like Charles a young man of good will, but his knowledge of the world and of European ways emphasizes the American's innocence. He becomes Charles's instructor, and his perceptive pupil matures

4. Even more relevant perhaps is a statement the author made to an interviewer in 1962 when asked about the relationship between Germans and *Ship of Fools:* " 'I believe,' Miss Porter said almost fiercely, 'that they are just as dangerous as they were, and the moment they get back their power they are going to do it again. This complacency about Germany is simply horrifying. People change in some ways, but they don't change basically. The Germans have taken the Jews as a kind of symbol, but they are against anybody and everybody, and they haven't changed a bit!' " (Quoted by Rochelle Girson in "The Author," *Saturday Review,* XLV [March 31, 1962], p. 15.)

fast. A passage near the end of the cabaret party reveals his new wisdom. He has just seen Lutte and feels strongly attracted to her:

And even at that moment, like the first symptoms of some fatal sickness, there stirred in him a most awful premonition of disaster, and his thoughts, blurred with drink and strangeness and the sound of half-understood tongues and the climate of remembered wrongs and hatreds, revolved dimly around vague remembered tales of Napoleon and Genghis Khan and Attila the Hun and all the Caesars and Alexander the Great and Darius and the dim Pharaohs and lost Babylon. He felt helpless, undefended, looked at the three strange faces near him and decided not to drink any more, for he must not be drunker than they; he trusted none of them.

(*LT*, 234)

Though he has been gradually prepared for this revelation, it is only when he feels himself most strongly attracted to Germany in the person of Lutte, the beautiful model, that he first senses his danger. He has already seen, in Rosa's special affection for Hans and her admiration for his *mensur* wound, that these Germans stick together; and he will soon have another lesson in the form of Lutte's preference for Hans over himself.

It gradually becomes clear that the characters of "The Leaning Tower" are designed with allegorical precision to represent larger political realities. Charles, the innocent American, thinks in terms of individuals rather than of nations. Certain that he will never be more than temporarily short of money, he yet cannot understand why the Germans consider him rich and dislike and exploit him accordingly. Except for the vague threats he is beginning to feel, he knows that his future is his own; he learns with surprise that Hans is content to follow his family's orders even in the matter of marriage. Throughout the story his individual experiences have generalizing overtones. In the multilingual Tadeusz he encounters the culture, historical sense, and disillusioned wisdom of Europe. Hans embodies the Germany of militarism, racist pride, and bitter resentment of defeat; his *mensur* wound, painful and festering, symbolizes well all these qualities and their combined unwholesomeness. The "amazing arrogance, pleasure, inexpressible vanity and self-satisfaction" (*LT,* 195) which Charles sees in the German's face when he speaks of his wound trouble him deeply. He sees the *mensur* custom as something which would be admired in no country but Germany, and he "rejects" the wound and all its meaning. It is one of the major causes of the ominous chill of death he feels in Berlin. Rosa is the Germany of sentimentalism and bitterly-felt poverty, strongly partial to the militaristic Hans. Lutte, the treacherous beauty certainly not typical of Germany yet a vessel of German pride, is also enamored of Hans. Otto Bussen represents the Germany of the scientist and scholar, and also of the peasant, driven to the point of suicide by the recent sufferings and present uneasiness of his country. He is, as Tadeusz points out, not very different from the peasants of other European nations. He is disdained by Hans and bullied by Rosa. Shy and devoted to study, he is capable of sudden transformation by the pleasures of beer and song. These characters contain other typical traits impossible to list here but clear in the story. In keeping with her usual practice, the author discusses the issues and meanings at length, usually through the mouths of characters.

Miss Porter directs much of her irony at the racial characteristics of the Germans. The following passage, in which Otto is speaking, is a sufficient example: " 'No matter how it came about,' he told them, 'the true great old Germanic type is lean and tall and fair as gods.' His forehead formed a deep wrinkle which sank to a meaty cleft between his brows. His small puffy eyes swam tenderly, the roll of fat across his collar flushed with emotion. 'We are not by any means all the pig type,' he said humbly, spreading his thick hands, 'though I know the foreign caricaturists make us all appear so' " (*LT,* 223-24).

The consciousness of death is an important thematic element in "The Leaning Tower," as it is in "Hacienda" and many other stories. Death is the ultimate meaning of the mysterious threat Charles feels in the air of Berlin and of the warlike instinct which seems to him to govern European developments. This latter point is made in one of his thoughts at the cabaret: "It seemed to him that the discussion was getting nowhere, and it reminded him of quarrels during his schooldays between the German boys and Mexican boys and the Kentucky boys; the Irish boys fought everybody, and Charles, who was partly Irish, remembered that he had done a good deal of fighting in which all sight of the original dispute had been lost in the simple love of violence" (*LT,* 225). Herr Bussen's suicide attempt concretely embodies the death theme and brings home to Charles the poverty and depression of the German people. It also illuminates character: Charles is concerned and practical enough to hurry out for medicine; Tadeusz is helpful and competent and the only person with the necessary insight to know with certainty that Bussen's act was deliberate; Rosa is emotional and possessive; Hans, unconcerned, leaves "coolly" to have his wound treated. It is at the news of the suicide attempt that Charles first feels the "chill and the knowledge of death" (*LT,* 245) which overcomes him at the end of the story.

"The Leaning Tower" belongs without doubt to the alpha branch of Miss Porter's work. Charles Upton is almost identical with Miranda in the essential qualities of artistic sensitivity, self-awareness, and insight into his surroundings, and like her he confronts the deepest mysteries. He is the fullest expression in all the stories of the alpha protagonist's artistic practice and point of view. His sketching is interchangeable with Miranda's writing in the sense that both involve an intensely aesthetic observation of other people, especially those most characteristic of the locale. There is nothing in the character of Charles which is essentially related to his masculinity except his brief and incidental interest in Lutte. It would seem that Miss Porter separated his identity from that of Miranda to enable her to deal with the German theme without the complications from the other stories which Miranda would necessarily bring with her. The use of a man in the part also provides a greater freedom of movement, facilitating contacts with the other typical characters with whom he must converse on more or less equal terms. The use of a woman in this typical-American role would have added numerous overtones without contributing to the central concern of the story. It can be said of "The Leaning Tower," as of some of the earlier stories, that it is more pattern than portrayal. Charles is present not primarily as an interesting and complex person but as a sensitive and intelligent observer. All the elements of the story— the simple and artificial plot, the diverse characters, the descriptions of setting—are subservient to theme. This theme is set forth clearly in conversations, corroborated by character and event, and embodied (with limited success) in a central symbol. In the Miranda stories, on the contrary, the theme is presented through the character of Miranda herself. The themes of all the other stories are personal, while that of "The Leaning Tower" is Miss Porter's one serious attempt to deal with a political subject. All these reasons and the additional one that Charles must show a naïveté not characteristic of Miranda, called for a male protagonist.

Different from Miranda in these necessary but superficial ways, Charles Upton yet has much in common with her. He is, aside from her and a few characters in *Ship of Fools*, the alpha protagonist whose biography is given in greatest detail. (Laura, of "Flowering Judas," ranks second in this respect.) This biography places Charles very close to the autobiographical Miranda. His home is San Antonio, Texas. Since he has to be rather young at the time of the story (1931), he is placed twelve to fourteen years behind Miranda, judging from the fact that when he was eight years old a "big war" was raging in Germany (*LT*, 152). His memories of his childhood home are for all practical purposes identical with hers. As he sits in a Berlin cafe he thinks, "Maybe I should have gone to Mexico. That's a good place for painters" (*LT*, 155). It can almost be said that Charles is unique among the alpha characters in the compassion he feels for people in difficulty; still, his interest in others seems to be, like Laura's and Miranda's, primarily aesthetic. He notices an emaciated beggar and "almost furtively" gives him a coin, then conceals himself and sketches the man (*LT*, 157). There is an interesting parallel between him and the heroine of "Theft": He "had never got into the habit of locking things" (*LT*, 176).

The aspect of the rejection theme most strongly emphasized in "The Leaning Tower" is, of course, the motif of oppression.

This thematic element is exactly parallel to the explicit theme of the story, the oppressiveness of pre-Nazi Germany. In terms of the other motifs of the theme, Charles escapes from the artistic barrenness of his home and country and, seeking the romantically ideal spot for his art work, goes to Berlin simply on the advice of his boyhood friend Kuno. The escape aspect of his trip to Europe is not emphasized in this story because it does not contribute to the explicit theme, which requires that Charles be seen as a representative and exponent of his country; yet he does advert to the fact that almost every American artist has gone to Europe. The few references to his family conform to the pattern by their negative tone. "He had thought, fitfully, of Kuno all that Christmas Eve, instead of his parents, who wrote long letters timed to reach him at the holiday saying how gloomy they would be without him. He had sent them a cable and had meant to think of them constantly, but he had not" (*LT,* 150). In Berlin he has been disillusioned, finding himself in another oppressive situation. He is comforted by the thought that he is relatively free to leave at any time and move on to other beckoning goals—Vienna, Rome, Paris—but his comfort is soon disturbed. He finds that the Berliners can impinge on his freedom by their demands that he show his papers or that he contract for his room for specified periods of time. Worse than this, he learns (and this is the essence of the central theme of the story—his initiation into the bitter knowledge of the mystery which is Germany) that there is no final escape for him. He is at the center of a number of concentric circles each of which is destructively oppressive—the hotel, Berlin, Europe, the world. Here are the last lines of the story: "There was something perishable but threatening, uneasy, hanging over his head or stirring angrily, dangerously, at his back. If he couldn't find out now what it was that troubled him so in this place, maybe he would never know. . . . But he didn't feel sorry for himself, and no crying jag or any other kind of jag would ever, in this world, do anything at all for him" (*LT,* 245-46). He has learned during one night in a "small, freshly painted, well lighted little place" (*LT,* 219) that the Europe which he had always considered so remote and peaceful is in reality a writhing tangle of hatred and violence, and that his own country, even the world, is part of this intricate network of evil.

The sense of isolation, that opposite side of the escape theme, would seem likely to predominate in the mind of a young man on his first visit abroad. Charles does feel this to some extent. He is lonely in crowds, and he pities the isolation of beggars. But usually his thoughts concern the oppressiveness of his situation. Almost every page of the story furnishes examples of the theme; the very language is filled with words which reflect it. Witness the opening lines: "Early one morning on his sixth day in Berlin, on the twenty-seventh of December, 1931, Charles Upton left his dull little hotel in Hedemanstrasse and escaped to the cafe across the street. The air of the hotel was mysteriously oppressive to him; a yellow-faced woman and an ill-tempered looking fat man were the proprietors, and they seemed to be in perpetual conspiracy. . . . His room was dark, airless, cold" (*LT,* 149). Darkness and cold, frequently emphasized, are objective correlatives of oppression, as is dullness—"The cafe was dull, too." The people, with their depressed air and hostile temper, are burdensome to Charles. A long string of salesladies and landladies impose upon him their greed and sentimentality so that he constantly feels guilty of some vague offense against them. The dull heaviness of the pig-like people weighs him down. After he escapes with great difficulty from his first hotel, he ends up in the barely tolerable house of Rosa Reichl, who annoys him by her intrusions into his privacy and tries to make him agree to stay for six months instead of three. Tadeusz, who is also conscious of the oppressiveness of the place, comments after Rosa has interrupted a conversation to tell them to go to bed, "You'd think we were living in a damnation jail, but all Berlin is just that" (*LT,* 199). Here is the real central image of the story: the damnation jail. Less explicit but much more effective than the artificial leaning tower symbol, it unites the motifs of oppression and death as they are often united in Miss Porter's work.

Berlin is oppressive for all the characters, even the Germans. No one praises Berlin, its weather, its culture, its dialect, or its people. All the outsiders seem to have come by accident like Charles, or under constraint, and to want to escape as soon as possible:

Hans said, "My father sent me here to see a doctor who is an old friend of his, but in ten days I shall be back in Heidelberg. The Polish fellow is a pianist so he came here because pianists seem to think old Schwartzkopf is the only Master. Herr Bussen, down the hall, he is Platt Deutsch to begin with and he lives in Dalmatia, so anything would perhaps be a change for the better to him. He thinks he is getting an education here and maybe he is. But look at you. A free man and you come to Berlin."

(*LT,* 191)

The nature of Berlin's effect on Charles is analyzed in great detail. He realizes that the weather, though unpleasant, is not the main trouble here. It is the faces, "with no eyes" and "shriveled as if they were gnawed hollow; or worse, faces sodden in fat with swollen eyelids in which the little no-eyes peered blindly as if all the food, the plates of boiled potatoes and pig's knuckles and cabbage fed to the wallowing body, had weighed it down and had done it no good" (*LT,* 184). Everywhere there is heaviness. Also, "the no-eyes in the faces of the women were too ready to shed tears" (*LT,* 184). There are the street vendors, silent, sullen, answering questions "as if in a burst of fury" (*LT,* 185). Houses and rooms are vulgarly ornate and cluttered with bric-a-brac. Rosa tells Charles that the happiest time of her life was spent in Italy; the value of the miniature leaning tower for her is its power to recall that distant time. The barber who cuts his hair speaks wistfully of Malaga. After the excitement over Herr Bussen's suicide attempt, Tadeusz suggests to Charles that they get drunk, then adds, "Seriously, I don't drink. But if I stayed too long in this place I would" (*LT,* 211). This provokes Charles into another attempt to analyze his impressions:

"It's getting me down, too, and I wish I knew why. Compared to really poor people, people I have seen, here and at home, even Herr Bussen is almost rich. Compared to even well-off people, I suppose I'm almost a pauper. But I never felt poor, I never was afraid of it. I always thought that if I really wanted money more than anything else, I could get it. But here—I don't know . . . everybody seems so *crowded,* somehow, so worried, and they can't get their minds off of money for a second."

(*LT,* 211)

Earlier, after an irritating talk with Herr Bussen, Charles had had similar thoughts. "The walls seemed to be closing in upon him, he imagined he could hear the breathing of those people in the other rooms, he smelt the iodoform on Hans' bandage, the spoiled sardines on Herr Bussen's breath, Rosa's sweetish female hysteria made him ill" (*LT,* 205). He gradually works off his anger by drawing caricatures of the people around him, beginning as he does so to feel more sympathetic toward them. "They were all good people, they were in terrible trouble, jammed up together in this little flat with not enough air or space or money, not enough of anything, no place to go, nothing to do but gnaw each other. I can always go home, he told himself, but why did I come here in the first place?" (*LT,* 205-6) It is impossible not to be struck by the feeling and imaginative vigor with which this author describes the hatefulness of being crowded.

The urge for escape always accompanies the sense of oppression, but escape is impossible for most of the people in the story. Real escape is, in fact, impossible for all of them, for the oppression which is now concentrated in Berlin is spreading to include the world. Even the Germans try unsatisfactory escapes—to the future, to the past, to study, to the mountains, to Hollywood—but all are at best temporary and despair prevails, even, apparently, over Charles. He does have a refuge from present troubles in his art, which is not an ignoble escape but a means whereby the artist transcends his personal concerns and achieves a deeper sympathy for others. It may start as venomous caricature but it requires a direct and unselfconscious gaze at the object which leads to understanding. The art theme is, however, only incidental in the story and seems to be swallowed up in the general despair. In his early dream of the burning house which looks like the leaning tower, Charles sees himself as escaping unharmed carrying a heavy suitcase containing "all the drawings he meant to do in his whole life" (*LT,* 188), but by the end of the story he has lost this naïve sense of detachment.

"The Leaning Tower" is not about art but about the modern world, and its message seems to be despair. Insofar as it is a political story its statement is largely justified by the war which followed; but the story never really functions on the political plane, and this fact is a key to its relative artistic failure. It conveys with strength the sense of strangeness and oppression suffered by an essentially isolated protagonist in an unfamiliar setting. It gives an impressionistic vision of Berlin but one marred by the tendentious distortions of caricature. It is unbalanced structurally by its subordination of every element to an overly ambitious semi-allegorical purpose. Awareness of the complex European situation, aside from theoretic discussion, never really enters the story. The strongly emphasized symbolic structure remains to a great extent emotionally uncharged, for the author's ability to concretize reality has never extended beyond the personal and immediate. It would seem that in "The Leaning Tower" Miss Porter has entrusted the creative act too extensively to the abstract intelligence, too little to that deep, inner way of working which has proved her only avenue to artistic success. That inner way of working, deeply personal as it is, deals in personal relationships and follows the pattern of the rejection theme.

4

The Miranda Stories

The Miranda stories contain Katherine Anne Porter's most personal work. For them she has created a type of thinly fictionalized autobiography different from the style of her other stories or that of any other author. The Miranda stories contain much of the author's best work, but they must be approached in their own proper way, not as one would approach a more conventional short story such as "Rope" or "He." The seven sketches—"The Source," "The Witness," "The Circus," "The Old Order," "The Last Leaf," "The Grave," "The Fig Tree"—and parts of "Old Mortality" are written in the form of a generalized narrative of recollection which reflects the orderly and apparently eternal quality of the old Southern life. These qualities are strongest in the first of the sketches, "The Source," which is built around the Grandmother and her annual whirlwind expedition from the town house to the old farm. "The Witness" and "The Last Leaf" are portraits of Uncle Jimbilly and Old Nannie, two aged family servants of the Grandmother's generation. Miranda plays the leading role in "The Circus,"

"The Grave," and "The Fig Tree," and appears incidentally elsewhere. As she progresses through the sketches their atmosphere changes. The impression of sacred order and decorum is somewhat diminished, and her reverence for the absolute authority of elders begins to waver. A comparison of the first sketch and the last reveals these changes symmetrically, as will be seen. Like most fiction about children or adolescents, the sketches constitute an initiation story. The three which feature Miranda record important discoveries about the elements of life—evil, sex, birth and death, the past, the insignificance of man.

The full pattern of the rejection theme does not appear in the sketches for they cover only the time of Miranda's girlhood, but the various motifs of the theme appear frequently in their language and the events they portray. The initiation process through which Miranda moves toward maturity is at the same time a preparation for the act of rejection by which she will before long declare her independence. In the early sketches she is just "one of the children." It is the Grandmother who dominates "The Source" and her servant Uncle Jimbilly who is "The Witness." In "The Circus" the Grandmother plays a lesser part but her authority is still evident. "The Old Order," the middle sketch of the seven, is a penetrating study of the Grandmother and of the society which produced her; it ends with her death, symbolic of the death of the old order. Old Nannie, her lifelong servant and companion, appears with her in that sketch and survives her to become "The Last Leaf." The last two sketches are devoted to Miranda. The sketches are not carefully chronological, for the Grandmother appears again in the last of them, "The Fig Tree," though the emphasis is on Miranda.

The first sketch portrays the Grandmother as the center of the family and its absolute authority. She appears in her elderly prime, still one of the absolutes around which the whole family revolves. "The Source" is a pleasant, nostalgic story of rural life in the old days. The farm, the source from which Miranda springs, is a microcosm of the Old South with its matriarchal domination; its loyal, undependable, comical Negroes; its orderly agrarian life. Although the author describes the Grandmother's domineering ways with gentle irony, it is clear that she has for her a respect and admiration with which she honors no other character in all her fiction, with the exception of Miranda. Not love—for she does not love any of them.

The style of "The Source" is perfectly sustained generalized narrative. There are no scenes, and the only plot is the rising and falling rhythm of the visit which unifies the sketch. Everything described is typical of all such visits; nothing is peculiar to one. The result of this technique is an impression of inviolable ritual order which exactly fits the situation, particularly as it is seen by the children. While the story is told as by an impersonal and slightly ironic observer, the point of view is subtly made to seem the children's by means of simple language, a semi-reverent attitude toward the Grandmother, and especially the four references to them. Each of the two sections opens with mention of the children. The first begins, "Once a year, in early summer, after school was closed and the children were to be sent to the farm, the Grandmother began to long for the country" (*LT*. 3); and the second, "If departure was a delightful adventure for the children, arriving at the farm was an event for Grandmother" (*LT*, 5). Their prompt obedience to her is explained as follows: "They loved their Grandmother; she was the only reality to them in a world that seemed otherwise without fixed authority or refuge, since their mother had died so early that only the eldest girl remembered her vaguely: just the same they felt that Grandmother was tyrant, and they wished to be free of her; so they were always pleased when, on a certain day, as a sign that her visit was drawing to an end, she would go out to the pasture and call her old saddle horse, Fiddler" (*LT*, 8). Although these references to the feelings of the children move the point of view toward them, they are left anonymous in this first sketch.

Accompanying the self-sufficient woman motif which dominates "The Source" are hints of the scorn for men which is its usual complement in the thematic pattern. Miranda and the other children never show much love or respect for their father. He is introduced as "her son, their father" (*LT*, 3), and is usually referred to condescendingly. It is clearly implied that he has little authority; it is the Grandmother who has a 'firm hold on family affairs" (*LT*, 3). A motif only remotely related to the rejection theme but prominent in the old order stories is the familiar Southern one of reverence for and attachment to the land as source and sustainer. With each visit to the farm the Grandmother feels "an indefinable sense of homecoming, not to the house but to the black, rich soft land and the human beings living on it" (*LT*, 5)—a somewhat aesthetic sense, incidentally. Among the other insights which the story furnishes into Southern culture is its reference to the "shabby old sets of Dickens, Scott, Thackeray, Dr. Johnson's dictionary, the volumes of Pope and Milton and Dante and Shakespeare" which were "dusted off and closed up carefully again" (*LT*, 7). The satisfaction shown in the annual cleaning rites recalls a lyric passage in "Hacienda":

Some day I shall make a poem to kittens washing themselves in the mornings; to Indians scrubbing their clothes to rags and their bodies to sleekness, with great slabs of sweet-smelling strong soap and wisps of henequen fiber, in the shade of trees, along river banks at midday; to horses rolling sprawling snorting rubbing themselves against the grass to cleanse their healthy hides; to naked children shouting in pools; to hens singing in their dust baths; to sober fathers of families forgetting themselves in song under the discreet flood of tap-water; to birds on the boughs ruffling and oiling their feathers in delight; to girls and boys arranging themselves like baskets of fruit for each other: to all thriving creatures making themselves cleanly and comely to the greater glory of life.

(*FJ*, 229-30)

This aesthetic love of purification is, as will be increasingly evident, closely related to the rejection theme. A large part of the meaning of "The Source" is just this pleasure in cleansing and renewal.

The shortest of the sketches, "The Witness," is a description of Uncle Jimbilly, an eccentric and picturesque old Negro who has been a family slave since the Grandmother's early days. Even more strictly than "The Source," this sketch adheres to the children's point of view. This is made clear by the extreme simplicity of the language and by such passages as the following, which, with skill and fine humor, records their thoughts as they sit listening to the old man's graphic descriptions of the horrors of slave days: "They knew, of course, that once upon a time Negroes had been slaves; but they had all been freed long ago and were now only servants. It was hard to realize that Uncle Jimbilly had been born in slavery, as the Negroes were always saying. The children thought that Uncle Jimbilly had got over his slavery very well. Since they had known him, he had never done a single thing that anyone told him to do" (*LT*, 15). The child's viewpoint is integral to the wonderfully graphic descriptions of the old man: "His hands were closed and stiff from gripping objects tightly, while he worked at them, and they could not open altogether even if a child took the thick black fingers and tried to turn them back. He hobbled on a stick; his purplish skull showed through patches in his wool, which had turned greenish gray and looked as if the moths had got at it" (*LT*, 13).

Miss Porter exhibits her usual talent for dialect: " 'Dey used to take 'em out and tie 'em down and whup 'em,' he muttered, 'wid gret big leather strops inch thick long as yo' ahm, wid round holes bored in 'em so's evey time dey hit 'em de hide and de meat done come off dey bones in little round chunks. And wen dey had whupped 'em wid de strop till dey backs was all raw and bloody, dey spread dry cawnshucks on dey backs and set 'em afire and pahched 'em, and den poured vinega all ovah 'em . . . Yassuh' " (*LT*, 14).

"The Witness" was called simply "Uncle Jimbilly" when it first appeared with "The Last Leaf" under the heading, "Two Plantation Portraits," in the *Virginia Quarterly Review* for January, 1935. The later title emphasizes the fact that the old Negro was a witness to the crime of the white man against the black in an earlier generation. His testimony is now delivered in a constant, barely audible mumble and is subject to fanciful exaggeration, yet this does not completely obscure its underlying seriousness, which even when conveyed in his "impersonal and faraway" tone causes the children "faint tinglings of embarrassment" (*LT*, 15). Uncle Jimbilly is a witness not only to slavery but to the past and its traditions—"He was very religious" (*LT*, 16)—and now he witnesses the early years of Miranda's life. It is in this brief sketch that she and her brother and sister are named and described. Maria is "a serious, prissy older girl of ten" with a "pleasant, mincing voice"; Paul is a "thoughtful sad looking boy of eight"; and Miranda a "quick flighty little girl of six" (*LT*, 14-15). Already Miranda is the spirited one, and her first stirrings of rejection may be seen here in the beginning of what will be a consistent absence of love in her references to the other members of her family. The "little quick one" is already living up to her name by showing an insistent desire to see and to know: She "wanted to know the worst" (*LT*, 15).

The South's ever-present sense of the past, only remote in "The Source," is here injected explicitly into the Miranda story. It will receive a more complex treatment in "The Old Order" and later stories. The children's practice of burying animals belongs to a motif that preoccupies the author in several stories —that of graves and excavations, with their implications of history and death—and is a clear link with the last of the sketches, "The Fig Tree."

Although "The Witness," primarily a character sketch, does not strongly embody any aspect of the rejection theme, echoes of it can be detected in the subject of slavery and the ubiquitous sense of death. The story also reflects the initiation theme, which is related to the pattern of rejection and disillusion. The descriptions of slavery give the children stirrings of guilt, and in the reference to Old Man Ronk they confront the mystery of human degradation. Uncle Jimbilly is here more a historical curiosity than the object of an Uncle Remus-type affection on the part of the children; but it is only later, in "The Last Leaf," that his embodiment of the theme of scorn for men is revealed through the contrast between his character and Old Nannie's, and her disdainful conduct toward him. It must be remembered here and in the discussion of each of the sketches that they function fully only when seen as parts of a whole. The present sketch contributes to the development of the rejection theme in ways which are not evident when it is studied alone.

"The Circus" is the first sketch in which Miranda plays a major part. In it she is quite young, and it records a stage in the process of her disillusionment or initiation into life. The largeness and intimacy of the family appear in the reunion which furnishes the occasion for attending the circus. It occupies "almost a whole section on one level" (*LT,* 21), but this mighty presence is only a backdrop for the painful experience Miranda undergoes as it were in solitude. In her fright at the clown's danger she derives no comfort from the fact that her family surrounds her. When the day's horrors return to her in a dream and she is "completely subjugated by her fears" (*LT,* 28), in her blind need for companionship she turns to the person nearest, Dicey, who is least bound to her by ties of blood and who stays with her more out of duty than affection. In other words, even while she is in the midst of her large and closely-knit family, Miranda is beginning, at this early age, and more instinctively than deliberately, to go her solitary way and endure her sufferings alone. This trend will never be reversed.

The author's careful adherence to the child's point of view is especially important in this story because its whole significance lies in the way things appear to Miranda. The dimensions, sounds, smells, and colors within the immense circus tent overwhelm her, forming a grotesque new world to contain the shattering experiences she is about to have. "An enormous brass band seemed to explode right at Miranda's ear. She jumped, quivered, thrilled blindly and almost forgot to breathe as sound and color and smell rushed together and poured through her skin and hair and beat in her head and hands and feet and pit of her stomach. . . . The flaring lights burned through her lids, a roar of laughter like rage drowned out the steady raging of the drums and horns" (*LT,* 23). She doesn't know the name "clown"; if she did she would not be so distressed at the antics of one. She sees him as "a creature in a blousy white overall with ruffles at the neck and ankles" (*LT,* 23). From the first he suggests death to her, with his "bone-white skull and chalk-white face" (*LT*, 23). Her innocent fancy is ready to accept a man walking on air, but when she sees that he is earthbound like other men and that his life depends on a tiny wire she is terrified. She takes things seriously:

He paused, slipped, the flapping white leg waved in space; he staggered, wobbled, slipped sidewise, plunged, and caught the wire with frantic knee, hanging there upside down, the other leg waving like a feeler above his head; slipped once more, caught by one frenzied heel, and swung back and forth like a scarf. . . The crowd roared with savage delight, shrieks of dreadful laughter like devils in delicious torment . . . The man on the wire, hanging by his foot, turned his head like a seal from side to side and blew sneering kisses from his cruel mouth.

(*LT*, 23-24)

A dwarf who suddenly assumes "a look of haughty, remote displeasure, a true grown-up look" (*LT*, 25), chills Miranda with "a new kind of fear" and a lesson in human deformity.

The explicit theme of "The Circus" is Miranda's initiation into a new dimension of experience and her failure to cope with it satisfactorily because of her inability to distinguish illusion from reality. Her slight brush with the mystery of sex in the form of boys looking up through the bleachers is also beyond her understanding at this early age. The result of her day at the circus is fear, which in itself is both ordeal and mystery—an initiation process and also a permanent and inseparable part of life. The episode reveals more fully Miranda's evolving character. Loyal to her name, she "could not look hard enough at everything." Even at the boys beneath the bleachers she "gazed and gazed, trying to understand it" (*LT*, 22). She is nervous, impressionable, sensitive above the average, and the circus experience has a profound effect on her. Previously she had been indifferent to the disfavor of most of her elders, but now she feels the need for protection and knows she must avoid offending those from whom she wants it. Miranda's circus experience leaves her more aware of self and ready to supply her own needs, and also quicker to detect illusion. It is a step toward that wisdom which lies at the end of a downward path.

This is the Grandmother's first circus too, and her attitude toward it reveals a wisdom and moral certitude lacking in the younger generation. She is the only one who at first opposes Miranda's going, and the outcome seems to prove her right. "Her son Harry," Miranda's father, continues to appear in an unfavorable light. Almost like another child, he teases Miranda and makes her cry. When he counters the Grandmother's criticism of the effect of circuses on the young by saying superficially, "This basket of young doesn't seem to be much damaged," she replies in words which demand respect: "The fruits of their present are in a future so far off, neither of us may live to know whether harm has been done or not. That is the trouble" (*LT*, 27). A lack of sympathy between Miranda and the other children is once more suggested by the way they tease her "with malicious eyes" and smile at her with pity, telling her all she has missed. The sense of loss is strong for Dicey as they leave the circus and later for Miranda when she hears all the wonders she has missed. "Ah, what she had not missed" (*LT*, 26). The sense of loss is also strong in the next sketch, but there it is the Grandmother's. Hardly in evidence in "The Circus," she returns to dominate "The Old Order," in which Miranda does not even appear.

"The Old Order" is the heart of the sketches. It is by far the longest of those that appeared in *The Leaning Tower* and occupies the middle position if "The Fig Tree" (the almost equal length of which may be owing to its later revision) be added as the last sketch. With a deeply penetrating glance it surveys the lives of the Grandmother and Old Nannie, who together typify their society. The title is taken from a poem no doubt popular in their day, Tennyson's *Idylls of the King:*

> The old order changeth, yielding place to new,
> And God fulfills Himself in many ways,
> Lest one good custom should corrupt the world.

Even during her life the Grandmother sees the old order crumbling, though she and Nannie are loath to admit it. She has seen how her children "went about their own affairs, scattering out and seeming to lose all that sense of family unity" so precious to her (*LT,* 55). An element of corruption has been passed from generation to generation. No matter how strictly they were raised, the children, especially the sons, usually turned out spoiled; and she saw "the confusion growing ever deeper" (*LT,* 51).

"The Old Order" is composed mostly of generalized narrative describing the long daily conversations between the aged Grandmother and her Negro companion. The style is quietly reminiscent with only touches of irony—not too unlike that of the essay in *The Days Before* entitled "Portrait: Old South." The old women have one topic.

They talked about the past, really—always about the past. Even the future seemed like something gone and done with when they spoke of it. It did not seem an extension of their past, but a repetition of it. They would agree that nothing remained of life as they had known it, the world was changing swiftly, but by the mysterious logic of hope they insisted that each change was probably the last; or if not, a series of changes might bring them, blessedly, back full-circle to the old ways they had known.

(*LT,* 35-36)

Occasionally their reminiscence slips into anecdote and this into dramatized scene. Only one scene is dramatized at length: the purchase of Nannie and her parents by the father of the Grandmother when the latter was "Miss Sophia Jane, a prissy, spoiled five-year-old" (*LT,* 39). This episode, important as marking the beginning of their relationship and also as a comment on slavery, is first described objectively, then seen from the point of view of Nannie, whose perfect memory for past scenes complements the Grandmother's recollection of dates.

The multiplicity of functions of the scene mentioned above is a good illustration of one of the finest qualities of this story and many of Miss Porter's other works: the economy with which they pack a richness of content into their limited space. It is difficult to believe that so much depth and detail could be included in slightly over twenty pages. Part of the explanation lies in the fact that each character and episode is typical. The ease with which the narrative maneuvers in time, furthermore, compresses history and gives an effect of fullness and complexity. A symbolic quality inheres not only in characters and events but also in certain objects. There is a natural symbolism in the old ladies' occupation of making patchwork out of old family finery. This work is a perfect objective equivalent of their conversation, which takes scattered events from memory, arranges them together in a "carefully disordered patchwork," and lays them away again, since they are of no use or interest to the younger generation. Patchwork covers are made to enshrine family relics, the most important of which—the holy of holies—is a rolling pin carved for his wife by their most illustrious ancestor. "This rolling pin was the Grandmother's irreplaceable treasure. She covered it with an extraordinarily complicated bit of patchwork, added golden tassels to the handles, and hung it in a conspicuous place in her room" (*LT,* 33).

Since the Grandmother personifies the old order, the author analyzes the entire culture by analyzing her. First of all, her external history is recorded in considerable detail. She was "the great-granddaughter of Kentucky's most famous pioneer" and the daughter of a "notably heroic captain in the War of 1812" (*LT,* 33). At seventeen she had been married to a second cousin, and she bore eleven children of whom nine survived. Her husband fought in the Civil War and died some years later of his wound. With his wife's money he had bought a sugar refinery in Louisiana, so after his death she moved there with her family. She bought a house and planted an orchard but soon saw that the refinery was a failure. Selling out at a loss she moved to Texas, where her husband had also bought land, taking her nine children, "the youngest about two, the eldest about seventeen years old; Nannie and her three sons, Uncle Jimbilly, and two other Negroes, all in good health, full of hope and greatly desiring to live" (*LT,* 53). The first years in Texas were hard. She built a large house and planted a farm. By the time her children began to marry she was able to start them off reasonably well with gifts of land and money. The children scattered and occasionally she visited them. When her son Harry's wife died at the birth of her third child, Miranda, the Grandmother raised the children. Before Miranda was nine years old the Grandmother died while on a visit to her third son and his family in far western Texas. She had spent a day working in the garden and "came into the house quite flushed and exhilarated, saying how well she felt in the bracing mountain air—and dropped dead over the doorsill" (*LT*, 56).

It is not these external events, however, which are the heart of "The Old Order." The sketch makes much more significant observations about the life of those days in the South by probing deeply into the heroine's mind and spirit, showing how she was formed at this deeper level by the events of her life and the culture in which she lived. The picture is not a pleasant one. Its external essentials are contained in a masterful summary early in the story:

Who knows why they loved their past? It had been bitter for them both, they had questioned the burdensome rule they lived by every day of their lives, but without rebellion and without expecting an answer. This unbroken thread of inquiry in their minds contained no doubt as to the utter rightness and justice of the basic laws of human existence, founded as they were on God's plan; but they wondered perpetually, with only a hint now and then to each other of the uneasiness of their hearts, how so much suffering and confusion could have been built up and maintained on such a foundation. The Grandmother's role was authority, she knew that; it was her duty to portion out activities, to urge or restrain where necessary, to teach morals, manners, and religion, to punish and reward her own household according to a fixed code. Her own doubts and hesitations she concealed, also, she reminded herself, as a matter of duty. Old Nannie had no ideas at all as to her place in the world. It had been assigned to her before birth, and for her daily rule she had all her life obeyed the authority nearest to her.

(*LT*, 36)

This was the old order. It was according to this scheme that the Grandmother herself had been raised, and she endeavored to impose it on the next generation, never doubting seriously that it was correct and indeed absolute. She could not help seeing that there were flaws. The children, for example, seldom seemed to turn out very well. She agreed in essence with Nannie's estimate of the younger generation: "Wuthless, shiftless lot, jes plain scum, Miss Sophia Jane; I cain't undahstand it aftah all the raisin' dey had" (*LT,* 38). But about the manner of this "raisin' " they admitted no doubts:

> They talked about religion, and the slack way the world was going nowadays, the decay of behavior, and about the younger children, whom these topics always brought at once to mind. On these subjects they were firm, critical, and unbewildered. They had received educations which furnished them an assured habit of mind about all the important appearances of life, and especially about the rearing of young. They relied with perfect acquiescence on the dogma that children were conceived in sin and brought forth in iniquity. Childhood was a long state of instruction and probation for adult life, which was in turn a long, severe, undeviating devotion to duty, the largest part of which consisted in bringing up children. The young were difficult, disobedient, and tireless in wrongdoing, apt to turn unkind and undutiful when they grew up, in spite of all one had done for them, or had tried to do: for small painful doubts rose in them now and again when they looked at their completed works.
>
> (*LT,* 38)

There is an indication of at least one of the flaws in the system in the description of the Grandmother's method of punishing her two sons who ran away during the "terrible second year in Texas." "Miss Sophia Jane went through the dreary ritual of discipline she thought appropriate to the occasion. She whipped them with her riding whip. Then she made them kneel down with her while she prayed for them, asking God to help them mend their ways and not be undutiful to their mother; her duty performed, she broke down and wept with her arms around them" (*LT,* 53-54). The author comments on the method's effectiveness. "They had endured their punishment stoically, because it would have been disgraceful to cry when a woman hit them, and besides, she did not hit very hard; they had knelt with her in a shamefaced gloom, because religious feeling was a female mystery which embarrassed them, but when they saw her tears they burst into loud bellows of repentance" (*LT,* 54).

Already their maleness has removed them almost completely from their mother's control.

The crucial question of slavery seems not to have bothered the Grandmother seriously. It was simply part of that eternal system which gave her only an occasional doubt. When Nannie asked, as she often did, why God was so hard on a certain race because of the color of its skin, and whether discrimination would continue in the next life, Miss Sophia Jane "was always brisk and opinionated about it: 'Nonsense! I tell you, God does not know whether a skin is black or white. He sees only souls. Don't be getting notions, Nannie—of course you're going to Heaven' " (*LT,* 51). Thus does she separate God completely from the social order. Nannie's views on slavery are quite superficial. "She was wounded not so much by her state of being as by the word describing it," and her first free act was to tell her mistress proudly, "I aim to stay wid you as long as you'll have me" (*LT,* 50). Nannie has lived with her mistress on "almost equal terms." In short, their relationship is typical of the best possible under the old order; yet the author makes clear her condemnation of slavery. It would be strange indeed if one who so bitterly detests oppression had not condemned it.

In portraying the type of woman who could live such a life, the story goes far beyond externals. As the woman is the center of the family and the family the basis of Southern society, so the center of the woman herself is her love. It is precisely here that Miss Porter finds the flaw around which everything crystallized: the Grandmother never achieved a real and satisfying union, spiritually or physically, with her husband. This failure and its implications are explored through the author's comment, dramatized, and powerfully symbolized. The Grandmother's attitudes toward marriage and sex are first revealed after the wedding of her youngest son, while she and Nannie are riding home. The sight of her self-possessed new daughter-in-law has led her to some apprehensive thoughts about the "new" woman who is "beginning to run wild, asking for the vote, leaving her home and going out in the world to earn her own living." "The Grandmother's narrow body shuddered to the bone at the thought of women so unsexing themselves; she emerged with a start from the dark reverie of foreboding thoughts which left a bitter taste in her throat" (*LT,* 45). The author's condemnation of this archaic view is obvious. Her own Miranda will soon be one of these "new women." Here, ironic light is directed at the fact that this old woman who is disapproving of others "unsexing" themselves has herself led an unsexed life and is by no means free from the subconscious effects of it. There follows a long discussion of various aspects of her sex life and marriage. Both she and Nannie were "married off" at the age of seventeen, neither marriage having the appearance of being based on love. The bearing of children was for them a "grim and terrible race of procreation, a child every sixteen months or so, with Nannie nursing both, and Sophia Jane, in dreadful discomfort, suppressing her milk with bandages and spirits of wine" (*LT,* 46). When Nannie almost died of puerperal fever, Sophia Jane nursed Nannie's child with her own, in spite of strong protests from husband and mother. "She had learned now that she was badly cheated in giving her children to another woman to feed; she resolved never again to be cheated in just that way. She sat nursing her child and her foster child, with a sensual warm pleasure she had not dreamed of, translating her natural physical relief into something holy, God-sent, amends from heaven for what she had suffered in childbed. Yes, and for what she missed in the marriage bed, for there also something had failed" (*LT,* 46-47). Here, certainly, is the crucial fact in the formation of this typical woman of the old order. The little satisfaction she does receive from the entire process of marriage and motherhood is related not to her husband but to her children. All else is pain and frustration, leading at best to indifference, at worst to a deep and ever-growing resentment against her husband and all men. With this as a foundation she is inclined never to excuse, always to exaggerate their faults. And of faults there are an abundance, since they have been spoiled by mothers who, like this one, let a compensatory sentimental love for their children undermine the strict code by which they attempted to raise them. But even the love which the Grandmother feels for the children, both white and black, whom she has nursed seems a strangely cold thing unlikely to violate her integrity. Its result is simply the spoiling of her own son and probably of the Negro boy too, for he "was brought up in the house as playmate for her son Stephen, and exempted from hard work all his life" (*LT,* 47).

The roots of her failure in the marriage bed, which extend far into the past, are traced to some extent in subsequent pages. During her late girlhood, while her officially affianced "lover" was away at school and on his travels, she was "gay and sweet and decorous, full of vanity and incredibly exalted daydreams which threatened now and again to cast her over the edge of some mysterious forbidden frenzy." This stage in her life is described delicately and profoundly.

She dreamed recurrently that she had lost her virginity (her virtue, she called it), her sole claim to regard, consideration, even to existence, and after frightful moral suffering which masked altogether her physical experience she would wake in a cold sweat, disordered and terrified. She had heard that her cousin Stephen was a little "wild," but that was to be expected. He was leading, no doubt, a dashing life full of manly indulgences, the sweet dark life of the knowledge of evil which caused her hair to crinkle on her scalp when she thought of it. Ah, the delicious, the free, the wonderful, the mysterious and terrible life of men! She thought about it a great deal. "Little daydreamer," her mother or father would say to her, surprising her in a brown study, eyes moist, lips smiling vaguely over her embroidery or her book, or with hands fallen on her lap, her face turned away to a blank wall. She memorized and saved for these moments scraps of high-minded poetry, which she instantly quoted at them when they offered her a penny for her thoughts; or she broke into a melancholy little song of some kind, a song she knew they liked. She would run to the piano and tinkle the tune out with one hand, saying, "I love this part best," leaving no doubt in their minds as to what her own had been occupied with. She lived her whole youth so, without once giving herself away; not until she was in middle age, her husband dead, her property dispersed, and she found herself with a houseful of children, making a new life for them in another place, with all the responsibilities of a man but with none of the privileges, did she finally emerge into something like an honest life: and yet, she was passionately honest. She had never been anything else.

(*LT,* 48-49)

This concentrated description of the inner life of a young girl of the old order indicates some of the ways in which her training distorted her developing instincts and helped prepare for a life of frustration: the absolute value placed on "virtue," irrecoverable once lost, by the code of Southern purity (for women); the air of mystery and evil, and the consequent fear and guilt, which resulted from the complete parental silence about sex; the sentimentalizing and falsifying of emotion caused by its forceful separation from reality. There is rich ambiguity in the statement that she lived her whole youth "without once giving herself away." She never gave away her innermost secrets even to herself, for the "dishonesty" which characterized her succeeding years was mostly unconscious. But the most important fact about this woman was that she never really gave herself away in love, with the result that her marriage was not an enrichment but a bitter violation of self, and hence necessarily a failure—one made doubly bitter by its destruction of her early unrealistic dreams. The Grandmother emerged from this failure cold and resentful toward men but with her natural strength and self-sufficiency redoubled, and it was upon this foundation that she built the partially honest life of her mature years. Only then did her inner motives become at least somewhat parallel to her outer, conscious life, which had always been "passionately honest" with an intense striving for outer truth deriving from her obscure inner sense of discord.

The Grandmother's transition to a more integrated life seems to have been related to the occasion when the two boys tried to run away. When they gave as their motive the desire to go to Louisiana to eat sugar cane, she suddenly realized how hard her children had been working and how hungry they were. With this thought "she felt her heart break in her breast." The author elaborates on the effects: "It was not that she was incapable of feeling afterward, for in a way she was more emotional, more quick, but griefs never again lasted with her so long as they had before. This day was the beginning of her spoiling her children and being afraid of them" (*LT*, 55). Apparently the increased "honesty" of her life was not so much a surface change as a hardening of those deep emotions involved in the sexual yearnings which had never been satisfied or even fully admitted. This profound disillusion with life seems to have weakened the emotional link which bound her to her children in a beneficent sternness so that afterwards she was activated by a shallower love, by awe at their separateness from her, and perhaps by a sense of guilt at the hardships she had necessarily inflicted upon them.

Whatever the exact development in her soul, she retained a hidden feeling that life had cheated her of something. This is revealed in the symbolism which concludes the description of her sexual fancies and repressions.

> Sitting under the trees with Nannie, both of them old and their long battle with life almost finished, she said, fingering a scrap of satin, "It was not fair that Sister Keziah should have had this ivory brocade for her wedding dress, and I had only dotted swiss . . ."
>
> "Times was harder when you got married, Missy," said Nannie. "Dat was de yeah all de crops failed."
>
> "And they failed ever afterward, it seems to me," said Grandmother.
>
> "Seems to me like," said Nannie, "dotted swiss was all the style when you got married."
>
> "I never cared for it," said Grandmother.
>
> (*LT*, 50)

"The Old Order" is the *locus classicus* for the characterization of the strong, independent woman and the concomitant motif of scorn for men. A particularly pure embodiment of these themes is found in the wedding of the Grandmother's youngest son to the daughter of a West Texas rancher. The Grandmother, riding home from the affair, has been thinking about losing another son—as usual, to a girl of whom she cannot fully approve. The author comments:

> The Grandmother had always had in mind the kind of wife each of her sons needed; she had tried to bring about better marriages for them than they had made for themselves. They had merely resented her interference in what they considered strictly their personal affairs. She did not realize that she had spoiled and pampered her youngest son until he was in all probability unfit to be any kind of a husband,

much less a good one. And there was something about her new daughter-in-law, a tall, handsome, firm-looking young woman, with a direct way of speaking, walking, talking, that seemed to promise that the spoiled Baby's days of clover were ended. The Grandmother was annoyed deeply at seeing how self-possessed the bride had been, how she had had her way about the wedding arrangements down to the last detail, how she glanced now and then at her new husband with calm, humorous, level eyes, as if she had already got him sized up.

(*LT,* 44-45)

The point here is not the function of this passage in the context of the story, but simply the zest with which the characterizations are made. And this is typical. Almost every woman the author portrays with real interest and fullness is "self-possessed," and most of her men, especially those associated with her major heroines, are spoiled babies. Miranda's attitudes toward men will be seen principally in "Old Mortality" and "Pale Horse, Pale Rider," but the Grandmother's is expounded here, and there is certainly no doubt about it. She was the center of authority and held full responsibility for "her tangled world, half white, half black, mingling steadily and the confusion growing ever deeper" (*LT,* 51); and the strain of worrying over whether the babies borne by the Negro women had been fathered by black men or white ended by giving her "a deeply grounded contempt for men. She could not help it, she despised men. She despised them and was ruled by them. Her husband threw away her dowry and her property in wild investments in strange territories: Louisiana, Texas; and without protest she watched him play away her substance like a gambler" (*LT,* 51-52). Later, when she "got the reins in her hands" (*LT,* 52), she let herself be persuaded into things by her sons, and "among them they managed to break up once more the stronghold she had built for the future of her family. They got from her their own start in life, came back for fresh help when they needed it, and were divided against each other" (*LT,* 52). The author goes to great lengths in joining the reaction against romantic Civil War literature. Her succinct comment on Miranda's grandfather and every other man who was wounded in the war is simply that they proved themselves "more heroic than wise" (*LT*, 52). When Grandmother's husband eventually died of the wound received in the war "she was bitterly outraged by his death almost as if he had willfully deserted her. She mourned for him at first with dry eyes, angrily" (*LT*, 53). Not only the Grandmother's opinion but the entire content of "The Old Order" follows this pattern which has been observed running through all the author's works. The only portrayals of men are the following: Sophia Jane's father and others, buying and selling slaves like animals; the old Judge presiding at the wedding, where he "reeked of corn liquor, swore by God every other breath," and offended Nannie by recalling her as a "strip of crowbait" (*LT*, 43); the Grandmother's two boys, running away from her; the son at whose home she was to die, consoling his wife by telling her that every change his mother has made will be restored to normal after she has gone. The heroine's dim view of the other sex is not limited to a few individuals or to one generation; she saw in her husband

all the faults she had most abhorred in her elder brother: lack of aim, failure to act at crises, a philosophic detachment from practical affairs, a tendency to set projects on foot and then leave them to perish or to be finished by someone else; and a profound conviction that everyone around him should be happy to wait upon him hand and foot. She had fought these fatal tendencies in her brother, within the bounds of wifely prudence she fought them in her husband, she was long after to fight them again in two of her sons and in several of her grandchildren. She gained no victory in any case, the selfish, careless unloving creatures lived and ended as they had begun.

(LT, 47-48)

The Grandmother's strength of character is emphasized repeatedly. Even early in her marriage she is described as "stubborn," having "already begun to develop her implicit character, which was altogether just, humane, proud, and simple" (*LT*, 46). She was not entirely without faults, however, as the author goes on to show: "She had many small vanities and weaknesses on the surface: a love of luxury and a tendency to resent criticism. This tendency was based on her feeling of superiority in judgment and sensibility to almost everyone around her. It made her very hard to manage. She had a quiet way of holding her ground which convinced her antagonist that she would really die, not just threaten to, rather than give way" (*LT,* 46). One wonders just which of her associates it was who rivaled her in judgment and sensibility.

The theme of the oppressive union is implicit throughout "The Old Order." The impression given is that the heroine found her society—that is, her family, "black and white," through her generation and the two following—predominantly burdensome, to use a mild term; and that it was only her great strength of character that enabled her to endure into a vigorous old age. Most oppressive of all was her own marriage, but from the beginning, at least in her deepest self, she "rejected" her husband. Before too many years she "escaped" from him by his death. She resented his leaving her his share of the work and his heritage of financial blunders, but that seems to have been almost the full extent of her feelings about him. In general, there is little evidence of love in "The Old Order." Certainly there is no instance of real love between two fully portrayed characters. The nearest thing to it is the companionship between the Grandmother and Nannie, and for this union the term "love" is explicitly rejected. Further light is thrown upon this companionship in the sketch which follows "The Old Order" and is closely related to it.

"The Last Leaf" is a pleasant, sympathetic portrait of Old Nannie, the last important survivor of the Grandmother's generation. Having by long and intimate association come to share some of the dignity of her mistress, she is here shown emerging into her "serene idleness" (*LT,* 60). This episode illustrates with perfect clarity the thematic pattern of the independent woman's escape by rejection of the oppressive union. On Nannie's simple level the oppression has been in the form of hard work which at last almost literally breaks her back. There is little love on either side. Though the children say, "We love you," they thoughtlessly continue to increase her burdens, comforting themselves with that sentimentality which in the old order was so frequently made to do for love. But

Nannie has finally reached that rare eminence at which she can be indifferent to love. The children, surprised and rather hurt by her sudden assertion of independence, find it "almost funny and certainly very sweet to see how she tried not to be too happy the day she left," but feel "rather put upon, just the same" (*LT,* 60).

"The Last Leaf" reveals how Nannie long ago made good her escape from another union which was, if not oppressive, at least indifferent to her. The man to whom she had been "married off" at the age of seventeen was Uncle Jimbilly. They had had thirteen children, nine of whom had died while they were still living in Kentucky, and after this period of reproduction had ended, the two had drifted apart. After Nannie has moved into her own cabin and is sitting on the porch smoking her pipe, Uncle Jimbilly wanders up and shows an inclination to stay. True to the pattern and to the example of her mistress, she turns him away with a rejection which seems to extend to the entire male sex: " 'I don' aim to pass my las' days waitin on no man, I've served my time, I've done my do, and dat's all.' So Uncle Jimbilly crept back up the hill and into his smoke-house attic, and never went near her again . . ." (*LT,* 63).

This sketch contains, in a few short but vivid details, almost the only physical description of Nannie. She is "tall and thin" with a "nobly modeled Negro face, worn to the bone and a thick fine sooty black" (*LT,* 59). It is mentioned that in former days, when Mister Harry argued with her about some petty thing, "she could always get the better of him by slapping her slatty old chest with the flat of her long hand and crying out: 'Why, Mister Harry, you, ain't you shamed to talk lak dat to me? I nuhsed you at dis bosom!' " (*LT,* 64) Much of the economical description of the old woman serves the purpose, in addition to describing her, of emphasizing her nobility and independence by alluding to her racial origins. "She was no more the faithful old servant Nannie, a freed slave: she was an aged Bantu woman of independent means, sitting on the steps, breathing the free air" (*LT,* 61).

"The Last Leaf" gives a new perspective to the sketches by

assuming, in a few short passages, the viewpoint of the children and of Harry, their father. The effect of this is a sense of the passing of time and of intimacy with, and sympathy for, the new generation, in spite of their faults. Their feelings are briefly mentioned when Nannie first announces her desire to move out. After she is gone they realize how much she has done for them because now "everything slackened, lost tone, went off edge. . . . They had not learned how to work for themselves, they were all lazy and incapable of sustained effort or planning. They had not been taught and they had not yet educated themselves" (*LT,* 61-62). In their little disputes in former days Harry had always given in to Nannie, crying,

"All right, Mammy, all right, for God's sake!"—precisely as he said it to his own mother, exploding in his natural irascibility as if he hoped to clear the air somewhat of the smothering matriarchal tyranny to which he had been delivered by the death of his father. Still he submitted, being of that latest generation of sons who acknowledged, however reluctantly, however bitterly, their mystical never to be forgiven debt to the womb that bore them, and the breast that suckled them.

(*LT,* 64-65)

These lines do not flatter Harry but they do arouse some sympathy for him. With this subtle shift in point of view it may be said that the dominance of the Grandmother has ended. In "The Grave" interest returns to Miranda, and with her it stays.

"The Grave" is the finest of the sketches. Like "The Circus" and "The Fig Tree," it recounts one episode in Miranda's life; but of the three "The Grave" is the most fully realized and richly suggestive. Though slightly longer than "The Circus," which covers perhaps half a day, it describes events which might easily have occurred within the space of an hour. These events are of the greatest simplicity, beautifully true to reality, and are portrayed with such minute honesty that they come closer to perfection than any other passage of comparable length in Miss Porter's writings. This sketch is the best example of her ability to find and present natural symbols. The truest meanings come not from contrived symbolism—even from such relatively modest symbols as the dove and the ring in "The Grave"—but from rightly selected and honestly, lovingly presented reality. In an early critical study of Miss Porter's work, Lodwick Hartley makes the following perceptive statement: "The greatest gift of Miss Porter is her consummate mastery of detail. Whatever may be her structural or emotional limitations, she has the uncanny power of evoking richness from minutiae. The gift is manifested everywhere in her work, but no more astonishing bit of observation can be found than in "The Grave," a simple and tremendously powerful little story of two children's contact with the mysteries of life and death."[1] He then quotes from the following passage describing the examination of the rabbit Miranda's brother has just shot:

The children knelt facing each other over the dead animal. Miranda watched admiringly while her brother stripped the skin away as if he were taking off a glove. The flayed flesh emerged dark scarlet, sleek, firm; Miranda with thumb and finger felt the long fine muscles with the silvery flat strips binding them to the joints. Brother lifted the oddly bloated belly. "Look," he said, in a low amazed voice. "It was going to have young ones."

Very carefully he slit the thin flesh from the center ribs to the flanks, and a scarlet bag appeared. He slit again and pulled the bag open, and there lay a bundle of tiny rabbits, each wrapped in a thin scarlet veil. The brother pulled these off and there they were, dark gray, their sleek wet down lying in minute even ripples, like a baby's head just washed, their unbelievably small delicate ears folded close, their little blind faces almost featureless.

(*LT,* 75-76)

Hartley justly observes, "Such an evocation of beauty from anatomical detail is not often excelled anywhere in the language." This scene, so graphically presented, is the heart of the story. It is imprinted on Miranda's mind as it is on the reader's and is revived for her with perfect clarity by the sight of pink candy rabbits in a Mexican market almost twenty years later. The first sentence, describing the kneeling children, frames the scene and suggests ritual, and the episode is precisely that—the ritual

1. "Katherine Anne Porter," *Sewanee Review,* XLVIII (April, 1940), 214.

of Miranda's entrance into maturity. This is unfolded as the scene continues. First she makes her act of acceptance, once again expressing the meaning of her name.

> Miranda said, "Oh, I want to *see*," under her breath. She looked and looked—excited but not frightened, for she was accustomed to the sight of animals killed in hunting—filled with pity and astonishment and a kind of shocked delight in the wonderful little creatures for their own sakes, they were so pretty. She touched one of them ever so carefully, "Ah, there's blood running over them," she said and began to tremble without knowing why. Yet she wanted most deeply to see and to know. Having seen, she felt at once as if she had known all along. The very memory of her former ignorance faded, she had always known just this.
>
> *(LT, 76)*

In one short lesson "the secret, formless intuitions in her own mind and body" (*LT*, 76-77) are crystallized in the knowledge of birth, and this knowledge is instantly filmed over with the chilling fixative of death. Death is the real meaning of this story; its title, as usual, fits it well. To Miranda, "quietly and terribly agitated," the vision becomes a "bloody heap" and she wants no part of it (*LT*, 77). The young rabbits are buried again in the tomb of their mother's body and Miranda, after thinking about "the whole worrisome affair with confused unhappiness" (*LT*, 77) for several days, lets it sink into her unconscious, its new "burial place." Later she recalls it in another setting of "mingled sweetness and corruption" and realizes for a painful moment that, lying all these years under a pleasant memory of "the time she and her brother had found treasure in the opened graves" (*LT*, 78), was this frozen vision of another open grave which had yielded up its ambiguous treasure—the knowledge of life and death.

"The Grave" achieves a universality of truth by which it seems to transcend the usual thematic preoccupations of its author. This brief moment in the life of the young heroine is one which she shares in some way with every girl. There are, however, some indications in the story of her special character, which is leading her toward her individual fate. The fundamental one is her strong desire to see, to know. This will impel her throughout life, leading her to other pains as it led her to this one. It is this search for experience which will take her to the "strange city of a strange country" where she will have a later vision of this scene. Elsewhere in the story the reader learns that she is rather unconventional for the time (1903) in her summer outfit of blue overalls, shirt, straw hat, and sandals, but this is in accord with her father's wishes, and it is her older sister Maria who is "the really independent and fearless one, in spite of her rather affected ways" (*LT,* 73). It is one of the early signs of Miranda's advance toward maturity that the possession of the gold ring found by Paul arouses in her a desire for more feminine clothing. Up to this time she hasn't cared for dolls and has liked to accompany her brother on hunting trips. She wasn't always a satisfactory companion, as we learn in a passage of charming humor:

She hardly ever hit any sort of mark. She had no proper sense of hunting at all. Her brother would be often completely disgusted with her. "You don't care whether you get your bird or not," he said. "That's no way to hunt." Miranda could not understand his indignation. She had seen him smash his hat and yell with fury when he had missed his aim. "What I like about shooting," said Miranda, with exasperating inconsequence, "is pulling the trigger and hearing the noise."

"Then, by golly," said Paul, "whyn't you go back to the range and shoot at bulls-eyes?"

"I'd just as soon," said Miranda, "only like this, we walk around more."

(*LT,* 72)

Another passage descriptive of her character has been misunderstood by some readers. It follows the statement that neighbor women were shocked by her boyish clothes. "Miranda, with her powerful social sense, which was like a fine set of antennae radiating from every pore of her skin, would feel ashamed because she knew well it was rude and ill-bred to shock anybody, even bad-tempered old crones, though she had faith in her father's judgment and was perfectly comfortable in the clothes" (*LT,* 74). This social sense of Miranda's will never lead her to adapt her conduct to the opinions of her neighbors, as this passage might seem to imply. Rather it is just one facet of her general sensitiveness to people and to reality, and an effect of her Southern training, which put great emphasis on social living. Later she will make this quite clear; but the Miranda of "The Grave" is not yet very much the strong, self-sufficient one who sees through and rejects the narrow and the oppressive. She is a little girl of nine. Likewise, her father and her brother are not the contemptible weaklings who usually surround Miranda and her self-assured counterparts. This story is too well-remembered, too close to reality, to be forced into a thematic mold.

The children's discovery of the old family graves in the first part of the story is closely related to their next experience. It adds the dimension of retrospective history to the day's revelations, just as Miranda's later recollection of the scene extends the story into the future. The gold ring, a relic of family femininity, is a gentle hint to the motherless girl that she must become a woman and begins her initiation into the mystery of all that is involved in that role. The ring awakes in Miranda "vague stirrings of desire for luxury and a grand way of living which could not take precise form in her imagination but were founded on family legend of past wealth and leisure" (*LT,* 74-75). The present reality is something quite different. "It was said the motherless family was running down, with the Grandmother no longer there to hold it together. It was known that she had discriminated against her son Harry in her will, and that he was in straits about money. Some of his old neighbors reflected with vicious satisfaction that now he would probably not be so stiff-necked, nor have any more high-stepping horses either. Miranda knew this, though she could not say how" (*LT,* 73). This is as far as the story goes in criticism of Miranda's father, and it indicates that these opinions are not yet hers. Similarly, there is little development of the theme of the oppressive union aside from this atmosphere of narrow, prying, unsympathetic neighbors, and this also is only beginning to dawn on Miranda. During the next nine years of her life she will come to find it unbearable, but at the present moment the dawning artist in her is completely occupied with "shocked delight in the wonderful little creatures for their own sakes, they were so pretty" (*LT*, 76); and the emerging woman in her, as she "scrambles out" with the dove of knowledge from the grave of her childhood, is spellbound by the mystery of life and death.

"The Fig Tree" is similar to "The Grave" in its emphasis on Miranda's initiation into life, but it differs from that sketch in several ways.[2] It is longer and more complex in plot, though even in "The Fig Tree" the narrated action is relatively simple. Miranda and her grandmother and father, with the servants, leave their house for the farm, to spend the remainder of the summer there. Just before their departure Miranda buries a dead chick near a fig tree and then thinks she hears it crying "Weep, weep" from the grave. Forced to leave immediately, she cries during the trip and asks fruitlessly to be taken back. They reach the farm and an unspecified length of time passes. Just before the return, Aunt Eliza, who has been the main attraction for Miranda, lets her look through her telescope at the moon and tells her that the sky contains "a million other worlds." The same evening, Miranda hears the cry of "Weep, weep" near another fig tree and is filled with joy when Aunt Eliza tells her the sound is made by tree frogs.

The central symbolic action of "The Fig Tree" is inferior to that of "The Grave," for it lacks the latter's natural unity and suggestive power and does not lend itself as well to vivid depiction. The juxtaposition of the buried chick and the sounds of

2. Katherine Anne Porter, "The Fig Tree," *Harper's Magazine*, CCXX (June, 1960), 55-59. Subsequent page references are to this source. "The Fig Tree" is typical of the sketches in that it is composed largely of generalized narrative and comments on many aspects of the life of the family. Chronologically it would have to be placed no later than "The Circus," since in it the Grandmother is still alive. Miranda's apparent age in this story would seem to place it near "The Circus" and before "The Grave," since the latter story, in which she is nine, indicates a greater understanding of death than does the present one. But it seems most fitting to place "The Fig Tree" last among the sketches, for it forms a balancing contrast with the first and it seems to carry Miranda further than do any of the others toward independence of the family and mature understanding of life.

the tree frogs savors somewhat of contrivance, as did the finding of the dove and the ring in the graves. Still there is considerable power in this symbolism, as also in that which is embodied in Great-Aunt Eliza. This monumental woman is for Miranda a sort of nature- or earth-goddess instructing her in the knowledge, but especially the mystery, of the universe. Miranda first sees her in an elevated position, halfway up a stepladder, giving directions about the telescope with which she would view the heavens. Even in this act Great-Aunt Eliza is violating the strict code of decorum represented by the Grandmother, and she continues to violate it at every turn. Miranda is at first disturbed by this revelation of a new set of values and by her discovery that someone can argue on equal terms and even find fault with the Grandmother, who has always been for her the absolute authority and the fixed center of life. But the knowledge which is at first disturbing proves in the end to be liberating. In this story Miranda is initiated into the awareness of the immensity of things. She learns not only that the world is large but that there are "a million other worlds." She finds that her grandmother is not the only world of values and that the different world of Aunt Eliza can exist separately from it and on equal terms. Eliza is "natural" in her scorn for manners as well as in her scientific investigations. Her universal vision is represented by the telescope, burning glass, and microscope with which she scans all things, from the largest to the smallest. The snuff which seems to permeate her with its color and odor is the symbol of her independence of the Grandmother's moral universe, and in its earthy color and origin, a reminder of her role as earth-goddess. She looms in Miranda's sight "like a mountain," and as she sits poring over some tiny object she looks "as if she were saying her prayers" at the shrine of nature (FT, 59).

It soon becomes evident that "The Fig Tree" is a clear embodiment of the rejection theme; the story's thematic pattern coincides almost perfectly with the rejection pattern, and many details of action and description, as well as the very language itself, reflect the theme and its motifs. Miranda's initiation into these new worlds is a liberation from the constriction of the old one. "The Grave" impressed upon her the fact that death is universal and may even short-circuit life by coinciding with birth. Thus that story became one of her first steps toward the sense of death as the ultimate and inescapable oppressor. "The Fig Tree," while it begins with the theme of death, reverses the direction of "The Grave" and carries Miranda toward a wider understanding of life. It is her ignorance of nature that causes the deep and urgent pain which oppresses her throughout most of the story, and it is the instruction of Aunt Eliza that liberates her from this oppression. This liberation is part of the intoxicating flood of knowledge which overwhelms Miranda in the final scene. True, as always, to her name, she has from the first held herself open to this new knowledge. On the first day at the farm she "stared fascinated at Great-Aunt Eliza until her eyes watered" (FT, 59). Throughout the summer she remains faithful to her new teacher.

> Yet Miranda almost forgot her usual interests, such as kittens and other little animals on the place, pigs, chickens, rabbits, anything at all so it was a baby and would let her pet and feed it, for Great-Aunt Eliza's ways and habits kept Miranda following her about, gazing, or sitting across the dinner table, gazing, for when Great-Aunt Eliza was not on the roof before her telescope, always just before daylight or just after dark, she was walking about with a microscope and a burning glass, peering closely at something she saw on a tree trunk, something she found in the grass.
>
> (FT, 59)

Finally Miranda's loyalty is richly rewarded. When, just before they are to return to town, Great-Aunt Eliza invites the children to look through her telescope, they are so awed they look at each other like strangers and cannot speak. The remainder of the story is so filled with meanings that it will be well to quote it in its entirety before discussing it.

> Miranda saw only a great pale flaring disk of cold light, but she knew it was the moon and called out in pure rapture, "Oh, it's like another world!"
>
> "Why of course, child," said Great-Aunt Eliza, in her growling voice, but kindly, "other worlds, a million other worlds."

"Like this one?" asked Miranda, timidly.

"Nobody knows, child . . ."

"Nobody knows, nobody knows," Miranda sang to a tune in her head, and when the others walked on, she was so dazzled with joy she fell back by herself, walking a little distance behind Great-Aunt Eliza's swinging lantern and her wide-swinging skirts. They took the dewy path through the fig grove, much like the one in town, with the early dew bringing out the sweet smell of the milky leaves. They passed a fig tree with low hanging branches, and Miranda reached up by habit and touched it with her fingers for luck. From the earth beneath her feet came a terrible, faint troubled sound. "Weep weep, weep weep" . . . murmured a little crying voice from the smothering earth, the grave.

Miranda bounded like a startled pony against the back of Great-Aunt Eliza's knees, crying out, "Oh, oh, oh, wait . . ."

"What on earth's the matter, child?"

"Miranda seized the warm snuffy hand held out to her and hung on hard. "Oh, there's something saying 'weep weep' out of the ground!"

Great-Aunt Eliza stooped, put her arm around Miranda and listened carefully, for a moment. "Hear them?" she said. "They're not in the ground at all. They are the first tree frogs, means it's going to rain," she said. "weep weep—hear them?"

Miranda took a deep trembling breath and heard them. They were in the trees. They walked on again, Miranda holding Great-Aunt Eliza's hand.

"Just think," said Great-Aunt Eliza, in her most scientific voice, "when tree frogs shed their skins, they pull them off over their heads like little shirts, and they eat them. Can you imagine? They have the prettiest little shapes you ever saw—I'll show you one sometime under the microscope."

"Thank you, Ma'am," Miranda remembered finally to say through her fog of bliss at hearing the tree frogs sing, "Weep weep . . ."

(FT, 59)

Miranda is filled with amazement at the humbling fact that ours is not the only world in the universe; but her sharpest rapture is at learning that there are mysteries which baffle even adults. Until this time she has been completely walled in by the certainties of the Grandmother (who, as we learn in "The Old Order," believed firmly that her duty was authority and kept her own nagging doubts strictly to herself), but now she receives au-

thoritative confirmation of the suspicion she has already felt—
that the world is too big and mysterious to be bounded by the
certainties of one person, even if that person is her Grandmother.
This is the thought that makes her break into inner song. It
is her song of liberation and it reminds the reader of Stephen's
song of liberation, though his is a much more bitter rejection
than hers. Miranda's new knowledge is an early step away
from the family and the society which will oppress her increasingly as she nears maturity. At present this separation is merely
suggested by the fact that, in her joy, she "fell back by herself,
walking a little distance behind."

Still at the back of Miranda's consciousness, even in this
joyful moment, is her concern for the buried chick, now become
only a vague uneasiness tinged with guilt. This concern, incidentally, reflects the ever-present oppression motif, for the
horror one feels at the thought of any living thing's being buried
alive results from unconsciously placing oneself in the same position, and Miranda, on the trip to the farm, showed her strong
revulsion at this thought. "Miranda's ears buzzed and she had
a dull round pain in her just under her front ribs. She had to go
back and let him out. He'd never get out by himself, all tangled
up in tissue paper and that shoebox. He'd never get out without
her" (FT, 57). Near the end of the story she again thinks she
hears weeping from "the smothering earth, the grave." The
motif appears frequently in "The Fig Tree." Miranda reveals
her special dislike for encumbrances of any kind by her approval
of the kittens' reactions to clothes. "Miranda hated dolls. She
never played with them. She always pulled the wigs off and
tied them on the kittens, like hats. The kittens pulled them off
instantly. It was fun. She put the doll clothes on the kittens and
it took any one of them just half a minute to get them all off
again. Kittens had sense" (FT, 58). As always, Miranda is
on the side of spirited self-assertion. Her sense of crisis when
the family's departure forces her to abandon the buried chick
is an early instance of family necessities calling her away from the
demands of her spirit. "She lagged and pulled backward,
looking over her shoulder, but her father hurried her toward the

carry-all" (FT, 57). The same family pressure appears in this earlier passage:

She'd have to hurry like anything to get him buried properly. Back into the house she went on tiptoe hoping not to be seen, for Grand-mother always asked: "Where are you going, child? What are you doing? What is that you're carrying? Where did you get it? Who gave you permission?" and after Miranda had explained all that, even if there turned out not to be anything wrong in it, nothing ever seemed so nice anymore. Besides it took forever to get away.

(FT, 56)

The very opening of the story shows Miranda's distaste for constraint.

Old Aunt Nannie had a habit of gripping with her knees to hold Miranda while she brushed her hair or buttoned her dress down the back. When Miranda wriggled, Aunt Nannie squeezed still harder, and Miranda wriggled more, but never enough to get away. Aunt Nannie gathered up Miranda's scalp lock firmly, snapped a rubber band around it, jammed a freshly starched white chambray bonnet over her ears and forehead, fastened the crown to the lock with a large safety pin, and said: "Got to hold you still someways. Here now, don't you take this off your head till the sun go down."

"I didn't want a bonnet, it's too hot, I wanted a hat," said Miranda.

(FT, 55)

Even the choice of verbs shows the author's preoccupation with pressure, force, constraint.

The fig tree which Miranda touches "for luck" binds the closing scene to the one in which she buried the dead chick under another fig tree. Both trees contain tree frogs, but only under the tutelage of Great-Aunt Eliza does Miranda recognize them for what they are: symbols of life and of the truths of nature.

Several details of the final scene are worthy of note. Eliza's question, "What on earth's the matter, child?" may be read as the earth-mother's expression of her willingness to explain any of the mysteries of her kingdom. At this invitation Miranda seizes the "warm, snuffy hand held out to her" and continues to hang on "hard" during the rest of the scene, showing her respect and insuring close communication with her teacher. Great-Aunt Eliza puts her arm around Miranda, but this embrace is not an irksome constraint; it is the prelude to the great revelation. Miranda concludes the ritual by thanking the earth-mother "through her fog of bliss at hearing the tree frogs sing, 'weep weep. . . .' "

It is interesting to see that the role of naturalist, which would seem so much more fitting in a man, is given by Miss Porter to a woman. Great-Aunt Eliza is now a version of the strong, self-sufficient woman, refreshingly different from the Grandmother but sharing to some extent, in spite of her habit of dipping snuff, in the awe which surrounds her generation in Miranda's eyes. By becoming her votary for a while, Miranda absorbs some of her love for nature and sense of mystery—qualities which will complement the less artistic ones she inherits from her Grandmother.

Significantly, this last of the sketches opens with Miranda being held by Aunt Nannie, the representative of the family, and closes with her holding tightly to Great-Aunt Eliza, who is not for her a representative of the family but a source of freedom and expansiveness. Miranda's grip signifies not so much love as liberation. Elsewhere in "The Fig Tree" the pattern of lovelessness continues to prevail. She is growing even more critical of her father. "Her father gave her the annoyed look he always gave her when he said something to upset her and then saw that she was upset. His words were kind but his voice scolded: 'Stop getting so excited, Baby, you know we wouldn't leave you for anything.' Miranda wanted to talk back: 'Then why did you say so?' " (FT, 57) Although Miranda's brother and sister are present in the sketch, they do not play an active part. The only reference to her relations with her sister is one which occurs in the passage recording Miranda's sudden disillusion at seeing her elders disagree.

Miranda, watching and listening—for everything in the world was strange to her and something she had to know about—saw two old women, who were proud of being grandmothers, who spoke to children always as if they knew best about everything and children knew nothing, and they told children all day long to come here, go there, do this, do not do that, and they were always right and children never were except when they did anything they were told right away without a word. And here they were bickering like two little girls at school, or even the way Miranda and her sister Maria bickered and nagged and picked on each other and said things on purpose to hurt each other's feelings.

(FT, 58)

"The Fig Tree," when viewed as the last of the sketches, compares interestingly with the first, as well as with "The Grave," which immediately precedes it. Both the first sketch and the last describe visits to the Grandmother's farm, but while the first emphasizes tradition and order, the last reveals disorder and points toward the disintegration of tradition. The emphasis of the sketches has completed its shift from the Grandmother to Miranda, and the latter is the center of the final story as the former was dominant in "The Source." There is a parallel between "The Fig Tree" and "The Grave" in the fact that in each story Miranda emerges from a grave into a new phase of her development. Her concrete emergence from the grave of her grandfather in the first symbolizes her advance from childhood toward maturity, with its bitter knowledge of death, the final oppressor. In the second, her spirit is released from the grave of ignorance and narrow limitations, just as it is released from the little grave under the fig tree where it has been imaginatively confined.

The *Leaning Tower* sketches were the last Miranda stories published, but in biographical order they are the first. In this group of closely related works the reader becomes acquainted with the social order in which Miranda spent her childhood, and with the Grandmother who symbolizes that order and plays an important part in Miranda's formation. Miranda herself is seen in the framework of her family and in her gradual initiation into life. This process of initiation dominates her portrayal in the sketches, which bring her only to the threshold of adolescence. "Old Mortality" will pick up the thread at this point and carry her to maturity. As is the case among the sketches, the link between them and the story is not made with extreme care, for each work stands to a great extent alone and has its own informing spirit. "Old Mortality" does in fact slightly overlap the sketches in the chronology of Miranda's life. In "The Grave" her age is given as nine, while at the beginning of "Old Mortality" she is eight. The latter work, furthermore, in its preoccupation with the enigmatic Amy, extends far into the semi-mythical past of the family and compresses time in an intricate manner quite distinct from the technique employed in the sketches. But, linking all the Miranda stories to one another and to every other work of fiction from Miss Porter's hand, is the rejection theme. It appears in their thematic structure, patent or submerged; it colors numerous minor themes and incidents and permeates even language and rhythm. It lies behind nearly every motif which recurs frequently in the stories and is almost certain to be found as the informing spirit of every portrayal of character or human relations that is done with thoroughness, sympathy, or force.

"Old Mortality," the story of Miranda's flight from her family, is divided into three approximately equal sections which could be entitled "Amy" (1885-1902), "Gabriel" (1904), and "Eva" (1912). In the three sections Miranda, whose life links them all, is eight, ten, and eighteen years of age. Published five years before the *Leaning Tower* sketches and differing considerably from them in tone and structure, "Old Mortality" is nevertheless a continuation of Miranda's education for life, which they began. If the sketches are stories of initiation, "Old Mortality" is more properly described as one of disillusion. The mysteries which Miranda encountered in the sketches were sometimes joyful, sometimes sorrowful, but always universal. In the next stage of her experience the lessons she learns are more uniformly bitter and more specialized in that they pertain to her particular society and her individual character. At first Miranda learns within her society and, though her isolation within it is quietly indicated, there are only hints that she will eventually repudiate it. In "Old Mortality" she begins and completes the repudiation. Beneath the intricate pattern of opposed value systems or myths which Robert Penn Warren has pointed out,[3] the basic movement of the story, to which all its parts contribute, is one of escape; and the closing pages, in which Miranda formulates to herself her beliefs and motives, contain the fullest expression of the rejection theme.

Each of the three sections of the story contributes in a distinct manner to its central theme. The first, in which Miranda learns the romantic legend of her Aunt Amy, succeeds remarkably for its brevity in evoking the atmosphere of the family, its narrowness and density, its oppressive moral surveillance, its morbid preoccupation with the past. In idealizing Amy as the embodiment of the myth, the family is unwittingly praising one whose very life condemns it and who resorted to death to escape from it. The contrasting life and escape of Eva is a reminder that the family is destructive in its cruelty as well as in its kindness. All this is grasped only remotely by the eight-year-old Miranda of the first section. At this stage her skepticism and that of her sister is limited to their awareness of the contrast between the romanticized picture of the family and its past given them by their elders, and the concrete evidence of fat female relatives, faded pictures, and moth-eaten finery. Warren characterizes the conflict as one of piety versus common sense. Piety wins at first. The girls can assimilate some contradictions, aided, as they are, by their youth and the numerous incitements to romanticism which surround them. "The visible remains were nothing; they were dust, perishable as the flesh; the features stamped on paper and metal were nothing, but their living memory enchanted the little girls" (*PH*, 8).

The second section contends with the first and negates it. The meeting with Uncle Gabriel brings home to the girls with shocking cogency the falsity of the family myth and its moral destructiveness. In this section Miranda, now ten years old, is already partially separated from the family, "immured" in

3. See "Katherine Anne Porter (Irony With a Center)," *Kenyon Review,* IV (Winter, 1942).

the New Orleans convent school from whose dullness she will eventually escape into marriage.

Section three, in which Miranda is eighteen and has completed her escape, brings her into contact with Cousin Eva, who furthers her disillusionment with Aunt Amy and completes her education in the destructiveness of the family. Miranda sees that Cousin Eva's avenue of escape is one she cannot follow, and the contrast between her father's cold reception of her and his warmth toward Eva reminds her that her rejection of the family has left her isolated. She reaffirms the rejection, accepts the isolation, and turns toward the future "in her hopefulness, her ignorance" (*PH*, 89).

The "discursiveness" and "anecdotal richness" with which Part I achieves the leisurely tone of a novel have been pointed out by Warren.[4] "Old Mortality" is a good example of Miss Porter's remarkable economy, through which the most casual-seeming passage has always a definite purpose, and usually several, in addition to its own particular value. Non-satiric humor, extremely rare in Miss Porter's work, furnishes perhaps the best example. There are several instances of it in "Old Mortality"; one will serve to illustrate their multi-purposiveness. It is the description of Great-Aunt Keziah, the fat Kentucky relative, and her husband's refusal to let her ride his good horses because, as he said, "My sentiments of chivalry are not dead in my bosom; but neither is my common sense, to say nothing of charity to our faithful dumb friends. And the greatest of these is charity" (*PH*, 5). In addition to its humor, this anecdote throws light on the code of chivalry and the realism of at least some of Miranda's relatives; more important, it serves as one of the instances of conflict in her mind between truth and family fable, the fable in this case being her father's statement that all the women in the family are slim. Among the other touches of humor in the story, the most delightful is the description, in Part II, of Miranda's ambition to be a jockey and someday "ride out, bouncing lightly with the other jockeys, and win a great race, and surprise everybody, her family most of all"

4. *Ibid.*, pp. 36-37.

(*PH*, 45). Even this episode is not without its functions in relation to drama and character portrayal.

The title of the story is taken from the poem which Gabriel writes, as if by inspiration, for Amy's tombstone:

> "She lives again who suffered life,
> Then suffered death, and now set free
> A singing angel, she forgets
> The griefs of old mortality."
>
> (*PH,* 17)

His poem has more meanings than he knows. Only a few elements in its complex significance can be pointed out here. In its romantic tone and facile faith, so unsuited to Amy, it reveals Gabriel's blind acceptance of his society's sentimentalism. The whole point of the story is the mortality which he and most others fail to see—the real meaning of the death of Amy, and the corruption and destructiveness of her society which it reveals. Miranda becomes increasingly aware of this mortality, aided especially by her meeting with Gabriel in Part II and her conversation with Eva in Part III. In his conventionally sentimental poem, Gabriel has unconsciously described Amy's life in terms of the rejection theme which really characterized it. She suffered the griefs of old mortality and set herself free, but not to enter a sentimental heaven which is just another part of the Southern myth which both she and Miranda have rejected; death is only death, as Miranda will learn in "Pale Horse, Pale Rider." The title of the story, containing all this ambiguity and more, serves as a reminder of the way in which tradition glosses over tragedy, covering corruption with lace and flowers.

"Old Mortality" opens with Miranda and her sister standing before a painting of their Aunt Amy. The central theme is presented immediately. "Quite often they wondered why everyone who looked at the picture said, 'How lovely'; and why everyone who had known her thought her so beautiful and charming"(*PH*, 3). The concrete evidence of the past does not agree with the version of it handed down by family tradition. Miranda feels only that her aunt was "spirited-looking" (*PH*, 3).

The dominant note in all the stories they hear about her is freedom of spirit, asserted in numerous ways and with impunity, for in her society beauty excused almost everything. Unconventionality was Amy's means of asserting herself, and there was no lack of narrow conventions against which to rebel. The whole oppressive world was personified for her in Gabriel, her second cousin, whose suit seemed to be backed by the whole moral pressure of the family will. She made it no secret that she found him dull and considered his world too narrow for her. When her mother commented to her that his frequent gifts were proof that she was always in his thoughts, she answered, "That's no place for me," but kept free even of her mother's understanding by speaking in a tone which "made it impossible to discover what she meant by what she said" (*PH*, 18). Amy's wedding dress, which the Grandmother shows to Miranda, typifies her character by its unconventionality, for "she would not wear white, nor a veil" (*PH*, 19). It also identifies Amy with the favorite romantic symbol of freedom: " 'Amy's wedding dress,' said the grandmother, unfurling an immense cloak of dove-colored cut velvet, spreading beside it a silvery-gray watered-silk frock, and a small gray velvet toque with a dark red breast of feathers" (*PH*, 19).

The mystery about Amy's death is willingly preserved by the romantic connivance of the family; but whether or not she committed suicide, as Eva flatly states, she gave every indication of willing and planning her death, for it was to be her means of escape. Her mother recalls, "One day when she was ill she said, 'Mammy, I'm not long for this world,' but not as if she meant it. I told her, 'You might live as long as anyone, if only you will be sensible.' 'That's the whole trouble,' said Amy. 'I feel sorry for Gabriel,' she told me. 'He doesn't know what he's asking for' " (*PH*, 19-20).

Amy would not obey her father or Gabriel even in small matters, so complete was her desire to be free of the code which they represented. She cut off her long beautiful hair because Gabriel complimented it, and she disobeyed with a vengeance her father's commands about modest dress. She delighted in

keeping alive and mysterious the question of what occurred between Raymond and herself at the dance to cause the "very
grave scandal" (*PH*, 22) which so upset Gabriel and the family
and sent brother Harry to his pleasant exile in Mexico. The
fever which was the first stage of her escape through death
began on the night of the dance, when after her brief campaign
against convention she was forced to return home immediately.
When her mother added her own rebuke at the shortness of her
dress Amy said, " 'Mammy, I'm sick of this world. I don't like
anything in it. It's so *dull*,' . . . and for a moment she looked
as if she might weep. She had never been tearful, even as a child,
and her mother was alarmed. It was then she discovered that
Amy had fever" (*PH*, 30). When Harry and his brothers left
for the Mexican border she escaped and accompanied them,
causing an even greater scandal and aggravating her fever. The
motifs of escape and oppression are evident in the lines which
follow this escapade.

> The scandal, Maria and Miranda gathered, had been pretty ter-
> rible. Amy simply took to bed and stayed there, and Harry had
> skipped out blithely to wait until the little affair blew over. The rest
> of the family had to receive visitors, write letters, go to church, return
> calls, and bear the whole brunt, as they expressed it. They sat in the
> twilight of scandal in their little world, holding themselves very
> rigidly, in a shared tension as if all their nerves began at a common
> center. This center had received a blow, and family nerves shud-
> dered, even into the farthest reaches of Kentucky.
>
> (*PH*, 32)

Before long Amy received a letter from Great-Great-Aunt Sally
Rhea written in "deep brown ink like dried blood, in a spidery
hand" (*PH*, 32). This relative, whose life had been one of
"vicious self-indulgent martyrdom to her faith," represents an
oppressive religion which was too much even for the family,
who had turned her religious career into a "comic legend" (*PH*,
33). Her advice was not calculated to appeal to Amy, whose
only response was to break into "her gay full laugh that always
caused everyone around her to laugh too, even before they
knew why" (*PH*, 33). She continued her life of gaiety and

dancing, and her illness became more serious. When certain that she was seriously ill, and perhaps out of sympathy for the long-suffering and recently disinherited Gabriel, she finally consented to marry him, suggesting they marry immediately for, "if we wait until after Lent, it may be too late" (*PH*, 36). Part I concludes with two letters which the Grandmother kept and Maria and Miranda read after they were grown. The first, from Amy on her honeymoon in New Orleans, hints that she will not live long. The second, from a nurse, describes her death only six weeks after her marriage. It implies rather clearly that she deliberately hastened it by taking an overdose of medicine.

Cousin Eva is another version of the strong, self-sufficient woman who escapes from the oppressive union, but in her case the entire process is in a minor key. She has felt the family at its most destructive in the sexual license and almost unbelievable cruelty of her mother, vices which her beauty and charm permitted her to indulge without the condemnation of the family. The early treatment she receives mars Eva for life and leads to Miranda's musing question, "Why was a strong character so deforming?" (*PH*, 78) Miranda, who "wanted to be strong," cannot admire her fully or emulate her. Still she must give her credit for the dreary victory she has won. Eva has directed her general resentment of oppression against one particular aspect of it, the limitation of women's legal rights. Miranda has little interest in this work but tells Eva sincerely, "I think it was brave of you, and I'm glad you did it, too. I loved your courage" (*PH*, 68-69). Although Eva possesses courage and some of its related virtues, she is deeply embittered by the cruelty of her mother and the family, filled with hatred and evil suspicions, and preoccupied with sex, though still quite naïve about it. She concentrates all this in her memory of Amy, who was cruel to her and who embodied all the graces she herself lacked. Her long devotion of hatred and her modern education enable Eva to see rather deeply into Amy and her romantic world, but her exaggeration of the evil in them forces Miranda to reject her view as equally romantic and to attempt to form her own from a balanced rejection of the two. She achieves no new theoretic synthesis, however; all that appears in the story is her rejection. Suddenly she is tired of "her intense Cousin Eva" (*PH*, 80). But Eva, excited by her own diatribe, goes on to reveal the real root of her bitterness—the family's teasing about her plainness. " 'Of course, you understand perfectly it was all in the very best humor, everybody was very amusing about it, no harm meant—oh, no, no harm at all. That is the hellish thing about it. It is that I can't forgive,' she cried out, and she twisted her hands together as if they were rags" (*PH*, 81). Exhausted, she concludes: " 'Ah, the family,' she said, releasing her breath and sitting back quietly, 'the whole hideous institution should be wiped from the face of the earth. It is the root of all human wrongs,' she ended, and relaxed, and her face became calm. She was trembling" (*PH*, 81). This passage, one of the most forceful in "Old Mortality," is an exact expression of the oppressive family motif. In Eva it is portrayed as an abnormal excess, but the important thing is to note once again with what vigor the author responds to this theme and to realize that, although their cases differ superficially in terms of the plot, Miranda is moved by exactly the same urge. Before long she too will be heard expressing it strongly.

"Old Mortality" confirms what the sketches revealed of Miranda's character and adds new detail. The following short passage tells much about her: "Miranda persisted through her childhood in believing, in spite of her smallness, thinness, her little snubby nose saddled with freckles, her speckled gray eyes and habitual tantrums, that by some miracle she would grow into a tall, cream-colored brunette, like cousin Isabel; she decided always to wear a trailing white satin gown. Maria, born sensible, had no such illusions" (*PH*, 9). Miranda is a determined idealist, romantic, imaginative, perceptive, independent, spirited. She will never lose any of these qualities. The author treats her with gentle irony but with obvious approval. The ironic distance will diminish as Miranda grows older, until only traces of it are in evidence at the end of "Old Mortality"; in "Pale Horse, Pale Rider" it will disappear completely. Like her Aunt Amy, Miranda detests dullness, and she seems to find little else at school. The sisters were "very dull good-natured women who managed to make the whole dormitory seem dull. All days and all things in the Convent of the Child Jesus were dull, in fact" (*PH,* 41). Miranda's efforts to liven up the place extend to falling flat on her face on the classroom floor during arithmetic class and refusing to rise until carried out. Her efforts, however, are fruitless, and the next that is heard of her academic career is that she ran away from school at the age of seventeen to get married. Although not fond of school, Miranda and her sister have always read "as naturally and constantly as ponies crop grass" (*PH,* 39), and Miranda continues to show evidence of her eager desire to see and to know. She can be quite stubborn in matters of truth, as she shows by asking her father twice, "Uncle Gabriel's a drunkard, isn't he?" in spite of his scolding and threats.

Miranda's gradual preparation for her eventual escape from the family takes the form, as has been seen, of a growing sense of oppression; it reflects two other motifs which are really aspects of this central one—the absence of love and scorn for men. It may be objected with some justice that in the treatment of Miranda and her family the presence of a basic love relationship is assumed. This is no doubt the case, but the point is simply that this love is not realized dramatically, not conveyed to the reader, whereas opposing forces are plentiful and powerful. In Miranda's case the motif of the strong, self-sufficient woman does not appear as explicitly as in the cases of other alpha heroines such as the Grandmother, for as Miranda grows into maturity the point of view in her stories becomes so close to her own that she is seldom described objectively. Her character is revealed primarily through her thoughts and actions, both of which are plentifully recorded, and in this manner she reveals herself to be the perfect embodiment of the rejection theme in both its positive and negative aspects.

The essential lovelessness of Miranda's family life is reflected in countless small details, most of which seem insignificant until one perceives the consistent pattern they form. Certainly the crucial fact here is that Miranda never knew her mother—

though there are few satisfactory mothers in the whole body of Miss Porter's work. Miranda's older sister Maria would seem to be one of the persons most likely to receive her affection, but virtually every joint reference to the two sisters gives evidence of antipathy. Several times Miranda refers to Maria as "too prissy for words." Their closest bond seems to be their fellowship in boredom at school. Aside from the portrayal of Gabriel there is little strong dramatization in "Old Mortality" of the motif of scorn for men; yet there are numerous small signs of it, especially in Miranda's attitude toward her father. Although he occupies a position of greater dignity here than in the sketches, where he was always subordinated to the Grandmother, his daughters show no real respect or love for him. His relation to them, in fact, seems strangely like that of a suitor who had better be on his toes if he wants to retain their approval. At his threat to punish Miranda's truth-telling about Gabriel's drunkenness the little girls "loosed their hands from his and moved away coldly, standing together in silence" (*PH,* 51). It may be said in general that of the men who appear or are mentioned in the story—Miranda's father, her grandfather, Uncle Gabriel, her unseen husband, assorted relatives and beaux —not one is presented as particularly admirable, good, strong, or beloved; whereas several of the women are distinctly admirable, at least in part. The closest the Miranda stories ever come to an expression of filial love is the rather long description (*PH,* 22-23) of Miranda's father as seen by the girls, in which he is presented as a "pleasant, everyday sort of father" who approves of them only if they are neat and well-behaved, and keeps them alert by laying intellectual traps for them. When Miranda arrives home for Gabriel's funeral, she seems to give some evidence of love for her father. She throws herself upon him but he holds her off, and she feels "the same painful dull jerk of the heart" (*PH,* 83) that she had felt before on similar occasions. Significantly, this episode is a completely negative one. The expression of love, quite similar, incidentally, to the one in "That Tree," is just a painful jerk of the heart, serving only to impress upon Miranda the completeness of her isolation.

It is called for by the plot but is not convincing because it goes against the whole emotional tendency of the story. Whatever she feels, it is not adequate to make her regret her escape. She walks along beside her father "feeling homeless, but not sorry for it" (*PH, 84*).

In keeping with Southern decorum there are no violent family quarrels in "Old Mortality"—"Nice people did not carry on quarrels before outsiders. Family quarrels were sacred, to be waged privately in fierce hissing whispers, low choked mutters and growls. If they did yell and stamp, it must be behind closed doors and windows" (*PH, 55-56*)—yet the terribly bitter scene in which Gabriel and his wife appear together places their marriage firmly in the tradition of "Rope," "That Tree," "The Downward Path to Wisdom," and "A Day's Work." When Miranda leaves she knows that Miss Honey hates them all. Another terrible instance of family bitterness is Eva's treatment by her mother, exemplified by the statement she often made in Eva's presence: "It's lucky for me my daughter is an old maid. She's not so apt to make a grandmother of me" (*PH, 12*). There is evidence of love in the description of Miranda's parents during their courtship, dancing at the ball which will soon be disrupted by Amy's scandal. In such cases as this where the assertion of love is inevitable—the best examples are in "Pale Horse, Pale Rider" and *Ship of Fools*—Miss Porter follows a set pattern. The young lovers are portrayed as in a dream world apart from reality and doomed to be short-lived. "Harry and Mariana, in conventional disguise of romance, irreproachably betrothed, safe in their happiness, were walzing slowly to their favorite song . . . a song of love and parting" (*PH, 26*). In fact they are parted almost immediately, and Harry goes off to a long and highly suspect exile in Mexico.

The story is, in general, accurately represented by the examples that have been cited. Miranda's family is characterized by coldness, mendacity, scorn for its men on the part of its women, close moral surveillance, a strict code of decorum, and innumerable relatives who are predominantly selfish, sentimental, cruel, unrealistic, clannish, provincial, and censorious. It is completely unimaginable that Miranda should remain in it.

Part III of "Old Mortality" completes Miranda's education in the nature of the family, and in its last pages dramatizes with great fullness her spiritual rejection of it. Miranda is on her way home for the funeral of Uncle Gabriel, who has, like his beloved Amy, escaped from an oppressive marriage to join his ideal lover in death. She follows the porter down the "stuffy" aisle of the sleeping-car between "dusty" green curtains, and meets Cousin Eva. The reader, following Miranda's thoughts during their conversation, learns her present attitude toward the family. "I suppose it would be pleasant if I could say something to make her believe that she and all of them would be lamented, but—but—" (*PH,* 68). Miranda defends Amy against Eva's attacks, partly because she is still young and a bit romantic, but especially because of the kinship she feels with her earlier counterpart. When she persists in this defense Cousin Eva insists, "you mustn't live in a romantic haze about life. You'll understand when you're married at any rate" (*PH,* 73). Then Miranda gives her and the reader a surprise:

"I'm married now, Cousin Eva," said Miranda, feeling for almost the first time that it might be an advantage, "nearly a year. I eloped from school." It seemed very unreal even as she said it, and seemed to have nothing at all to do with the future; still, it was important, it must be declared, it was a situation in life which people seemed to be most exacting about, and the only feeling she could rouse in herself about it was an immense weariness as if it were an illness that she might one day hope to recover from.

(*PH,* 73-74)

It now becomes ironically evident that of the two it is Eva who is more enslaved to the code, for all her independent life, and more naïve about sex. She is genuinely repelled by the news that Miranda has eloped. When she tells the girl, "If you had been my child I should have brought you home and spanked you," Miranda laughs out, then replies, "And you must know I should have just gone straight out again, through the nearest window, . . . If I went the first time, why not the second?" (*PH,*

74) By now she has made it perfectly clear that her motive in eloping was not the acceptance of love but the rejection of oppression.

Eva goes on disclosing her own soul by criticizing Amy, and when she finishes giving Miranda "the other side of the story" (*PH,* 82), grows calm with spent feeling. Before leaving her Miranda gives her an impulsive kiss, and the sudden tears in the old woman's eyes are a hint of the need for love which lies beneath her bitterness. The next few lines, an excellent example of Miss Porter's great skill at compression, bring them to their destination: "Miranda fell asleep while she was getting off her clothes. Instantly it was morning again. She was still trying to close her suitcase when the train pulled into the small station, and there on the platform she saw her father, looking tired and anxious, his hat pulled over his eyes. She rapped on the window to catch his attention, then ran out and threw herself upon him" (*PH,* 82). Miranda is immediately closed out by her father's cold reception and his warmth toward Eva. Uncharacteristically, Eva warms up to him in return, for "she liked Harry, she always had liked him" (*PH,* 84). They speak briefly of Gabriel. " 'Oh, Gabriel wouldn't mind, he'd like seeing you cheerful. Gabriel was the cheerfulest cuss I ever saw, when we were young. Life for Gabriel,' said Father, 'was just one perpetual picnic.' 'Poor fellow,' said Cousin Eva. 'Poor old Gabriel,' said Father, heavily' " (*PH,* 70). Impelled by the falsity of this, Miranda confirms her rejection of the family, though not without expressing hope of eventual forgiveness. The author retreats momentarily to a more objective distance. "Surely old people cannot hold their grudges forever because the young want to live, too, she thought, in her arrogance, her pride" (*PH,* 84). This line will be echoed at the end of the story.

At this point Miranda begins the meditation which constitutes her personal declaration of independence. "I will make my own mistakes, not yours; I cannot depend upon you beyond a certain point, why depend at all? There was something more beyond, but this was the first step to take, and she took it" (*PH,* 84-85). The whole story of her life up to this point has been designed to show just how little one really can depend upon their world for truth or a moral code and how little love there is to bind her to them. She walks along with her two companions who have forgotten her in their comfortable talk of common memories. " 'It is I who have no place,' thought Miranda. 'Where are my own people and my own time?' She resented, slowly and deeply and in profound silence, the presence of these aliens who lectured and admonished her, who loved her with bitterness and denied her the right to look at the world with her own eyes, who demanded that she accept their version of life and yet could not tell her the truth, not in the smallest thing' " (*PH*, 85). She is well along on her own downward path to wisdom. " 'I hate them both,' her most inner and secret mind said plainly. *'I will be free of them, I shall not even remember them'* " (*PH*, 85-86). She refuses to sit with her father and Eva during the ride home. As she listens to them speaking of familiar things with childlike gaiety and freshness, she feels stifled.

Miranda could not hear the stories above the noisy motor, but she felt she knew them well, or stories like them. She knew too many stories like them, she wanted something new of her own. The language was familiar to them, but not to her, not any more. The house, her father had said, was full. It would be full of cousins, many of them strangers. Would there be any young cousins there, to whom she could talk about things they both knew? She felt a vague distaste for seeing cousins. There were too many of them and her blood rebelled against the ties of blood. She was sick to death of cousins.
(*PH*, 86-87)

Miranda is being driven by an impulse stronger than the reasons she can find to justify it. If it were not for all the earlier stories which have prepared for this repudiation, the force of her feelings would certainly seem inexplicable. This observation applies even more strongly to her next thoughts. Already the pattern has begun to form. Once the first overt escape has been made, there can be no end to it. "She did not want any more ties with this house, she was going to leave it, and she was not going back to her husband's family either. She would have no more bonds that smothered her in love and hatred. She knew now why she had run away to marriage, and she knew that she was going to run away from marriage, and she was not going to stay in any place, with anyone, that threatened to forbid her making her own discoveries, that said 'No' to her" (*PH*, 87). Miranda will never learn that there is no love which does not require sacrifice, because in her world she has never found enough good in love to justify even the least patience with sacrifice. Love to her is a romantic ideal, and her romantic ideals began crumbling years before. Thus unconsciously handicapped, she stands on the threshold of life. "Oh, what is life, she asked herself in desperate seriousness, in those childish unanswerable words, and what shall I do with it? It is something of my own, she thought in a fury of jealous possessiveness, what shall I make of it?" (*PH*, 87) Here the author intrudes to point out that Miranda is far too naïve in thinking that her life is something she can shape and control by a series of "acts of the will directed towards a definite end" (*PH*, 87). She has been given this simplified belief by her early training. She has also been assured that there are good and evil ends between which one must make a choice.

But what was good, and what was evil? I hate love, she thought, as if this were the answer, I hate loving and being loved, I hate it. And her disturbed and seething mind received a shock of comfort from this sudden collapse of an old painful structure of distorted images and misconceptions. "You don't know anything about it," said Miranda to herself, with extraordinary clearness as if she were an elder admonishing some younger misguided creature. "You have to find out about it." (*PH*, 87-88)

Like Stephen, she finds comfort in the sudden rejection of love. Not only does she reject persons; she rejects the entire scale of values through which persons have imposed on her. Considering the kind of love she has experienced, her rejection would seem to be justified. After this liberation she is uncertain of her next step.

There are questions to be asked first, she thought, but who will answer them? No one, or there will be too many answers, none of them right. What is the truth, she asked herself as intently as if the question had never been asked, the truth, even about the smallest, the least important of all the things I must find out? and where shall I begin to look for it? Her mind closed stubbornly against remembering, not the past but the legend of the past, other people's memory of the past, at which she had spent her life peering in wonder like a child at a magic-lantern show.

(*PH,* 88)

She is left, she feels, with nothing of the past and nothing in the present except her unattached self. Necessarily, she turns to the future.

Ah, but there is my own life to come yet, she thought, my own life now and beyond. I don't want any promises, I won't have false hopes, I won't be romantic about myself. I can't live in their world any longer, she told herself, listening to the voices back of her. Let them tell their stories to each other. Let them go on explaining how things happened. I don't care. At least I can know the truth about what happens to me, she assured herself silently, making a promise to herself, in her hopefulness, her ignorance.

(*PH,* 88-89)

Miranda is more romantic than she realizes with her vision of unobstructed autonomy and self-sufficiency, her ignorance of self-deceit and the deceit of life; but though the author steps back once again to observe her heroine's limitations of vision, she finds in her no limitation of spirit; and that, to her, is the essential.

The pages just examined contain the author's most explicit and thorough statement of the rejection theme. It bears an obvious relation to the rejection elements in the other stories, but there are differences just as obvious—differences in time and place, in personal character, in the nature of the oppression and the escape, in the attitude taken by the author toward the protagonist. It is these very differences which make so striking the omnipresence of the rejection pattern in Miss Porter's work. There is a world of difference between Miranda in "Old Mortality" and Ninette in "Magic" or Rosaleen in "The Cracked Looking-Glass" or Charles Upton in "The Leaning Tower"— yet they are all impelled by the same strong urge to escape, and with varying degrees of success, go about their individual ways of trying to satisfy it. The theme will take yet another form in the final Miranda story.

In "Pale Horse, Pale Rider," the story of Miranda is concluded. This is true not only in the sense that in it she is most advanced in age; twenty-four is not, after all, a very advanced age. It is true primarily because in this story she undergoes a physical and spiritual harrowing which leaves her with literally no future. It is easy to understand why Miss Porter has selected this as her best work, for in it she has tried, and with remarkable success, to record an experience which was quite possibly the most important of her life. For "Pale Horse, Pale Rider," in its central experience of near-fatal illness, is autobiographical.[5] At the time of the story Miranda is working for a newspaper in Denver and contracts influenza in the epidemic of 1918. The story is a record of her illness and narrow escape from death. It is also—and the degree to which Miss Porter is aware of this must remain problematical—the key to all the author's work, for it contains the archetypal pattern of the rejection theme.

The technical skill exhibited in "Pale Horse, Pale Rider" can hardly be praised too highly. Miss Porter's ability to represent the physical and mental sensations of dream and delirium has been seen in "Flowering Judas" and "The Jilting of Granny Weatherall," but in this story she achieves her most sustained intensity and poetic beauty. Qualities observable here as in any of her works are mastery of sentence and paragraph rhythm, vivid powers of description, and extreme compression, power, and swiftness. Smooth and rapid transitions from one state of consciousness to another are often effected through the use of association. The end of the vision of the pale horseman furnishes a good example: "She pulled Graylie up, rose in her stirrups and shouted, I'm not going with you this time—ride on! Without pausing or turning his head the stranger rode on. Graylie's ribs heaved under her, her own ribs rose and fell, Oh,

5. Evidence for this statement is given later in the present discussion. For another of Miss Porter's references to the illness on which Miranda's is based, see the interview with Barbara Thompson in *Paris Review*, XXIX (Winter-Spring, 1963), 97. This passage is quoted in Chapter Six below.

why am I so tired, I must wake up. 'But let me get a fine yawn first,' she said, opening her eyes and stretching, 'a slap of cold water in my face, for I've been talking in my sleep again, I heard myself but what was I saying?' " (*PH,* 181-82) Ribs furnish the association in this case; the switch from dream speech to waking speech is quietly indicated by quotation marks. Whatever remains to be said of other aspects of "Pale Horse, Pale Rider," it must first be acknowledged that the brilliance of its prose style is almost its dominant element, raising it above even the usual high level of the author's stylistic performance.

"Pale Horse, Pale Rider" is, at least superficially, quite different from the other Miranda stories. To begin with, it is filled with the peculiar atmosphere which characterized the United States during the First World War, with its sentimental patriotism, its distorted vision of the enemy, its sometimes brutal pressures for comformity. This is the only story in which Miranda is mature and in which her mind is entered through a variety of stream-of-consciousness technique. The six years which have passed since her conversation with her Cousin Eva in "Old Mortality" have wrought many changes in this young woman. Even as the story opens she is much more aware of the deceits of life than she was when last seen. In her dream of the pale rider, she tells herself that early morning is best for her "because trees are trees in one stroke, stones are stones set in shades known to be grass, there are no false shapes or surmises" (*PH,* 180). Frequent illness is one of the teachers from whom she has learned. "As for herself, she had had too many pains to mention, so she did not mention them. After working for three years on a morning newspaper she had an illusion of maturity and experience; but it was fatigue merely, she decided, from keeping what she had been brought up to believe were unnatural hours, eating casually at dirty little restaurants, drinking bad coffee all night, and smoking too much" (*PH,* 198). In rejecting the rigid world of her youth, she has rejected all that went with it, from its religion to its timetable. She has not, however, abandoned her vague ideal of happiness or her insistent demand for truth. With stern honesty she sees through almost every sort of sham, even in herself. She is repelled by the snob and the phoney and she finds them everywhere, especially among men. It is her sensitive desire for truth that causes her to reject the visits to military hospitals as futile, and to write honest drama reviews which return to haunt her. It makes her reflect, while listening to a pompous dollar-a-year man speaking of patriotism and democracy, "Coal, oil, iron, gold, international finance, why don't you tell us about them, you little liar?" (*PH*, 222) "Pale Horse, Pale Rider" seems different from the earlier work, finally, in being a love story, which would certainly set it apart from the other Miranda stories. But the difference is more apparent than real. Once it is realized that this is primarily a story not of love but of death, there is no difficulty in seeing its relation to the other stories about Miranda, for they are all about death.

It is difficult and sometimes futile to measure the degree of "reality" of a character in a literary work, but in this case the point is of importance; for the basis of the statement that this is hardly a love story is the fact that Adam is hardly real. The alpha heroine has never been portrayed in a real love relationship or even a real friendship with any person, male or female. The nearest approximation to love is the heroine's unhappy early marriage in "Old Mortality," an event which has no concrete reality in the story. The essential falsity of the love elements in the implicit Miranda stories "Theft" and "Flowering Judas" has been observed, and it will be enlightening to keep the latter story in mind during the examination of the present one, for there is a strong parallel between the romantic loves of Laura and Miranda. It seems that whenever the possibility of a love affair arises for the alpha heroine, there arises an opposed force adequate to nip it in the bud. "Pale Horse, Pale Rider" is the most striking example of this. It will be recalled that the alpha stories and almost all the others have been characterized by a marked absence of love in every human relationship. In the present story, the first which portrays Miranda in the everyday social and business world, she is almost necessarily on friendly terms with some of her fellow workers; but these friendships do not affect her deeply, and it is interesting to note that even in the most intimate of them, those with Towney and Chuck, she keeps her distance by mental criticism of each at some point in the story. Furthermore, most of the characters who appear incidentally—the socialites at the army hospital, the landlady, the nun on the telephone—are predominantly unpleasant. War and plague reveal not nobility but meanness. Even the doctors and nurses who save Miranda's life are sinister and repugnant to her.

All this is explained by the fact that the rejection theme simply excludes fulfillment through love. Here it must once again be recalled that this thematic pattern does not always coincide with the plot but in some stories underlies it, impressing itself more or less consciously and explicitly on the surface pattern. Consequently, where the plot parallels the rejection theme it is strong, but where it deviates it is lacking in fictional reality and emotional force. Wherever love, which is not an element of the pattern, seems to appear, it is closely related to that sense of disillusion and loss which *is* an element of the pattern; and upon examination the emotional force will be found to result from the latter element, not the former. These qualifications must be observed with special care in reading this story. Certainly it is, at least on the surface, intended by the author and accepted by the reader as a love story. More precisely, it is a story of romantic love—of that kind of devotion which remains strongly self-centered even in its yearning for the beloved, to whom it is attracted principally by external qualities. The hectic superficiality of this particular love affair is to a great extent justified by the imminence of separation and death, as well as by the youth, independence, and rather Bohemian existence of the heroine. Nevertheless—and this point is central to the present discussion—such a relationship may be completely devoid of that genuine human love which exerts a profound influence on the individual, opening him up to intimate communion with another. It is on the basis of this understanding of love that "Pale Horse, Pale Rider" may be denied the status of love story.

Miranda's steady pursuit of the rejection pattern, her search for experience in a state of constantly affirmed independence, has not made for a happy life, as she reveals when she thinks herself near death: " 'You'd get the notion I had a very sad life,' she said, 'and perhaps it was, but I'd be glad enough to have it now. If I could have it back, it would be easy to be happy about almost anything at all. That's not true, but that's the way I feel now.' After a pause, she said, 'There's nothing to tell, after all, if it ends now, for all this time I was getting ready for something that was going to happen later, when the time came. So now it's nothing much' " (*PH*, 237). The nature of this elusive "something" will be revealed in the vision she has in the depth of her illness. The irony of Miranda's life is that it is her constant rejection of others that robs her of possible bliss. This nihilistic tendency is always present in the alpha heroine, and determining the author's attitude toward it in the various stories brings one close to her fundamental view of reality. "Pale Horse, Pale Rider" is the story in which her attitude appears in its broadest implications. Hence it is the most important source of evidence for an evaluation of Miss Porter's fictional world.

As in "Flowering Judas," the principal factor undermining love is the presence of death. Miranda sees Adam as condemned to death from the beginning. "She liked him, she liked him, and there was more than this but it was no good even imagining, because he was not for her nor for any woman, being beyond experience already, committed without any knowledge or act of his own to death" (*PH*, 205). Miranda had met Adam only a few days before, when he moved into an apartment near hers. He was on leave only "because his outfit expected to be sent over shortly": " 'Came in to make my will,' he told Miranda, 'and get a supply of toothbrushes and razor blades' " (*PH*, 197). Their strolls are punctuated by pauses for funeral processions. Death is present in the city and in the nearby army camp to which Adam is subject to immediate summons. They discuss it.

"I wonder," said Miranda. "How did you manage to get an extension of leave?"

"They just gave it," said Adam, "for no reason. The men are

dying like flies out there, anyway. This funny new disease. Simply knocks you into a cocked hat."

"It seems to be a plague," said Miranda, "something out of the Middle Ages. Did you ever see so many funerals, ever?"

"Never did. Well, let's be strong minded and not have any of it. I've got four days more straight from the blue and not a blade of grass must grow under our feet. What about tonight?"

(PH, 200)

This proximate danger of death is superimposed upon the threat of war death for Adam; and Miranda herself is already under the shadow, with only the tenuous authority of a dream to assure her that she will emerge safely. The dream of the pale horseman marks the beginning of her illness, which overcomes her quickly, stealing most of the little time she has with Adam and making her love doubly fragile. Early in the story, while she is sitting with Chuck at a dull play, she tells him that she is going to leave the paper. Then, like Mr. Thompson in "Noon Wine" when he is about to escape by means of suicide, she thinks, "This is the beginning of the end of something. Something terrible is going to happen to me. I shan't need bread and butter where I'm going. . . . Oh, Adam, I hope I see you once more before I go under with whatever is the matter with me" (*PH,* 215-16).

Adam is made unreal for Miranda not only by the threat of death which hangs over him but also by the manner in which he is portrayed. It is interesting to note that in this story, just as in every other alpha story in which the heroine is supposedly in love—"Theft," "Flowering Judas," "Old Mortality"—she is first presented for a time in the isolation which is her natural state; it is only later, and always with surprise, that the reader learns of the existence of a lover. This is another indication of the lovers' fundamental unsubstantiality. It is clear that Miss Porter consciously employs in this story some elements of the Eden myth, with its overtones of knowledge and love leading to death. The only aspect of the story in which the myth functions vitally is in the portrayal of the hero as an Adamic figure. He is the innocent young man, ideally beautiful, strong, and healthy—that is, unreal. He is "tall and heavily muscled in the shoulders, narrow in the waist and flanks" (*PH*, 197), and we are repeatedly told that he has "never had a pain in his life" (*PH*, 198). He looks clear and fresh to Miranda, "like a fine healthy apple" (*PH*, 198). Wearing his new tailor-made uniform he is "all olive and tan and tawny, hay colored and sand colored from hair to boots" (*PH*, 196). Characteristics frequently noted in the alpha heroine are a distant, artistic manner of looking at people and an aesthetic love of cleanness. These descriptions of Adam suggest that Miranda's reaction to him is primarily aesthetic. Other examples are plentiful. She observes that his eyes are "pale tan with orange flecks in them" and that his hair is "the color of a haystack when you turn the weathered top back to the clear straw beneath" (*PH*, 199). This straw man of hers gives off "whiffs of tobacco smoke, a manly smell of scentless soap, freshly cleaned leather and freshly washed skin" (*PH*, 225). One can hardly miss the special fittingness of her assertion, "Adam, I think you're very beautiful" (*PH*, 236). Miranda's aesthetic approach to people is perfectly illustrated by the hospital episode in which she flees in shame from an embittered soldier and then looks through a window at him, noticing his young face, sharp features, and hands, which "were not laborer's hands but not well-cared-for hands either. They were good useful properly shaped hands, lying there on the coverlet" (*PH*, 193).[6]

Adam, far from being a human lover who might successfully cross Miranda's barrier of isolation, is just another of her illusions of happiness. He is in a sense dead from the beginning of the story and is regarded by Miranda largely in an aesthetic manner which implies a certain distance between viewer and object. And there are other indications. To a great extent Adam

6. An aesthetic emphasis also marks Miranda's antipathies. She says of dollar-a-year men, "I hate those potbellied baldheads, too fat, too old, too cowardly, to go to war themselves, they know they're safe; it's you they are sending instead—" (*PH*, 223). She describes one of this breed as follows: "He was an ordinary man past middle life, with a neat little melon buttoned into his trousers and waistcoat, an opinionated tight mouth, a face and figure in which nothing could be read save the inept sensual record of fifty years" (*PH*, 221). In Adam Miranda admires beauty; in other men she scorns its absence. The implied valuation of masculine reality is obvious.

is just a reflection of Miranda's mind, a voice playing with her the game of cynicism. "Their smiles approved of each other, they felt they had got the right tone, they were taking the war properly" (*PH*, 201). In other respects he is simply a pleasant complement to her, as in his ruddy health, his masculine distaste for reading, his boyish desire to show her what kind of a person he is when he "has his machinery with him" (*PH*, 209). Adam makes no demands upon Miranda and even dies a ritual death for her preservation. Like Laura, Miranda provides the means of her lover's death, which suggests that he is only a creature of her mind and hints in a veiled way that she is rejecting him.

Before Miranda's prostration, her relationship with Adam seems to find its fullest expression in dancing. This appears in the following passage, which contains several relevant details:

> Strolling, keeping step, his stout polished well-made boots setting themselves down firmly beside her thin-soled black suede, they put off as long as they could the end of their moment together, and kept up as well as they could their small talk that flew back and forth over little grooves worn in the thin upper surface of the brain, things you could say and hear clink reassuringly at once without disturbing the radiance which played and darted about the simple and lovely miracle of being two persons named Adam and Miranda, twenty-four years old each, alive and on the earth at the same moment: "Are you in the mood for dancing, Miranda?" and "I'm always in the mood for dancing, Adam!" but there were things in the way, the day that ended with dancing was a long way to go.
>
> (*PH*, 198)

Note here the impersonal aesthetic pleasure in Adam's company, the superficial small talk that comprises so much of their conversation (they never disagree), and the element of oppression in Miranda's consciousness of innumerable impediments to her bliss. It will also be noted that their love is implied with delicate circumlocution, an approach well suited to their sophistication and the fragile, dream-like quality of this brief romance. When Adam, boy-like, tells Miranda about his "machinery," she reflects: "She felt she knew pretty well what kind of person he was, and would have liked to tell him that if he thought he had left himself at home in a boat or an automobile, he was much mistaken" (*PH*, 209). The assertions of their love are largely confined to such coy evasions. This technique of understatement can be extremely effective, but only when the reality alluded to has been "proved" in other ways. A careful examination of "Pale Horse, Pale Rider" shows that here this is not the case.

Miranda's unconscious evasion of commitment by concentration on romantic aesthetic detail and the shortness of time is evident in the following thoughts and memories which run through her mind in the newspaper office:

Miranda wished to stop hearing, and talking, she wished to think for just five minutes of her own about Adam, really to think about him, but there was no time. She had seen him first ten days ago, and since then they had been crossing streets together, darting between trucks and limousines and pushcarts and farm wagons; he had waited for her in doorways and in little restaurants that smelled of stale frying fat; they had eaten and danced to the urgent whine and bray of jazz orchestras, they had sat in dull theaters because Miranda was there to write a piece about the play. Once they had gone to the mountains and, leaving the car, had climbed a stony trail, and had come out on a ledge upon a flat stone, where they sat and watched the lights change on a valley landscape that was, no doubt, Miranda said, quite apocryphal—"We need not believe it, but it is fine poetry," she told him; they had leaned their shoulders together, and sat quite still, watching.

(*PH*, 207)

Miranda's isolation and the dancing motif may be seen in another illuminating passage:

When the tune changed to "Madelon," Adam said, "Let's dance." It was a tawdry little place, crowded and hot and full of smoke, but there was nothing better. The music was gay; and life is completely crazy anyway, thought Miranda, so what does it matter? This is what we have, Adam and I, this is all we're going to get, this is the way it is with us. She wanted to say, "Adam, come out of your dream and listen to me. I have pains in my chest and my head and my heart and they're real. I am in pain all over, and you are in such danger as I can't bear to think about, and why can we not save each other?"

(*PH*, 226)

But Adam cannot come out of his dream for he is a dream; there can be no real contact between him and the realities of her life. Miranda, detached as ever, hugs to herself in a tawdry make-believe world her last illusion of happiness, this unreal lover who is "the only really pleasant thought" (*PH*, 194) she can find. One thinks of Amy's flippant remark in "Old Mortality": "What I really need is a good dancing partner to guide me through life, that's the match I'm looking for" (*PH*, 21).[7] Even when she is closest to Adam in the delicate equilibrium of dancing, Miranda cannot elude the ambiguous sense of her own isolation. She envies the young lovers she sees sitting "quietly together . . . while they looked into the hell they shared," for "no matter what kind of hell, it was theirs, they were together" (*PH*, 227). She has a constant fear of not seeing Adam again, for "every step they took towards each other seemed perilous, drawing them apart instead of together, as a swimmer in spite of his most determined strokes is yet drawn slowly backward by the tide"—and yet she looks at him with eyes "steady and non-committal," and tells herself, in spite of herself, "I don't want to love, not Adam, there is no time and we are not ready for it and yet this is all we have—"(*PH*, 219). At his nearness "a deep tremor set up in Miranda, and she set about resisting herself methodically as if she were closing windows and doors and fastening down curtains against a rising storm" (*PH*, 220). The ambiguity of Miranda's attitude, with its blend of acceptance and rejection, is a reminder that her love story, while partially convincing as romantic tragedy, is nevertheless, on the level of realized human experience, perfectly compatible with the pattern of rejection. Life will never give her enough "time" to love.

It is only when Miranda has slipped into the timeless half-world of her illness that she seems to capitulate. " 'Adam,' she said out of the heavy soft darkness that drew her down, down, 'I love you, and I was hoping you would say that to me, too.'

He lay down beside her with his arm under her shoulder,

7. There is a remarkable similarity between Miranda's Adam-as-dancing-partner and the "good-looking, gold-braided young officer" who plays a similar role for Mrs. Treadwell. See *Ship of Fools*, page 434, and the discussion of that passage in Chapter Five below.

and pressed his smooth face against hers, his mouth moved towards her mouth and stopped. 'Can you hear what I am saying? . . . What do you think I have been trying to tell you all this time?' " (*PH*, 241) She sees him clearly only for an instant; then he soothes her to sleep with the words, "I love you." She dreams that she is the cause of his death, and when she wakes he leaves "for five minutes" and she never sees him again. This apparent tragic parting of two lovers is in reality rather thoroughly undermined by the tendencies of the rejection theme. Adam, of course, fulfils the role of ideal lover, then disappears. Miranda arrives at her apparent self-commitment only at the moment of parting when it need have no consequences whatever. She is not even in full control of herself when she vows her love, and her final grasping at the vanishing ideal will serve only to deepen the bitterness of the disillusion with life which is to follow.

If it requires a careful reading to see that "Pale Horse, Pale Rider" is not a genuine love story, there is no such difficulty involved in seeing that it is a story of death. Death is in the very title, which as usual points directly at the heart of the work. The story opens with Miranda's dream of the pale rider, whose lineaments seem derived from the South's romantic dream of the Civil War. The reader of the earlier Miranda stories knows that she has always been preoccupied with death, and the pale rider is presented as an acquaintance of her childhood. "And the stranger? Where is that lank greenish stranger I remember hanging about the place, welcomed by my grandfather, my great-aunt, my five times removed cousin, my decrepit hound and my silver kitten? Why did they take to him, I wonder? And where are they now? Yet I saw him pass the window in the evening" (*PH*, 180). Death is the ultimate oppression, and in this last Miranda story more than in any other, it hovers behind the immediate oppressions which surround the heroine. On waking from the dream she first becomes clearly aware of her headache, and this headache blends with another nagging preoccupation—the war. "Slowly, unwillingly, Miranda drew herself up inch by inch out of the pit of sleep, waited in a daze for life to begin again. A single word struck in her mind, a gong of warning, reminding her for the day long what she forgot happily in sleep, and only in sleep. The war, said the gong, and she shook her head" (*PH*, 182). She recalls another daily irritation: "Dangling her feet idly with their slippers hanging, she was reminded of the way all sorts of persons sat upon her desk at the newspaper office. Every day she found someone there, sitting upon her desk instead of the chair provided, dangling his legs, eyes roving, full of his important affairs, waiting to pounce about something or other. '*Why* won't they sit in the chair? Should I put a sign on it, saying, "For God's sake, sit here"?' " (*PH*, 182) Miranda finds her mind working "in a continual effort to bring together and unite firmly the disturbing oppositions in her day-to-day existence, where survival, she could see clearly, had become a series of feats of sleight of hand" (*PH*, 182-83). In a conversation with Adam she voices her hatred for the war, which she sees, characteristically, as a series of oppressions inflicted upon herself. "The worst of war is the fear and suspicion and the awful expression in all the eyes you meet . . . as if they had pulled down the shutters over their minds and their hearts and were peering out at you, ready to leap if you make one gesture or say one word they do not understand instantly. It frightens me; I live in fear too, and no one should have to live in fear." (*PH*, 223-24). She is currently being subjected to a particularly odious invasion of her liberty in the form of patriotic persecution by the Lusk Committee, whose representatives try to intimidate her into buying a Liberty Bond which she cannot afford. The visit of these dignitaries, combining as it does the two motifs of oppression and scorn for men, calls forth the author's best efforts:

The two men slid off the desk, leaving some of her papers rumpled, and the oldish man had inquired why she had not bought a Liberty Bond. Miranda had looked at him then, and got a poor impression. He was a pursy-faced man, gross-mouthed, with little lightless eyes, and Miranda wondered why nearly all of those selected to do the war work at home were of his sort . . . "Look here," he asked her, "do you know there's a war, or don't you?" . . . "Yeah," said the younger man in a nasty way, "the war." Miranda, startled by the tone, met his eyes; his stare was really stony, really viciously cold, the kind of thing you might expect to meet behind a pistol on a deserted corner. This expression gave temporary meaning to a set of features otherwise nondescript, the face of those men who have no business of their own. . . . (they had stood there cawing back and forth over her head) . . .

Miranda, desperately silent, had thought, "Suppose I were not a coward, but said what I really thought? Suppose I said to hell with this filthy war? Suppose I asked that little thug, What's the matter with you, why aren't you rotting in Belleau Wood? I wish you were . . ."

(*PH,* 184-86)

In this episode, in the portrayals of the small-time actor and the dollar-a-year man, and in other passages where the plot gives free rein to the motif, we find the familiar acid etchings of contemptible males. Miranda never fails to criticize, at least mildly, every man with whom she comes in contact. Of Bill, her city editor, she tolerantly observes that "He would never be more than fourteen years old if he lived for a century" (*PH,* 211), and she studies Chuck's pathetic efforts to conceal the fact that he "had a bad lung and didn't care for sports" (*PH,* 212). At times she even regards the admirable Adam as a child, another of the indications that she is managing to keep her distance. She thinks patronizingly about his fondness for "machinery," and on another occasion her thoughts run as follows: "No, there was no resentment or revolt in him. Pure, she thought, all the way through, flawless, complete, as the sacrificial lamb must be. The sacrificial lamb strode along casually, accommodating his long pace to hers, keeping her on the inside of the walk in the good American style, helping her across street corners as if she were a cripple—'I hope we don't come to a mud puddle, he'll carry me over it.' " (*PH,* 224).

Miranda is aware that she is about to undergo some profound ordeal, perhaps even death, and she has a painful certainty that death will soon take Adam from her; yet she seems more preoccupied with her present difficulties and her desire to escape with him than with the threat of her own death. This is not surprising, for her desire to escape is fundamentally an unconscious desire for death. This is clearly revealed in her thoughts. Early in the story, while bathing, "Miranda turned over in the soothing water, and wished she might fall asleep there, to wake up only when it was time to sleep again" (*PH,* 188). As her headache grows worse and the noises of the newspaper office more irritating, she tells Adam that she longs to sit in a park or drive to the mountains. He suggests tomorrow, and she answers, "Yes, tomorrow, unless something else happens. I'd like to run away; let's both" (*PH,* 202). Later, after a disturbing encounter with an actor she has criticized, she tells Chuck, "There's too much of everything in this world just now. I'd like to sit down here on the curb, Chuck, and die, and never again see—I wish I could lose my memory and forget my own name . . . I wish—" (*PH,* 214). The ambiguity in Miranda's attitude toward death appears in the dream of the pale rider, which is a link with her early life. She dreams that she is in her childhood home, preparing to escape from the house for an early morning ride.

> Now I must get up and go while they are all quiet. Where are my things? Things have a will of their own in this place and hide where they like. Daylight will strike a sudden blow on the roof startling them all up to their feet; faces will beam asking, Where are you going, What are you doing, What are you thinking, How do you feel, Why do you say such things, What do you mean? No more sleep. Where are my boots and what horse shall I ride? Fiddler or Graylie or Miss Lucy with the long nose and the wicked eye? How I have loved this house in the morning before we are all awake and tangled together like badly cast fishing lines. Too many people have been born here, and have wept too much here, and have laughed too much, and have been too angry and outrageous with each other here. Too many have died in this bed already, there are far too many ancestral bones propped up on the mantelpieces, there have been too damned many antimacassars in this house, she said loudly, and oh, what accumulation of storied dust never allowed to settle in peace for one moment.
>
> (*PH,* 179-80)

From here the dream goes on to the vision of the pale rider, after which she wakes to the oppressions of the war and of life. The romantic childhood image of death and the childhood sense of oppression blend into the present sense of death and oppression, and this early dream anticipates and contrasts importantly with Miranda's approaching vision of death and paradise. All the important strands in the story and in her entire life will be brought together in the visions of Miranda's illness.

From the moment Adam departs and the interns take Miranda away, her love affair becomes simply and inevitably a lost ideal, like Laura's love in "Flowering Judas," or that of the heroine in "Theft," or Granny Weatherall's love for the man who jilted her, or Charles Upton's dream of a romantic Berlin. The sense of loss has a validity which the love affair did not, for to the author loss is real. The motif has appeared earlier in the story as a foreshadowing of what is to come. Once, upon leaving her room for a meeting with Adam, Miranda "stood undecided a moment possessed by the notion that she had forgotten something she would miss seriously later on" (*PH*, 195). This feeling remains in the back of the reader's mind, without any specific applicability, until it blends with the heroine's final sense of deprivation. Even in the opening dream there is mention of Miranda's ambivalent poverty, with the emphasis this time on her contentment with it. Death has taken everyone from her and she thinks, "What else besides them did I have in the world? Nothing. Nothing is mine, I have only nothing but it is enough, it is beautiful and it is all mine. Do I even walk about in my own skin or is it something I have borrowed to spare my modesty?" (*PH*, 180) At the end of the story, even the humble flesh will be sadly diminished.

The ever-present thought of war and death is given its bitterness by its threat of deprivation. On one occasion Miranda "closed her eyes and faced for one instant that was a lifetime the certain, the overwhelming and awful knowledge that there was nothing at all ahead for Adam and for her. Nothing. She opened her eyes and held her hands together palms up, gazing at them and trying to understand oblivion" (*PH*, 217). Later, as her body undergoes alternating chills and fever, her mind wanders into delirium. Her first thought is a death wish, veiled in the imagery of whiteness which will later envelop her. "I wish I were in the cold mountains in the snow, that's what I should like best; and all about her rose the measured ranges of the Rockies wearing their perpetual snow, their majestic blue laurels of cloud, chilling her to the bone with their sharp breath" (*PH,* 231). Her mind then swings in contrast to her childhood home, which she loves, one notes, not for human but for aesthetic reasons.

Oh, no, I must have warmth—and her memory turned and roved after another place she had known first and loved best, that now she could see only in drifting fragments of palm and cedar, dark shadows and a sky that warmed without dazzling, as this strange sky had dazzled without warming her; there was the long slow wavering of gray moss in the drowsy oak shade, the spacious hovering of buzzards overhead, the smell of crushed water herbs along a bank, and without warning a broad tranquil river into which flowed all the rivers she had known.

(*PH,* 231)

As her preoccupation with death forces itself into the dream, she sees a ship beside her bed and behind it a Rousseauistic archetypal jungle, "a writhing terribly alive and secret place of death, creeping with tangles of spotted serpents, rainbow-colored birds with malign eyes, leopards with humanly wise faces and extravagantly crested lions; screaming long-armed monkeys tumbling among broad fleshy leaves that glowed with sulphur-colored light and exuded the ichor of death, and rotting trunks of unfamiliar trees sprawled in crawling slime" (*PH,* 232). She gaily boards the ship and sails into the jungle, where she is suddenly beset from all sides by the fears that have been troubling her waking hours. "The air trembled with the shattering scream and the hoarse bellow of voices all crying together, rolling and colliding above her like ragged storm clouds, and the words became two words only rising and falling and clamoring about her head. Danger, danger, danger, the voices said, and War, war, war" (*PH,* 232). This dream is the second in a series of four which Miranda has during the story. In one respect these four dreams constitute a progressive purification of her idea of death. In the first she saw it in the form of a not completely unpleasant figure derived from romantic childhood memories. The second presents death more realistically in terms of fearfulness and corruption, but it also employs imagery accumulated during her life. The third dream, that of the flying arrows, brings her closer to the essence of death by presenting it as the privation of all her happiness (in the form of Adam). The symbolism is simpler than before and the realization stronger. In the fourth dream Miranda will see death as it were face to face, with imagery of the utmost simplicity. This imagery, like that of the pale rider, will be drawn from her childhood, but this time from her earliest and most fundamental images, not the romantic superficialities of her communal mythology. This last dream must be approached by way of the events leading to it and studied carefully, for it is the most important episode in all of Miss Porter's work and the key to the rejection theme which underlies everything she has written.

When Miranda asks about Adam she is told he left a note and will be back tomorrow. She does not believe this, and when the note is read cannot grasp "the dancing words that just escaped as she almost touched them" (*PH,* 247). She sinks deeper into silent whiteness, the color of death and privation, which first surrounded her when the white-clad Dr. Hildesheim wrapped her in a white blanket. "The white walls rose sheer as cliffs, a dozen frosted moons followed each other in perfect self-possession down a white lane and dropped mutely one by one into a snowy abyss" (*PH,* 247). She sees a corpse wrapped in white with a large stiff bow "like merry rabbit ears" taken away, and is then surrounded by a white fog which conceals within it all the sufferings of the world, and fears it "might part at any moment and loose the horde of human torments" (*PH,* 248-49). In this fog she sees two white-clad executioners hurrying toward death a pitiable old man who is trying to explain "in a high weeping voice" that "The crime of which he was accused did not merit the punishment he was about to receive" (*PH,* 249). This, incidentally, is a concise statement of Miranda's view of life. The following lines expand upon it:

"The road to death is a long march beset with all evils, and the heart fails little by little at each new terror, the bones rebel at each step, the mind sets up its own bitter resistance and to what end? The barriers sink one by one, and no covering of the eyes shuts out the landscape of disaster, nor the sight of crimes committed there" (*PH*, 249). In a sort of sinister political cartoon she sees Dr. Hildesheim, "his face a skull beneath his German helmet, carrying a naked infant writhing on the point of his bayonet, and a huge stone pot marked Poison in Gothic letters. He stopped before the well that Miranda remembered in a pasture on her father's farm, a well once dry but now bubbling with living water, and into its pure depths he threw the child and the poison, and the violated water sank back soundlessly into the earth" (*PH*, 249-50). In this juxtaposition of old and recent images she sees the war, and the doctor who has taken her from her lover, poisoning the new source of happiness and vitality which she has just found—her ideal love for Adam. Significantly, the vitality is not derived from the lover but seems to have been potentially present in her own nature. She screams abuse at the doctor and then is haunted by the guilt of her injustice. Her consciousness is split, half suffering and half observing. She wakes and sees the nurse's hands and knows they are hands but also says, "to me they are white tarantulas, don't touch me" (*PH*, 251). She fears to close her eyes lest she see worse things, but once again "the midnight of her internal torment closed about her" (*PH*, 251). She now has her last and most terrifying vision of death. All the words and almost all the images she has used to describe it fade away.

She lay on a narrow ledge over a pit that she knew to be bottomless, though she could not comprehend it; the ledge was her childhood dream of danger, and she strained back against a reassuring wall of granite at her shoulders, staring into the pit, thinking. There it is, there it is at last, it is very simple; and soft carefully shaped words like oblivion and eternity are curtains hung before nothing at all. I shall not know when it happens, I shall not feel or remember, why can't I consent now, I am lost, there is no hope for me. Look, she told herself, there it is, that is death and there is nothing to fear. But she could not consent, still shrinking stiffly against the granite

wall that was her childhood dream of safety, breathing slowly for
fear of squandering breath, saying desperately, Look, don't be afraid,
it is nothing, it is only eternity.

(*PH,* 251-52)

With this tremendous vision of the void Miranda has come to
the limit of her world. Her lifelong need for truth has at last
been satisfied, and the truth is nothing. No longer will there be
"tough filaments of memory and hope pulling taut backwards
and forwards holding her upright between them" (*PH,* 241),
for now there can be no hope, and memory is only pain. But
even now the life within her refuses to surrender. Her mind
continues seeking and undergoes a further purification of images.

Granite walls, whirlpools, stars are things. None of them is death,
nor the image of it. Death is death, said Miranda, and for the dead
it has no attributes. Silenced she sank easily through deeps under
deeps of darkness until she lay like a stone at the farthest bottom of
life, knowing herself to be blind, deaf, speechless, no longer aware
of the members of her own body, entirely withdrawn from all human
concerns, yet alive with a peculiar lucidity and coherence; all notions
of the mind, the reasonable inquiries of doubt, all ties of blood and
the desires of the heart, dissolved and fell away from her, and there
remained of her only a minute fiercely burning particle of being
that knew itself alone, that relied upon nothing beyond itself for its
strength; not susceptible to any appeal or inducement, being itself
composed entirely of one single motive, the stubborn will to live.
This fiery motionless particle set itself unaided to resist destruction,
to survive and to be in its own madness of being, motiveless and
planless beyond that one essential end. Trust me, the hard unwinking
angry point of light said. Trust me. I stay.

(*PH,* 252-53)

The final realization that death is unknowable comforts the
questing mind, which is now content to cease its anxious
wrestling with images and sink into darkness. The observing
half, meanwhile, goes on watching. Even it is still bound to
images, but now the image has reached the ultimate simplicity,
signifying only existence. As in the case of Granny Weatherall,
it is the traditional one of light. Miranda has now reached the
lowest point in her physical life.

The vision, like Miranda's life, is marked by a fundamental ambivalence. There is the instinct of rejection, which is a flight from all known reality and hence toward death, but there is also a tenacious instinct of life doing battle with it. She wants to fall into the abyss, yet she does not. This time the choice is not in her hands; she may not reject life as she rejected family, society, husband. Here the outcome rests, ironically, with Dr. Hildesheim. Yet the tension here is great. Her downward path represents a disengagement which Miranda has always sought— from "all human concerns," from painful thoughts, doubts, and desires, from "all ties of blood"—but when this progressive liberation brings her to the last single point of light, she cannot reject it as easily for it is herself. In fact, this existence as an unwinking angry point of light is the goal she has always sought. This stubborn flame possesses the qualities of the strong, self-sufficient heroine—qualities which Miranda cannot help but admire, as she admired them, through connaturality, in her Grandmother. The entire bent of her life has led her toward a likeness with this being that "relied upon nothing beyond itself for its strength, . . . composed entirely of one single motive, the stubborn will to live"—but such a life can exist only on the threshold of death.

From this point of light poised between life and death there now grows, like a soap bubble balanced on a razor's edge, the vision of Miranda's paradise. This vision marks a culmination in her life as well as in this most crucial of her stories. The importance of the scene in Miss Porter's eyes is indicated by some biographical details furnished by her friend Glenway Wescott:

It pleases me to recall a conversation that I had with Katherine Anne while she was writing "Pale Horse, Pale Rider" and was having trouble with a passage in it toward the end in which Miranda, desperately ill, almost dead, was to see heaven. She told me that she herself, at the end of World War I, had experienced this part of what she had created this heroine to experience and to make manifest; and because, no doubt, it really was heaven, she found herself unable to re-see it with her lively, healthy eyes. . . . With characteristic, somewhat superficial helpfulness I proposed to my dear friend and rival, "Why not at that point just write a page about your inability to recede, your impotence to write? . . . Let each one of your readers fill in the kind of heaven that his particular life has prepared him to go to, when his turn comes. . . . Katherine Anne did not take to this suggestion. She let "Pale Horse" go for another year, and turned to other work. . . .

In due course, "Pale Horse, Pale Rider" appeared in book form, in 1939, with the vision worth a year's waiting: "thinned to a fine radiance, spread like a great fan, and curved out into a curved rainbow."[8]

Every reader will share Wescott's gratitude for his friend's perseverance, and the reader aware of the importance of this scene in relation to Miss Porter's fiction as well as her life will not be surprised at it. Wescott is right, of course; this is no theological heaven but precisely the kind of heaven that Miranda's particular life has prepared her to go to when her turn comes. It is the ideal she has unconsciously been seeking with all the force of her being. Consequently it is also the standard by which she has judged life and inevitably found it wanting.

The passage should be seen in its entirety. It follows the lines, "Trust me, the hard unwinking angry point of light said. Trust me. I stay":

At once it grew, flattened, thinned to a fine radiance, spread like a great fan and curved out into a rainbow through which Miranda, enchanted, altogether believing, looked upon a deep clear landscape of sea and sand, of soft meadow and sky, freshly washed and glistening with transparencies of blue. Why, of course, of course, said Miranda, without surprise but with serene rapture as if some promise made to her had been kept long after she had ceased to hope for it. She rose from her narrow ledge and ran lightly through the tall portals of the great bow that arched in its splendor over the burning blue of the sea and the cool green of the meadow on either hand.

The small waves rolled in and over unhurriedly, lapped upon the sand in silence and retreated; the grasses flurried before a breeze that made no sound. Moving towards her leisurely as clouds through the shimmering air came a great company of human beings, and Miranda saw in an amazement of joy that they were all the living she had known. Their faces were transfigured, each in its own

8. *Images of Truth: Remembrances and Criticism* (New York, 1962), pp. 37-38.

beauty, beyond what she remembered of them, their eyes clear and untroubled as good weather, and they cast no shadows. They were pure identities and she knew them every one without calling their names or remembering what relation she bore to them. They surrounded her smoothly on silent feet, then turned their entranced faces again towards the sea, and she moved among them easily as a wave among waves. The drifting circle widened, separated, and each figure was alone but not solitary; Miranda, alone too, questioning nothing, desiring nothing, in the quietude of her ecstasy, stayed where she was, eyes fixed on the overwhelming deep sky where it was always morning.

(*PH,* 253-54)

Thus Miranda, whose eyes have never stopped seeking truth and some beauty beyond it, finally enters her brave new world. In it she finds perfected the beauties she has loved—meadows, the sea, the freshness of morning. But most significant are the people, now not "tangled together like badly cast fishing lines," but surrounding her in a perfect equilibrium of nearness and remoteness, communion and solitude. Far more beautiful than that forgotten Adam who dimly prefigured them, they are purified of the abrasive human traits which made them burdensome to Miranda. Her joy is perfect, but it cannot last. This heaven elaborated out of the tiny flame of an impossible desire is visible only when every trace of the distorted, painful, oppressive world of reality has been refined away. But Miranda must now be drawn back up into that bitter world. "Lying at ease, arms under her head, in the prodigal warmth which flowed evenly from sea and sky and meadow, within touch but not touching the serenely smiling familiar beings about her, Miranda felt without warning a vague tremor of apprehension, some small flick of distrust in her joy; a thin frost touched the edges of this confident tranquility; something, somebody, was missing, she had lost something, she had left something valuable in another country, oh, what could it be?" (*PH,* 254)

The familiar sense of loss occurs in a context which reveals what had always been its deepest meaning: "There are no trees, no trees here, she said in fright, I have left something unfinished. A thought struggled at the back of her mind, came clearly as a voice in her ear. Where are the dead? We have forgotten the dead, oh, the dead, where are they? At once as if a curtain had fallen, the bright landscape faded, she was alone in a strange stony place of bitter cold, picking her way along a steep path of slippery snow, calling out, Oh, I must go back! But in what direction?" (*PH,* 254-55) The flaw, first noticed as an imperfection in the natural verisimilitude of the scene, quickly becomes known as a radical defect in the plan: its failure to account for death, the root of Miranda's sense of loss. She is still on this side of death; and death, as she has seen, is oblivion. Her paradise was an illusion projected upon an uncertain future by the light of her desire, refracted through the crabbed, inadequate forms of reality. Its vanishing is her final disillusion, and the terrible irony of her return to consciousness is almost beyond description.

Pain returned, a terrible compelling pain running through her veins like heavy fire, the stench of corruption filled her nostrils, the sweetish sickening smell of rotting flesh and pus; she opened her eyes and saw pale light through a coarse white cloth over her face, knew that the smell of death was in her own body, and struggled to lift her hand. The cloth was drawn away; she saw Miss Tanner filling a hypodermic needle in her methodical expert way, and heard Dr. Hildesheim saying, "I think that will do the trick. Try another."[9]

(*PH,* 255)

The story of Miranda is over. After "Pale Horse, Pale Rider" there can be nothing more to tell. She has learned that the promise made to her will not be kept. The dissatisfaction, sense

9. In *Images of Truth* Wescott records an episode from Miss Porter's early life which may have some significance here. He says that "when she was a girl somewhere in the South, she had to spend months and months in a sanitarium with a grave pulmonary illness, diagnosed as one of the baffling, uncommon forms of tuberculosis. She was too ill to have visitors. Letters also evidently were overstimulating and exhausting. Even books seemed not good for her; her reading had to be rationed, just a few pages at a time. Then it was discovered that the intense restlessness of her bright eyes gazing at the ceiling, examining and re-examining the furniture, staring at the solitude, gave her a temperature. Her doctor therefore prescribed that a restful green baize cloth be placed over her face for an hour or two every morning and every afternoon, as one covers the cage of a canary when one doesn't want it to sing. . . . That was only the beginning of a lifetime of delicate health and indomitable strength" (p. 29).

of loss, and threat of death which have clouded her life now darken it completely. The imagery in the remainder of the story will be marked by lack of color and imperfection of form. The walls of her room, once white, are now "a soiled gray." And both Miranda and the reader know, even before reading the letter bearing the news, that Adam is dead. She is now doubly confirmed in her life-long isolation.

After her wasting illness, Miranda's disgusted rejection includes even her own body. It is "a curious monster," she reflects, "no place to live in, how could anyone feel at home there? Is it possible I can ever accustom myself to this place?" (*PH,* 257) She feels now in the world, as Charles Upton in Berlin and Laura in Mexico felt after vainly seeking their ideals there, like "an alien who does not like the country in which he finds himself, . . . does not mean to live there and yet is helpless, unable to leave it at his will" (*PH,* 257-58). She now finds oppressive "the precise machine of the hospital, the whole humane conviction and custom of society" which set her "once more safely in the road that would lead her again to death" (*PH,* 260). Now there can be no escape. Her friends come to cheer her and she feigns cheer, for "it will not do to betray the conspiracy and tamper with the courage of the living; there is nothing better than to be alive, everyone has agreed on that" (*PH,* 260). Realizing that she cares for no one, "her hardened, indifferent heart shuddered in despair at itself, because before it had been tender and capable of love" (*PH,* 261). Whatever love there was in Miranda's earlier life is now, like her fragile love for Adam, utterly dead. At the loss of her paradise the heart in her bosom has broken, as did that of her Grandmother, leaving her incapable of deep feeling. Her life now, also like her Grandmother's, must be one of stern and futile endurance.

She returns to the routine of living. There is a hint of the instinct of rejection in her request for "gray suede gauntlets without straps, . . . gray sheer stockings without clocks"—as Towney says, "Everything without something so that it will be almost impossible to get" (*PH,* 262). She tells herself that she will eventually be again at home in life, but the reader knows she never has been. She thinks of Adam, declares her love for him, and sees his ghost, "the last intolerable cheat of her heart" (*PH*, 264); but now, after her vision of paradise, the love plot stands exposed in its essential shallowness. The dim anticipation of paradise that Miranda saw in Adam has been swallowed up by the direct vision. The thought of him now is only part of the sense of loss. But she warns herself not to think of the all that is lost, and with a courage that demands admiration turns again toward life—not this time as at the end of "Old Mortality," in "her hopefulness, her ignorance," for she has learned that only ignorance can justify hopefulness. As ever, she will be the strong, self-sufficient woman, but now there will be no meaning beyond her strength, no hope.

5

Ship of Fools

※

In her introduction to Eudora Welty's "A Curtain of Green" (1941), Katherine Anne Porter speaks of what she considers one of the hazards of the writer's trade: "But there is a trap lying just ahead, and all short-story writers know what it is—The Novel. That novel which every publisher hopes to obtain from every short-story writer of any gifts at all, and who finally does obtain it, nine times out of ten. Already publishers have told her, 'Give us first a novel, and then we will publish your short stories.' "[1] As usual Miss Porter speaks from her own experience. But in her case, as one would expect, the compulsion came from within; for she has never been one to obey publishers or anyone else where her art is concerned. She herself tells, in an interview with Elizabeth Janeway, how the novel forced itself upon her:

I wrote the first and last pages in 1940 in Louisiana. It was to be another short novel, like the three in "Pale Horse, Pale Rider." I

1. *The Days Before* (New York: Harcourt, Brace and Company, 1952), p. 105.

wrote those very quickly after I came back from Europe. Of course, I'd been making notes for years. But I wrote them each in a week—no, a week for "Old Mortality" and "Noon Wine," nine days for "Pale Horse, Pale Rider." Then I started "Ship of Fools," and wrote straight ahead, fifty pages very quickly, before I realized that it was going to be something else, something long. But none of that fifty pages is lost.[2]

Even though no outside agent coerced her into it, *Ship of Fools* did prove to be in some respects a trap for Katherine Anne Porter. She seems to have felt this acutely in 1941 when she was still in the early throes of trying to finish the expanding novel which had so soon got out of hand. She began it in the brief period of creativity which produced some of her finest work, but it was just at that time that her talent—which had never been suited to long novels—began to decline, or better, to contract. The only important short works which lay ahead were "The Downward Path" and "A Day's Work," two extremely narrow studies in bitterness; the strange, subjective, and unsuccessful "Leaning Tower"; and the brilliant sketches, which were the product of an autobiographical regression and a further narrowing of vision down to the inner core of memory. In short, narrowness and rejection were becoming increasingly dominant, and the ungainly novel went counter to the prevailing trends. The situation was not at all auspicious for beginning a work which would attempt to be broad in scope and objective in view, and the outcome has shown that the obstacles largely prevailed.

The voyage of *Ship of Fools* was a long and halting one: "1932: Paris, Rambouillet, Davosplatz, Salzburg, Munich, New York, Mulhocaway, Rosemont: 1962; Yaddo, August, 1941; Pigeon Cove, August, 1961." As Miss Porter states on an introductory page, it was in 1932 that she read Sebastian Brant's *Das Narrenschiff* with the memory of her first European voyage (Veracruz to Bremerhaven in 1931) still fresh in her mind. This was also the year in which she began taking notes for the novel, though there were some years after 1932 when she

2. *The New York Times Book Review,* April 1, 1962, p. 5.

"didn't touch it."[3] Glenway Wescott, in *Images of Truth,* gives the following detail: *"Ship of Fools* began with a sea voyage that she took in 1931 and specifically, she says, with an account of it in a letter to her friend and fellow writer, Caroline Gordon."[4] The delay during the early years may be attributed largely to numerous interruptions, several of which Wescott lists: frequent illness, an extremely full and sociable life, financial difficulties, lectures and university teaching, non-fiction writing, an unsettled world situation, difficulties in her personal life, difficulties within the novel itself—in short, a great deal of "heartbreak and travail."[5] In spite of her avowed rejection of literary companionship and interdependence and her oft-expressed desire for free time to devote to her writing, Miss Porter has, almost compulsively, it would seem, stayed in the literary limelight. For this reason, and because of the high quality of her early work, the forthcoming novel which she first announced in 1940 was awaited with a variety of feelings and an abundance of publicity. Several portions of it were published over a number of years in various periodicals.[6] In his review of the book Mark Schorer comments, "This novel has been famous for years. It has been awaited through an entire literary generation. Publishers and foundations, like many once hopeful readers, long ago gave it up."[7] It was principally the sustained effort of the late 1950's that finally brought the book to completion. During this period the author lived in a country home in Connecticut where, as Wescott quotes her, she stayed "on guard and secretive and solitary as a woodchuck peeping out of its hidey-hole."[8]

3. *Ibid.*
4. *Ibid.,* p. 47.
5. *Ibid.,* p. 46.
6. Edward Schwartz, "Katherine Anne Porter: A Critical Bibliography," *Bulletin of the New York Public Library,* LVII (May, 1953), 211-47, lists the following: "Embarkation," *Sewanee Review,* LX (January, 1947), 1-23; "The Exile," *Harper's Magazine,* CCI (December, 1950), 70-78; "The High Sea," *Partisan Review,* XII (Fall, 1945), 514-49; "Kein Haus, Keine Heimat," *Sewanee Review,* LII (October, 1944), 465-82; "The Prisoner," *Harper's Magazine,* CCI (October, 1950), 88-96; "The Strangers," *Accent,* VI (Summer, 1946), 211-29; "Under Weigh," *Harper's Magazine,* CCI (November, 1950), 80-88.
7. *The New York Times Book Review,* April 1, 1962, p. 1.
8. *Images of Truth: Remembrances and Criticism* (New York, 1962), p. 47.

In a prefatory comment, Miss Porter states explicitly that her novel employs the "simple almost universal image of the ship of this world on its voyage to eternity." This allegorical meaning is applied to the voyage as a whole rather than to specific details of it. The limited extent to which individual characters are given allegorical significance may be illustrated by the portrayal of the captain, the character who lends himself most readily to this purpose. Some attention has obviously been given to emphasizing his role as the "God" of his little world. Early in the voyage he remains hidden because, as he later informs his table companions, the innumerable responsibilities of getting the ship underway require his undivided attention. Whatever subtlety there is in this parallel is dissipated when he appears. His face is "that of a pompous minor god: a god who had grown somewhat petulant and more than a little mean in his efforts to maintain his authority" (*SF*, 94-95). In view of the kind of universe presented by the author in this book and in her earlier works, it is clear that this weak, pompous ruler is intended to represent the stern fundamentalist God of her early religious training as envisioned by the artist-intellectual of today. Eventually it is admitted that he simply hates all passengers. Throughout the book his false front conceals fear and weakness, and on the night of the fiesta, when the evil Spanish dancers take over the captain's table, he is driven into hiding. There may even be an irreverent allusion to the doctrines of the generation of the Word and the Incarnation in this line which follows a description of the captain's ill-humored face: "It was as if his own nature had shaped his face to match itself" (*SF*, 95).

While the captain represents the closest approach to allegory in the portrayal of individual character, the *Vera* is meant, in a general way, to present the truth about the world. The great majority of its passengers are poor, crowded, and without hope of betterment. When asked about them, the officers reply that "they had no idea who the steerage passengers were, nor why there were so many, nor what their situation was precisely, except that anyone could see they were of the lowest class. No doubt everything would be known in time" (*SF*, 58). These people seem to present a vague threat to the passengers who gaze down at them like visitors at a zoo, but the latter put their faith in the captain's ability to keep the lower classes under control. Various races and types are included among the travelers, as well as some unspecified miscellaneous freight. It is not a pleasure cruise, and the honest *Vera* is far from ideal. It is a small ship, "like a prison almost," and considerably the worse for wear. A middling ship, it carries a middling sort of passenger. The doctor reflects that it is simply a microcosm of life: he has seen all these people before. Freytag notes that "people on voyage mostly went on behaving as if they were on dry land, and there is simply not room for it on a ship. Every smallest act shows up more clearly and looks worse, because it has lost its background" (*SF,* 132). The author's identification of the ship with the world has serious implications, for it is a claim that the picture presented is a balanced and reasonably complete one. Miss Porter has confirmed this intention. It is the sum, she has said, "of what I know about human nature, the fatalities of life and the perils of human relationships. Everything I was able to express I put in it."[9] Whatever else may be said about the book, it must be judged in the light of this claim.

Ship of Fools is a novel only in one of the broader senses of that protean term, for, as Mark Schorer says in his review of the book, it has "no plot, not even, really, a story."[10] Its magnitude lies not in the long, intricate plot of the classic novel but in the fact that it portrays over forty characters, many of them at considerable length, through a loose and leisurely accumulation of data provided by dramatization of their actions, penetration of their thoughts, and commentary on their backgrounds. Miss Porter has spoken of the book in terms of scenes written when she could "see" them and then arranged in order with connecting bridges.[11] The dining room, with its captain's table and descending hierarchical order, is the one setting in which all the passengers gather and the tensions between them

9. Rochelle Girson, "The Author," *Saturday Review,* XLV (March 31, 1962), 15.

10. Schorer, *The New York Times Book Review,* p. 1.

11. Janeway, *The New York Times Book Review,* pp. 4-5.

take visible form. Their other encounters are in smaller groups on the deck or in their cabins, and some of them are frequently presented alone. Below the passenger deck is the steerage, into which are crowded "eight hundred and seventy-six souls: Spaniards, men, women, children, workers in the sugar fields of Cuba, being deported back to the Canaries and to various parts of Spain (wherever they came from) after the failure of the sugar market" (*SF,* xii). The novel is given clear-cut unity by the convention of the sea voyage, but within that unity there is only the simplest structure. There are three parts, "Embarkation" (68 pages), "High Sea" (292 pages), and "The Harbors" (136 pages), each possessing a somewhat distinctive mood established primarily through the abundance of concrete detail related to each stage of the voyage. What the story contains of plot consists of gradual developments in the relations, mostly casual, between passengers. A fiesta given near the end of the voyage by the zarzuela troupe fulfils several purposes, the most important of which is to provide a climax in the development of the social pattern. The fiesta is first mentioned about midway through the book, and it takes place just before arrival at the first port of destination. On the night of the fiesta many of the forces which have been building up are released in bursts of passion and violence. The social structure of the little world is upset and the forces of evil reign. After this climax, interest drops off quickly. Contrary to common practice, the arrivals at destination are dull, gloomy, anticlimactic. The book closes as David and Jenny, neither of whom desired it, land in a Germany of darkness, cold, and menacing evil.

The style of *Ship of Fools* is generally smooth and competent, adhering to the literal concreteness which is characteristic of the traditional novel. Wescott speaks of reading long sections without encountering a metaphor. Perhaps necessarily, the style of the novel lacks the flexibility and brilliant intensity that characterizes that of most of the stories. These familiar qualities do appear, however, in the leisurely and sharply detailed description of Veracruz which opens the novel.[12] In a

12. It will be remembered that the opening section of *Ship of Fools* was written at the time of the *Pale Horse, Pale Rider* stories.

manner reminiscent of "Hacienda," Miss Porter richly documents the lassitude, corruption, and general disorder of the Mexican seaport town. The powerful effect is obtained largely through animal and animal-human imagery, which she has used frequently for similar purposes, though never so strongly as here.

A woman reached her bare arm out of the window to the parrot and gave him a rotten-ripe banana. The parrot, with a little croak of thanks, took it in one claw and ate, fixing a hard dangerous eye on the monkey, who chattered with greed and fear. The cat, who despised them both and feared neither because he was free to fight or run as he chose, was roused by the smell of the raw, tainted meat hanging in chunks in the small butcher's stand below him. Presently he slid over the sill and dropped in silence upon the offal at the butcher's feet. A mangy dog leaped snarling at the cat, and there was a fine, yelping, hissing race between them to the nearest tree in the square, where the cat clawed his way out of danger and the dog, in his blindness of fury, stumbled across the abused feet of the Indian on the bench. The Indian seemed hardly to move, yet with perfect swiftness and economy swung his leg from the knee and planted a kick with the hard edge of his sandal in the dog's lean ribs. The dog, howling all the way, rushed back to the butcher's stand.

(SF, 5-6)

If the line between human and animal is thin in this passage, it disappears in the next.

The beggar who came to the terrace every morning in time for the early traffic appeared around the corner shambling and crawling, the stumps of his four limbs bound in leather and twine. He had been in early life so intricately maimed and deformed by a master of the art, in preparation for his calling, he had little resemblance to any human being. Dumb, half blind, he approached with nose almost to sidewalk as if he followed the trail of a smell, stopping now and then to rest, wagging his hideous shock head from side to side slowly in unbearable suffering. The men at the table glanced at him as if he were a dog too repulsive even to kick, and he waited patiently beside each one for the sound of the small copper coins dropped into the gaping leather bag around his neck. When one of the men held out to him the half of a squeezed lime, he sat back on his haunches, opened his dreadful mouth to receive the fruit, and dropped down again, his jaws working. He crawled then across the street to the square, and lay down under the trees behind the little Indian, who did not turn his head.

(SF, 4-5)

The passengers who will form the cast of the novel are introduced in this setting, and the point of view of the natives is adopted in order to make them appear as unpleasant as possible.

"Well," said the desk clerk to the waiters nearest him, "here come our burros again." The waiters, dangling their greasy rags, aimed spiteful stares meant to be noticed at the badly assorted lot of human beings who took silent possession of the terrace, slumping about the tables and sitting there aimlessly as if they were already shipwrecked. There, again, was the unreasonably fat woman with legs like tree trunks, her fat husband in the dusty black suit and their fat white bulldog. . . . The ridiculous woman had kissed the beast on his wet nose before turning him over to the boy who tied him up in the kitchen patio for the night. . . .

A tall thin young woman—a leggy "girl" with a tiny, close-cropped head waving on her long neck, a limp green frock flapping about her calves—strode in screaming like a peahen in German at her companion, a little dumpling of a man, pink and pig-snouted.

(SF, 11-12)

After the precise depiction of the seaport and the vivid introduction of most of the characters, the focus blurs somewhat and there is little of such sharp visual imagery in the remainder of the book. The emphasis shifts to the inner natures of individuals and the interactions between them.

The large structural framework and plain, functional style of *Ship of Fools* would have lent themselves well to the depiction in depth of a wide variety of characters, on the order of Dickens or Tolstoy, or to the accumulation of a rich complexity of people and things in the style of Saul Bellow's *The Adventures of Augie March.* The talent of Katherine Anne Porter, however, is not of this comprehensive kind. Like these other novelists, Miss Porter deals with human life and human relations—but the scale on which she comprehends them is severely limited. *Ship of Fools* represents an effort to force a large structure into a small thematic frame. The resulting distortion is centered, as one would expect, in the portrayal of character. Miss Porter's characters are not free even to be fully human. That is to say, the limitations imposed on them are not the deep and mysterious limitations characteristic of real life, limitations partly external and partly springing in an obscure manner from the depths of the individual nature. The bounds imposed upon her characters are narrow, and to the reader of Miss Porter's earlier work, not particularly mysterious. Comparison of *Ship of Fools* with the earlier work is valid, for Miss Porter's outlook has not changed. There is, in fact, an introspective quality in it which prevents change. Extended over the broad expanse of the novel, the narrowness of Miss Porter's human spectrum results in a monotonous repetition of a few themes and leads to the complaint of numerous readers that little remains to be learned about the characters after the first hundred pages. In the light of these facts it is not surprising to hear Miss Porter say in a recent interview, of the voyage which inspired *Ship of Fools,* "I don't think I spoke a half-dozen words to anybody."[13]

One of the strongest factors in the uniformity of character portrayal in *Ship of Fools* is the all-pervasive ironic voice of the narrator. Mark Schorer comes close to the point: "If, like Brant's book, hers moves constantly from character to character, the dramatic point of view continually shifting, yet the controlling point of view, her perfectly poised ironical intelligence, is constant and in complete authority."[14] Miss Porter's ironic intelligence is indeed constantly present, either in direct comment on the more despicable characters or in indirect comment on them and on life in general through the minds of the few characters with whom she is truly sympathetic. It is as if there were in her some strong compulsion to be constantly proving a point, to be explaining and re-explaining herself through every character, every scene, every sentence. She is not capable of leaving her characters free to act and to change. Her scorn for the majority of them, usually tiresome, occasionally takes the form of skillful parody. A fine instance of this is the mock-serious description of Herr Rieber's amorous campaign against Lizzi Spockenkieker.

13. *Paris Review* (Winter-Spring, 1963), p. 112.
14. Schorer, *The New York Times Book Review,* p. 5.

Herr Rieber had wound himself up to a state of decision regarding Fraulein Lizzi Spockenkieker. First, she was not a Fraulein at all, but a woman of worldly experience; and though Herr Rieber liked nothing better than a proper amount of feminine coquetry and playful resistance, still, carried beyond certain bounds, they became mockery and downright insolence which no man worthy of the name would endure from any woman, no, not if she were Helen of Troy herself! In this frame of mind he took her arm after dinner and guided her for their stroll. While listening to music, he drew her up the stairs to the boat deck, and led her, with the silent intentness of a man bent on crime, to the dark side of the ship's funnel. He gave his prey no warning, no moment in which to smack his face or flee, he seized Lizzi low around her shoulders, hoping to pin her arms to her ribs, and snatching her to him, he opened his mouth for a ravenous kiss.

It was like embracing a windmill. Lizzi uttered a curious tight squeal, and her long arms gathered him in around his heaving middle. Her thin wide mouth gaped alarmingly and her sharp teeth gleamed even in the dimness. She gave him a good push and they fell backward clutched together, her long active legs overwhelmed him, she rolled him over flat on his back and for a moment her sharp hipbones ground his belly cruelly. Herr Rieber had one flash of amazed delight at the undreamed-of warmth of her response, then in panic realized that unless he recovered himself instantly, the situation would be irremediably out of his control.

He braced himself to reverse the unnatural posture of affairs, and attempted to roll into the proper position of masculine supremacy, but Lizzi was spread upon him like a fallen tent full of poles, her teeth now set grimly in his jowl, just under his jawbone. Pain took precedence of all other sensations in Herr Rieber's being; silently with tears in his eyes he fought to free himself.

(*SF*, 284)

Here, as everywhere else in the novel, the humor is never pure comedy, always satire. Mark Schorer's apparent determination to praise the book has led him to make, among numerous perceptive remarks, the following statement:

If, as a conceptual convenience, Miss Porter has associated her novel with a medieval tradition of peculiarly harsh and not very witty satire, there is nothing (or almost nothing) harsh in her book. There is much that is comic, much even that is hilarious, and everything throughout is always flashing into brilliance through the illuminations of this great ironic style. At the same time, almost everything that is comic is simultaneously pathetic; what is funny is also sad, moving to the point of pain, nearly of heartbreak.[15]

On the contrary, there is little in the book that is not harsh; its title is quite appropriate. True, much great comedy is sad, pathetic, painful, even heartbreaking; but it is fundamentally joyful and expansive, flowing from a basic acceptance of reality. If its tone is constantly a blend of indignation and scorn we may as well call it by its true name, satire. Glenway Wescott, by no means a harsh critic, remarks, "It occurs to me that there is a minimum of laughter of any kind in *Ship of Fools*."[16] He concludes that humor, while "powerful" in Miss Porter's letters, is "distilled out of her fiction, for fiction's sake."[17] He does not give any examples of this humor in her letters, but on the previous page he speaks of their "formidable wit, which may have troubled some people," refraining from illustrating it because "hers is a type of humor that cannot be appreciated if the target is veiled."[18] This last observation applies perfectly to the novel. Every trace of humor has a target.

The constant ironic presence of the author is only one aspect of a fundamental constriction of human nature in *Ship of Fools*. As Granville Hicks observes, if the characters are presented with great care and remarkable insight, this insight turns up a remarkably dull and uniform product.[19] To get at the root cause of the novel's narrowed vision, we must return to the rejection theme. One characteristic of the rejection pattern which was sometimes partially concealed in the short fiction but appears with painful clarity in *Ship of Fools* is its utter lovelessness. If not one character of all the forty or more portrayed is capable, in spite of the selfishness and self-delusion in human na-

15. *Ibid.* The severe limitations of *Ship of Fools* were missed or ignored to a remarkable degree by most of the early reviewers. Their myopia, while it may be attributed in large part to gallantry and to the influence of Miss Porter's reputation, nevertheless verges on critical irresponsibility.

16. *Images of Truth*, p. 49.

17. *Ibid.*

18. *Ibid.*, pp. 48-49.

19. See his review of the novel in *The Saturday Review*, XLV (March 31, 1962), 15.

ture, of mature, reasonably generous and stable love—or even of friendship—then the novel's world is, to say the least, incomplete.

A relatively new facet of the rejection theme exposed in the novel, and another source of shallowness in character portrayal, is the treatment of evil both in the abstract and in the concrete. This longest and latest of Miss Porter's works, attempting as it does to give her "last word" about life, devotes considerable attention to this important concept. Evil is, indeed, overwhelmingly present in the novel; no critic, however cheerful, has failed to see this. Miss Porter has spoken of the evil in the book, and it is the subject of much meditation and discussion among the characters, particularly Dr. Schumann. It is not, however, very clearly defined. Various kinds of sexual promiscuity prevail; it is in this form that evil makes strong assaults on the moral certainties of the doctor, who is the voice of traditional morality in the book and the only one seriously concerned with it. As a matter of fact, however, the only form in which evil appears in the novel as powerfully revolting and destructive is that of oppression—of pain inflicted upon individuals by their own natures or by others. Prostitution and pimping are practiced by the most completely evil of them, but their evilness makes itself strongly felt only in their calculated aggression against others. Miss Porter has described her book as "the story of the criminal collusion of good people—people who are harmless—with evil."[20] The principal form this collusion takes is that of the weak or unwitting co-operation of the more stupid Germans in the social persecution of Freytag. Miss Porter's understanding of evil is extremely personal. Traditional moral standards are to some extent taken for granted, but where the factor of violation of the individual's rights is not present, standards seem to shade off into unreality. This places *Ship of Fools* directly in the tradition of the rejection theme, in which all evil takes the form of oppression. This subjective view of morality seems to be confirmed by another statement of the author's. "In response to a comment that the novel's outlook

20. Girson, "The Author," *Sat. Rev.*, p. 15.

seemed rather bleak, Miss Porter protested, 'I don't think that this is a pessimistic book at all. I am not trying to make anybody out a saint or a sinner, but just showing human beings with failings and prejudices or with burdens a little more than they can bear, burdens that have made them what they are and through which they are trying to struggle. Some of them make it and some of them don't.' "[21] The important terms here are "failings and prejudices" (tendencies to oppress others) and "burdens" (internal or external oppressions). Miss Porter adds, in speaking of collusion with evil, "It happens through inertia, lack of seeing what is going on before their eyes" (the exact antithesis of the qualities of the alpha heroine). While moral speculation is carried to no great length even in Dr. Schumann's meditations, the novel presents enough of the complexity of life to start numerous lines of reasoning. It seems, for example, to emphasize the malice of fate by pointing to the suffering that can result from simple misunderstanding. Immediately after Freytag is informed that he has been moved away from the captain's table because his wife is Jewish, the following episode takes place: "He felt quite light and hollow with rage, and hardly knew how he reached the upper deck again; when that doleful little Baumgartner family, with its sickroom air, walking in a huddle, murmured among themselves at him '*Guten Morgen . . . Grüss Gott . . . Haben Sie gut geschlafen?*' he rudely passed them by, and hurt their feelings badly, and never knew it" (*SF*, 239). There are at least five such accidents, simply gratuitous little abrasions adding to the burden of the numerous wounds which are inflicted deliberately.

Miss Porter is not seriously concerned with tracking these or other clues down to their general meanings, for she is not a philosophical writer any more than she is a political writer. Artistically, she sees life in terms of the individual and his immediate relations with other individuals and the world; and, as numerous critics have pointed out, she is scrupulously devoted to portraying life as she sees it, concretely. The critic who attempts to pursue her philosophical or political conclusions

21. *Ibid.*

is likely to find himself either building on scanty foundations and out into a void, or confusing Miss Porter's fictional world with his own idea of the real world. The critic's job is to describe the thematic pattern which actually vivifies her fictional world, a world to which even such generalizations as "evil" and "guilt" seem rather foreign.

The standards by which Katherine Anne Porter's characters are judged are not those of good and evil, but those of truthfulness and self-delusion. To Miss Porter, truth is not a philosophical concept but an index of the individual's awareness of his immediate circumstances, including memory and sense of the future. It is a lack of this awareness, she seems to say, which leads one to "evil"—that is, oppression of others. Miranda, and other characters in proportion as they resemble her, are pre-eminent in truth-fullness and hence "good" to others. Viewed in this way, such goodness as there is in Miss Porter's fiction is seen to be purely negative, for it results from the heroine's tendency to move away from others rather than toward them.

While Miranda does not appear in *Ship of Fools,* there are several characters in the novel who share her characteristics in varying degrees. There are also characters—the vast majority, in fact—who do not share them in the least and therefore correspond to the beta characters of the earlier fiction. In short, the same classification of characters which marked the early works obtains as well in *Ship of Fools,* though the large number of characters in the novel and the technical innovations in the manner of their portrayal make it necessary to examine with some care the way in which they conform to the ever-present pattern. Such an examination, involving as it does the rejection theme as a whole and also the manner of its incorporation into the novel, is the most illuminating way to approach *Ship of Fools;* for this work, like everything else Miss Porter has written, is completely governed by the rejection theme.

In the short fiction, identification of alpha works was relatively easy, the criterion being the presence of Miranda or another strongly autobiographical protagonist, usually feminine, who was analogous to her. In all the alpha stories the dramatic point of view, usually a concomitant of rounded development of a character and reader-identification with him, was restricted to the central protagonist. In *Ship of Fools,* on the other hand, the dramatic point of view is fragmented, distributed among all the major characters and some of the minor ones. A passage of Wescott's is of interest in this connection:

I can think of only one possible reason for anyone's not liking this book: just at the start the characters are almost too strong; one shrinks from them a little. No, you may say, I do not wish to spend another page with this smug glutton, or this hypochondriacal drunkard, or this lachrymose widow; no, not another word out of that girl in the green dress! But presently, having read a certain number of pages, you feel a grudging sympathy with one and all, or a rueful empathy, or at least solidarity, as a fellow human being.

I told Katherine Anne this one day on the telephone, and she said, "I promised myself solemnly: in this book I will not load the dice. We all do it, even you have done it; and so have I in my day, as you well know. But this time, I resolved, everyone was to have his say. I would not take sides. I was on everyone's side."

At that point I had reached only about page 100, and I replied to her, "Yes, my dear, but it might also be said that you are on no one's side."

This evidently surprised her a bit but she took it kindly.[22]

Being on a character's side would seem to mean portraying him sympathetically. One of the strongest technical means of doing this is adopting his dramatic point of view, and this Miss Porter has scrupulously done for a large number of the passengers on her ship. The reader sees through the eyes of even the animalistic Pepe for a short while (*SF,* 223). Does this mean that the author's sympathy is equally distributed among the characters? Obviously not. The efforts she makes to treat each character fairly contribute to the fullness of the various portrayals and hence to the artistic stature of the book as a whole, but it would be neither possible nor desirable for her to show equal concern for, say, the utterly degenerate Pepe, the weak, foolish Denny, and the wise and noble Doctor Schumann. In reality, the constantly controlling point of view is, as Schorer has said, the

22. *Images of Truth,* p. 53.

author's ironic mind; and this mind classifies the characters rather clearly. Most important are Mrs. Treadwell, Jenny and David, and Dr. Schumann. Each of these occupies the dramatic point of view for long periods of time. La Condesa is also of major importance for her own unique reasons, but she is seen mostly from the Doctor's point of view because her importance is primarily in relation to him and also because she is to be kept relatively remote and mysterious. Freytag may be classed with another group, of slightly less importance, which includes Denny and Lowenthal and perhaps Hansen, Frau Rittersdorf, and Captain Thiele.

Wescott makes some important observations about the characters. He concedes that there are some who "really are hateful or at least horrifying" and specifies Herr Graf, Concha, Ric and Rac, Herr Glocken, and the fat man in the cherry-colored shirt. Then he continues:

But these grotesque personages are on the very outer edges of the book; a little closer to our humanity than the professor's wife's vomiting white bulldog, but not much. They make a frame around the more important, less anomalous portraits; a baroque or rococo frame. This also differentiates Katherine Anne's novel from other novels of the grand-hotel type. She is not mainly interested in the patchwork and variegation of human nature. What fires and polarizes her mind are the themes (as I have said), the elements, the universal characteristics: mutual unkindness of lovers, gluttony and alcoholism, snobbery and conformism, and political power, even that inevitably wielded by the captain of a ship at sea, and bourgeoisie versus destitution, and immaturity versus senility—with scarcely ever a word about any of these subjects in the abstract, not a bit of intellectuality per se; only intelligence, constantly arising afresh from observation.[23]

He is correct in noting that the emphasis in the book is not on the variety of human nature but on certain motifs, led by mutual unkindness of lovers. Furthermore, each of the elements he mentions is in reality an aspect of the rejection theme as it is embodied in the present work. More specifically, each may be viewed as arising from an oppressive union of predominantly

23. *Ibid.*, pp. 54-55.

beta characters, or from the forced companionship of the voyage itself. Conflict between lovers needs no introduction, and the incompatibility of youth and age is seen primarily in the relationship between Herr Graf and Johann, one of the clearest examples in all the works of the mutually destructive union. The political power wielded by the captain is most strongly felt in his official persecution of Freytag and his despotic treatment of the poor. In both cases the emphasis is on the oppression suffered, not on an abstract consideration of the many-sided and fundamentally just nature of authority. Several characteristics of the poor steerage passengers are shown, but the main impact of their presence is a sense of their physically and spiritually oppressed condition as contrasted with that of the bourgeoisie. There is also the vague oppression their presence imposes on the latter—and, finally, the spirit of human dignity which the poor manage to retain in spite of oppression. Snobbery and conformism are the two basic elements in the Germans' tyranny over Jews. Alcoholism functions principally as a method of escape from boredom, pain, and unpleasant human relationships; and also as a habit which makes some individuals unpleasant to others—as Denny to Mrs. Treadwell, David to Jenny and Freytag, and Herr Baumgartner to his family. In sum, the critic might well have gone on to the more significant conclusion that what really "fires and polarizes" this author's mind is the sense of oppression and the more or less successful urge to escape from it. Seen in this light, characters and their relationships may be recognized for what they really are: elements in a narrow and inflexible pattern—a pattern seemingly imposed on the author herself by her inner response to life.

When asked by Rochelle Girson with which of the characters in *Ship of Fools* she identified herself, Miss Porter replied, "I am nowhere and everywhere. I am the captain and the seasick bulldog and the man in the cherry-colored shirt who sings and the devilish children and all of the women and lots of the men. . . . You know, I got attached to my gang on the boat. I hated to give them up."[24] The generality of the statement

24. Girson, "The Author," *Sat. Rev.*, p. 15.

should not be allowed to hide its significance. An author is, of course, in some way present in every one of his creations; still, there are great differences in the degrees of subjectivity of various works of fiction. In spite of the assertions of some critics as to the great objectivity of Miss Porter's work, it can hardly be too strongly emphasized that in one crucially important way it is highly subjective. One might put it this way: There is a more profound difference between the two brothers in the parable of the prodigal son, even though their characterization is of the utmost simplicity, than between any two of the more fully developed characters in *Ship of Fools,* including those of different sexes. The view of life and pattern of conduct which characterize each of the important individuals on the ship are those of Miranda: a sense of oppression, the instinct of rejection, and some degree of success in escaping into the ambivalent state of independence-isolation. In some of the characters this pattern lies below the surface and may even oppose certain forces in the plot, just as it did in some of the short fiction—but its signs are everywhere. Preoccupation with old age and death, and the sense of loss, motifs integrally related to the rejection theme, are in abundant evidence in the portrayals of the major characters. Those, on the other hand, who fail to reach the alpha class are, to the extent of that failure, related to the beta characters of the earlier works. Life is oppressive for them also, but because of their deficiencies of intelligence, strength, sensibility, they are incapable of escaping from their oppressive unions and so remain subject to burdens of the grosser sort—nagging wives, fatuous husbands, dominating parents, alcoholism, and so on almost without limit. Several of the important characters will be examined in detail, but first a few words must be said about the rejection theme in the work as a whole.

On the subject of oppression in *Ship of Fools* one hardly knows where to start. It is everywhere. The motif of the oppressive union and its corollary, the desire for escape, can be found reflected in language, imagery, situation or explicit statement on literally almost every page. The novel opens with the observation that "The port town of Veracruz is a little purgatory between land and sea for the traveler" (*SF*, 3). Indifference and antagonism are keynotes struck at the very beginning and echoing throughout. Here, also from the opening page, is some commentary on the Veracruzanos:

> There is maybe a small sign of uneasiness in this pugnacious assertion of high breeding; in this and in the methodical brutality of their common behavior towards the travelers who must pass through their hands to reach the temporary haven of some ship in harbor. The travelers wish only to be carried away from the place, and the Veracruzanos wish only to see the last of them; but not until every possible toll, fee, extortion, and bribe due to the town and its citizens has been extracted.
>
> (*SF*, 3-4)

In the next few pages this statement is documented in overpowering detail. The voyage itself is both an escape and a movement toward new disillusions, and the ship says nothing more clearly about the world it symbolizes than that it is oppressive. Its passengers are aboard only by necessity and few are certain of their destination. The passageways are stuffy and the cabins are even more so, both physically and psychologically. True to the pattern, every marriage is predominantly unhappy, and only inferior characters are portrayed in stable unions. The happiness of the newlyweds, apparently an exception, is, as in similar cases in "Old Mortality" and "Pale Horse, Pale Rider," only a temporary romantic euphoria, remote from the surrounding reality and based primarily on the first strong waves of sexual pleasure which will inevitably soon diminish. The union between Jenny and David, both of whom are to some extent alpha characters, is mutually destructive; and that between Dr. Schumann and La Condesa is, in a subtler way, equally so. Cabin-mates are uniformly burdensome to each other. Aside from the newlyweds and from the families, who have their own intramural miseries, the only ones who show no mutual repugnance are the priests, the Cuban students, and the zarzuela company, all of them inhumanly homogeneous in their various ways.

Words like "stifling," "stuffy," and "smothered" appear frequently. Mrs. Treadwell, especially, is constantly rushing to a porthole for a breath of fresh air. Body odors and the various strong perfumes and disinfectants employed by the passengers add to the physical sense of oppression. The motif of oppression is not limited to the principal characters but appears in such secondary ones as the purser. "It was the hour for his nap, and yet he must be humoring this fool. He said politely, 'Let us go,' and restrained, no doubt to his own permanent moral injury, a very pure, laudable impulse to spread his huge fat hand over Herr Rieber's red, sweating face and push, hard" (*SF*, 252). Herr Lowenthal, the Jew, is especially conscious of oppression, from which his only escape is insensitivity and cleverness. "Ah, he needed to be more careful and clever than he was—he suffered waves of fright sometimes because he feared he was not clever enough, they would play him a trick someday and he would not know until it was too late. It occurred to him often that he was living in a world so dangerous he wondered how he dared to go to sleep at night" (*SF*, 97). Even Jenny, sometimes so sympathetic to others, sums up the situation as follows: "Everybody looks tired. It's just the same as we were in Veracruz, or in Havana. We all remember we're strangers and don't like each other. We're all on our way somewhere else and we'll be glad to see the last of each other. God, I'd hate to think I'd ever get even a postcard from anybody on this ship again, as long as I live!" (*SF*, 400-1) Mark Schorer puts all this concisely:

Most of the major characters are presented in groups, chiefly family groups, each group with its own problem or project, and then there are a few solitary figures wandering the decks in isolation. And while the various groups become acquainted with one another and each reacts critically to the others and all interact, they are in fact all isolated. When they are not indifferent to one another, they are impelled by active hostility or chill malice. When they appear, within the groups, to be loving one another, they are usually destroying one another and themselves, if they have not already done so.[25]

25. Schorer, *The New York Times Book Review*, p. 5.

An interesting note about the cases in which "they appear to be loving one another" is the fact, already seen in earlier works, especially "Pale Horse, Pale Rider," that the supposed lover's reactions to his beloved are usually aesthetic rather than properly human. This is true not only of the artists, Jenny and David, but of others as well. Freytag, early in the story, thinks of his absent wife chiefly in terms of her physical beauty. To Jenny "he described her coloring, very dear to his taste: wheat blonde, rosy-faced, true Rhine-maiden sort of girl; and told again her charming name. 'Mary Champagne,' he said, fondly. 'I think I fell in love first with her name' " (*SF,* 90-91). Only later does he gradually advert to her other qualities, which are dominated by intelligence and a bitterly sharp tongue; he also gradually allows himself to resent and be unfaithful to her. The aesthetic approach is taken toward the newlyweds. They are "both very beautiful in pure white" (*SF,* 86), and Jenny remarks to Freytag, "Aren't they lovely together, really?" He answers that the bride "has just the right look, somehow. . . . Eden just after the Fall. That little interval between the Fall and the driving out by that tricky jealous vengeful old God. . . . Anyone who doesn't know that, once in a lifetime, once anyway —and maybe it doesn't happen oftener—is unlucky, no matter what else good may happen to him" (*SF,* 91-92). His words remind the reader of the evanescence of married happiness and of God's resemblance to Captain Thiele. The thoughts of Jenny and David about each other, at those rare times when love seems to predominate, are heavily weighted with admiration of face or figure. Another method of evading love is illustrated in a reference to Freytag's feeling for Mary: "Yet he and Mary fell in love, and so honestly and surely in love, it was like knocking down a hornet's nest" (*SF,* 63). Immediately the emphasis is shifted to the persecution they suffered at the hands of their families. The final impression left by the passage is one not of love but of the cruelty of relatives and the lovers' pleasure at escaping. In short, love is presented in *Ship of Fools* as fundamentally unreal. Thus the only possible real escape from a world of oppression is firmly closed off.

Mrs. Treadwell is the individual in *Ship of Fools* most familiar to the reader of the Miranda and implicit-Miranda stories. She resembles especially the heroine of "Theft." Her very name suggests circumspection with its ambivalent nature, partly admirable, partly impoverishing. That the author views her sympathetically is evident from the first. She is the only passenger described almost exclusively in favorable terms. "An inconspicuous slender woman in early middle age, conventionally dressed in dark blue linen, with a wide blue hat shading her black hair and small, rather pretty face and intent dark blue eyes, regarded the Spaniards with some distaste while raising the short sleeve over her right arm, to glance again at the place where the beggar woman had pinched her" (*SF*, 14). She has Miranda's inquiring eyes and also her instinctive distaste for human contact. When first seen she is looking with unbelief at the bruise which represents an intolerable aggression such as she tries determinedly to avoid, then tries to reject as something unreal which could never happen to her. She is in Miranda's natural state, isolation, and the reader learns only later that she has left a husband who was flagrantly unfaithful and so jealous that he used to beat her until her nose bled. Throughout the story she is seen as charming, intelligent, and sophisticated. Her only possible fault is the subtle one of rejection, which she herself sees and judges at least as harshly as does anyone else. The sections devoted to her are especially full of the imagery of rejection. One such passage occurs while she is in her cabin, listening perforce to the inanely malicious gossip of her annoying cabin-mate, Lizzi. She has, characteristically, been playing solitaire and asking herself why she had not stayed in Paris, which was "delicious" even in August, in order to be "safe from the sort of people she seemed to meet up with almost anywhere else" (*SF*, 207). After listening to the irritating jabber as long as she can stand it,

Mrs. Treadwell threw off the gabbling Fury-like echoes, got up suddenly shaking out her long gown and went to the porthole. The pure cool air bathed her face, she opened her mouth to breathe more freely, feeling soiled by what she had listened to in that cabin. The sea and the sky were almost one in the vast darkness, the waves just beneath rolled and washed back upon themselves in white foam in the rayed lights from the ship.

(*SF,* 207-8)

The sense of confinement and revulsion is extremely vivid, and the passage illustrates the familiar motifs of desire for cleansing and resort to impersonal beauty. Mrs. Treadwell's instinct of rejection is to a great extent shown as a hard-won means of self-defense against a ready involvement with others which has brought her only disillusion and suffering. There is, however, little evidence in the novel of her sympathy for others, except, perhaps, very briefly during her first contacts with Freytag. At any rate, her condition is ambiguous; and its ultimate meaning, which the author as usual takes no pains to formulate, seems to be that life is particularly miserable for the most admirable people.

Like Miranda, Mrs. Treadwell, seeking an impossible ideal of happiness, has rejected the world of her childhood. The lines immediately following the passage just quoted comprise one of her most serious meditations on life.

What am I to do, she asked herself, where am I to go? Life, death, she thought in cloudy fear, for she was not able to face the small immediate situations which might demand decision, action, settlement no matter how temporary. Her very vagueness frightened her, for life and death, rightly understood, were ominous dreadful words, and she would never understand them. Life, as she had been taught in her youth, was meant to be pleasant, generous, simple. The future was a clear space of pure, silvery blue, like the sky over Paris in good weather, . . . all clean and crisp as the blue tissue paper in which all the white things of her childhood had been folded, to keep them white, to make them whiter, to give them icy-blue whiteness. She was always going to be gay and free, later, when she was rid of nurses and school was over, and there was always to be love—always love.

Well, well, she said, drawing in her head, Life has been in fact quite disagreeable if not sordid in spots. If anybody called me a lady tramp I hope I should not have my feelings hurt. Nasty things have happened to me often and they were every one my own fault. I put myself in their way, not even knowing they were there, at first.

And later when I knew, I always thought, But this is not real, of course. This is not Life, naturally. . . .

Yet, here I am cooped up in a dingy little cabin with a vulgar woman who will come in presently and begin talking about her "affairs." She is a woman I would never have in my house except to dress my hair or to fit a new frock; and I sit here smelling her horrible perfumes and sleeping in the same room with her; and I have drunk too much wine and played thirty games of solitaire without winning once. Because otherwise life—this life, this is life, this beastly little business here and now—would be too dreary and disgusting to be got through with another moment. . . .

(SF, 208-9)

Like her prototype, she rejects her childhood world because she feels it did not tell her the truth. She has never found in life the "icy-blue whiteness" that she was led to expect. Like Miranda at the end of "Pale Horse, Pale Rider," she finds her whites a dirty gray. If she has not been given as harrowing an experience as Miranda's brush with death and paradise to justify her totally negative view of life, she has at least been given a vicious husband and countless other unspecified sufferings, and a beggar woman has given her a completely intolerable pinch on the arm. Events during the voyage are likewise calculated to justify Mrs. Treadwell's rejection of people. When she lets down her guard slightly before the attractive Freytag, he immediately burdens her with his secret sufferings and then his bitter resentment. The showdown scene between them finds her again in full retreat:

"I shouldn't have tried to talk about it," he said, with some underlying resentment, "I should never say anything about it."

"Perhaps you are right," said Mrs. Treadwell, thinking, What do you expect of me? What can I do? She moved to put her tray aside. He took it from her and set it on the deck beside his own. They rose. . . . Mrs. Treadwell moved away again, from the threat of human nearness, of feeling. If she stayed to listen, she knew she would weaken little by little, she would warm up in spite of herself, perhaps in the end identify herself with the other, take on his griefs and wrongs, and if it came to that, feel finally guilty as if she herself had caused them; yes, and he would believe it too, and blame her freely. It had happened too often, could she not learn at last? All of it was no good, neither for confidant nor listener. There was no cure, no comfort, tears change nothing and words can never get at the truth. No, don't tell me any more about yourself, I am not listening, you cannot force my attention. I don't want to know you, and I will not know you. Let me alone.

(SF, 142)

This fear of her sympathetic heart is not convincing. If this heroine is fated ever to find the truth she seeks, she is quite certain it will not be through human relations. Granville Hicks has noted the resulting pessimistic atmosphere in arriving at his predominantly unfavorable verdict on *Ship of Fools.*

> The voyage ends, and the passengers go their ways, completely unchanged by anything that has happened. . . . Even Mrs. Treadwell seems to have learned nothing about herself that will make any difference in her life. . . .
> What, then, are we to conclude that Miss Porter is saying about the voyage of life? Is it that there is no possibility of change, no hope of redemption? . . . Miss Porter is saying something about the voyage of life, and what she is saying is somber indeed.
> Perhaps that is why the novel, for all its lucidity and all its insights, leaves the reader a little cold. There is in it, so far as I can see, no sense of human possibility. Although we have known her people uncommonly well, we watch unconcerned as, in the curiously muted ending, they drift away from us.[26]

If he were more aware of the rejection theme, the critic would have no need to wonder at Mrs. Treadwell's continued progress along the downward path or to speculate about the possibility of redemption in this fictional world. What the author has to say about life has already been seen in Miranda.

Just as Mrs. Treadwell has an impossible ideal of happiness, so she also has an impossible ideal of self-sufficiency. While most people accept in principle the necessity of a certain involvement with society, whether they like it or not, this proud heroine sees herself as essentially separate from society and feels that every unpleasant contact with it is "her own fault" because she might have avoided it. She negates both the unpleasantness of the world and her own involvement in it by

26. Review of *SF* in *Sat. Rev.,* p. 16.

telling herself "This is not life," even though each encounter with reality impresses more strongly upon her the realization that this "beastly little business here and now" is life after all. Still she continues to regard the voyage of life and all human contact as something "to be fled from, lightly from point to point," in the hope that "moment by moment she would find a split second of relief from boredom in the very act of flight which gave her the fleeting illusion of invisibility" (*SF*, 30). Ceaselessly and hopelessly, she looks for an ideal life that will combine perfect isolation with the company of perfectly beautiful people in a completely purified, blue and icy white world. The reader of the last Miranda story knows where this world is to be found.

The dissatisfaction accompanying Mrs. Treadwell's rejection takes the familiar form of a sense of loss. Once, when searching for her ticket (symbolic of her entire life-voyage), she peers into her handbag "without expectation" and asks, "wherever do things go?" (*SF*, 137) This and several other motifs are concentrated in her meditation on her forty-sixth birthday (*SF*, 252-53). It is not the first she has spent "alone on a train or a ship," and she is feeling her age as a "downright affront to her aesthetic sense." She muses on the hazards of woman's middle life, when the lower instincts "take alarm for fear they have missed something, are hot for marginal enjoyments," and when hearts grow cold or "go overripe and pulpy," and "women especially, one is told, so often lose their modesty, their grace. They become shrill, or run to fat, or turn to beanpoles." Suddenly she feels "Time itself as a great spider spinning a thick dusty web around her life, winding and winding until it covered all—the light is shut out and the pulse shrivels and the breath is slowly smothered off—Death, death! she said, and her fright was as simple and overwhelming as her fear of the dark when a child." She recalls the "pleasant nonsense" talked by her elders about "growing old gracefully," then escapes to the rail and thinks, "such a little ship, like a prison almost, so few places to go"—and leans there "breathing the sweet cool wind," wishing she knew "somebody to watch clouds with." (In a moment Freytag will appear; she will innocently ask him to watch clouds with her; and he will flood her with his bitter resentment at her unwitting offense against him.) Here together are isolation, the sense of loss, the aesthetic attitude toward life, preoccupation with age and death, rejection of early teachings, and oppression both physical and spiritual.

The motif of scorn for men is not as clear-cut in *Ship of Fools* as in the short fiction, for among the numerous characters in the novel are several men who share alpha characteristics; and the author has, as she reminded Wescott, permitted each to hold the dramatic point of view for a time. The tendency is, however, freely exercised upon such characters as Herr Rieber, Captain Thiele, Professor Hutten, Herr Baumgartner, Herr Graf, Herr Lowenthal, the male dancers, the Cuban medical students, the priests, Arne Hansen, William Denny, and David Scott; though the motif is obscured somewhat by the fact that several feminine characters receive almost equal scorn. In the earlier alpha works the general rule is that the heroine, and women in general, are superior to men; in the novel other criteria sometimes supersede the masculine-feminine one. The principal cleavage is between major characters, male or female (but all related to Miranda), and secondary characters, all of whom tend to be caricatures or grotesques.

Scorn for men is seen in its purest form through the eyes of Mrs. Treadwell, the closest counterpart of Miranda; and the supreme climax of the motif is her assault on Denny with the heel of her slipper, an episode so bizarre and powerfully dramatized that it catches the special attention of every reader. Circumstances are arranged to justify the act. Mrs. Treadwell has painted her face to resemble Amparo's (a far-fetched coincidence), and Denny mistakes her room for the dancer's. He is undeniably a lout and Mrs. Treadwell's patience has been sorely tried; both are so drunk they cannot remember on the following morning what has happened. But all these preparations fail to conceal the gratuitous ferocity and sober thoroughness of Mrs. Treadwell's mutilation of the drunken Denny. The scene immediately following their encounter is profoundly suggestive.

Still in an alcoholic fog, Mrs. Treadwell seems to enjoy her only really happy moment in the entire book. "In her joy and excitement, she snatched off her bloodstained sandal and kissed it" (*SF*, 466). She smiles delightedly at her hideous wicked face, which seems to reveal "something sinister" in her character. Just before Denny's arrival she had been caring for Lizzi, who had been made hysterical by the shameful conduct of her porcine lover, Herr Rieber (a hysteria not clearly motivated, incidentally). When Lizzi moaned, "Oh, the brute, the savage, the beast," Mrs. Treadwell "repressed her airy impulse to ask, 'Which one of them?'" (*SF*, 463) Her general detestation of man has forced her into a temporary alliance with the "vulgar woman" she so thoroughly scorns. Denny's blundering intrusion has been basically a savage sexual attack, in the course of which he "gave a twist to her front, which wrenched her breast so painfully she almost went off balance" (*SF*, 464). But this proud, strong woman will never completely lose her balance, least of all at the hands of a man. She chastises the representative of the enemy sex, treading him under her heel like a serpent, so to speak, then returns to her bed in girlish innocence. "Blissfully she sang a tuneless song under her breath as she tied her Alice in Wonderland hair ribbon and slipped into her white satin gown with the bishop sleeves. She was folding herself into bed like a good little girl who has finished her prayers . . ." (*SF*, 466). The blissful song sung to oneself marks here, as in "The Downward Path to Wisdom" and "The Fig Tree," a triumph of rejection by the alpha protagonist. The imagery of the scene shows clearly that the root of Mrs. Treadwell's hatred for men is her resentment, shared with her more frankly puritanical counterparts in the Old Order and with the wives in "That Tree" and "A Day's Work," at man's violation of her virginity and the solitary integrity it symbolizes so organically. She complained much earlier in the book that her husband "preferred sleeping with any chance slut" rather than with her, though she tried hard to be "slut enough to please him" (*SF*, 141).

Mrs. Treadwell is not, of course, fully conscious of all this. In her day-to-day life she wants to be admired, sent flowers, taken to the theater, and—especially—danced with. Since, like Amy and Miranda, she needs a good dancing partner to lead her through the voyage, she selects the best-looking of the ship's officers, a man with whom there is little danger of involvement. A passage late in the novel is extremely important in her characterization, revealing as it does some of her deepest motivations. She has been dancing with the fat purser, who has just asked her to join him in a glass of wine.

But providentially her good-looking, gold-braided young officer intervened, and with a deferential bow to the purser, took her away again. He had a smooth fair face with no expression at all, she observed, none. He was as sleek, neat, immaculately correct and inhuman-looking as if he were poured into a mold. He danced with waxlike smoothness, with small even steps accommodated to hers, holding her at an unfashionable, formal distance, as if he had been trained at her own dancing school. "Why, he's young enough to be my son," she could not help thinking, "and he reminds me of my grandfather." She decided this was no real drawback, settled into the leisurely spin of his style and began to enjoy the floating lightness and the pleasant male nearness, no weight and no burden but only a presence. She closed her eyes a moment and danced in lulling darkness, with a diffused tenderness for this wraith who guided her with light fingers at waist and palm, the lover who had danced with her in her daydreams long before she had danced with any man. Opening her eyes, she found him watching her face with a peculiar intentness unexpected and disturbing. Was it her imagination, instructed in the ways of the lurking animal, was it her own seeking eyes? Or was it really a goatish gleam?"

(*SF*, 434)

This excerpt is, first of all, immensely valuable as a footnote to "Pale Horse, Pale Rider." The unreal young officer is Miranda's Adam, though the plot of the earlier story did not permit such frankness about his unreality. With this partner Mrs. Treadwell, like Miranda, escapes to a "lulling darkness" in which she can enjoy her closest approach to the ideal state, "pleasant male nearness, no weight and no burden but only a presence" (Miranda's paradise). She can feel superior to this dull man who is young enough to be her son, yet safe in his grandfatherly embrace, for he is as harmless as the dream-partner who did not in the least violate the innocence of her girlish heart. But as always, there is a flaw; suddenly she sees "the lurking animal," "the goatish gleam." The episode comes to its inevitable conclusion a short time later. As they stroll on deck after an informal tour of the ship, the officer embraces and kisses her violently.

Mrs. Treadwell shuddered at the same unpleasant sensation of being bitten, of the blood being drawn by suction to her mouth that had revolted her in the past, and she drew away, turned her head outward, refused, and defended herself by a passivity that dismayed and enraged him.

He drew his head back, lifted his elbow and swept her hair back with his forearm, and she saw the sweat standing on his forehead. "I have been looking at you, thinking about you, for a long time," he said, harshly. "You never noticed me, no not even when we danced—why not? Now you will not kiss me—why not? . . . Do you want me to beg you? to say I love you? I never knew what people meant by that word."

"Don't say it, don't say it, I cannot bear the sound of it . . ."

His face, manner, mood, all shifted with the same violence, from erotic impetuosity to sheer pettiness. "Then why did you come with me, why did you encourage me to kiss you?"

Mrs. Treadwell drew away altogether, stood back facing him. "And now for the first lovers' quarrel," she said outrageously and laughed with a somewhat extreme amusement. What a young face he had; she saw him as if for the first time—smooth and lineless, clear features, tightly drawn, with angry vanity in the set of the mouth, a burning uneasiness in the eyes."

(*SF*, 460-61)

At last the old scorn for childlike, goatlike man and the sophisticated, fastidious passivity are exposed for the defensive weapons they really are. The genteel Mrs. Treadwell joins the ranks of the alpha heroines, aligned in the instinctive campaign of frigidity which they have waged against their men. This core of revulsion, thinned, flattened, and elaborated into the pattern of the rejection theme, continues to impel this heroine, even when hope is lost, on a search which is much more deeply romantic than she seems to realize. The self-distaste which has always lain deeply hidden within the core of rejection now becomes more pronounced in Mrs. Treadwell, as it did in Miranda after her great disillusion:

A small deep wandering sensation of disgust, self-distaste came with these straying thoughts. She remembered as in a dream again her despairs, her long weeping, her incurable grief over the failure of love or what she had been told was love, and the ruin of her hopes —what hopes? She could not remember—and what had it been but the childish refusal to admit and accept on some term or other the difference between what one hoped was true and what one discovers to be the mere laws of the human condition? She had been hurt, she had recovered, and what had it all been but a foolish piece of romantic carelessness? She stood up to take a deep breath and walk around the stuffy room.

(*SF*, 481)

When she leaves the *Vera* she does not even look back.

The character of Jenny Brown is most profitably studied in the composite she forms with her pseudo-lover, David Scott. It is when viewed as modified by David that she most closely resembles the alpha protagonist, but even individually she is in some ways closer to Miranda than is Mrs. Treadwell. Her early life, for example, closely resembles Miranda's (and, incidentally, in its artistic flight, resembles even more closely Miss Porter's own as she has described it elsewhere).[27]

Though David never believed it, no matter what she told him, Jenny had, in a mid-Southern state, a small but pertinacious family of brothers, sisters, aunts, uncles, cousins, even a small niece and nephew, the quite most conventional assortment, really; and she was fond of them all, in a baffled, detached sort of way. . . . they presented to her the impermeable front of what she called "the family attitude"—suspicion of the worst based on insufficient knowledge of her life, and moral disapproval based firmly on their general knowledge of the weakness of human nature. . . . wouldn't their blood run cold if they could only know the facts? Ah well, the family can get under your skin with little needles and scalpels if you venture too

27. See Edward Schwartz, "The Way of Dissent: Katherine Anne Porter's Critical Position," *Western Humanities Review*, VIII (1954), 119-30. Miss Porter is quoted as saying she escaped the South "because I didn't want to be regarded as a freak. That was how they regarded a woman who wanted to write. . . . When I left, they were all certain I was going to live an immoral life" (p. 120).

near them: they attach suckers to you and draw your blood from every pore if you don't watch out. But that didn't keep you from loving them, nor them from loving you, with that strange longing, demanding, hopeless tenderness and bitterness, wound into each other in a net of living nerves.

It was no question at all whether they were the kin you would have chosen, would have preferred, at any rate; they were the family you belonged to, and there you were, stuck for good, for life and for eternity itself, no doubt. . . . she could not live near her family because she was afraid of their weaknesses and faults—they were also her own; and most of their virtues repelled her even more than their faults. She had spent years of strategic warfare trying to beat those people out of her life; then more years trying to ignore them; to forget them; to hate them; and in the end she loved them as she knew well she was meant in simple nature to do, and acknowledged it; it brought her no peace, and yet it put a certain solid ground under her feet. . . . They were the family and she was the stray sheep; they never let her forget it, they were full of malice and resentment they could not hide, and they invented little slanders about her among themselves to justify their view of what they called her "desertion."

And moreover, they couldn't be fooled for a moment with all that nonsense about wanting to paint, to be an "artist." A young woman of good family leaves her home and place for only one reason: she means to lead a shameless abandoned life where her relatives and her society cannot restrain or punish her. Artist indeed! What was to stop her painting at home in the back garden?
(*SF*, 185-87)

In a general way this all applies perfectly to Miranda, except that in her case there is not such a clear assertion of love. Jenny's painting and Miranda's writing are interchangeable. Both are "artistic" in their whole approach to life. Mrs. Treadwell, incidentally, shares this characteristic in the sense that her deepest pleasures are of an aesthetic, not a social nature; she does not long for Paris because she has friends or lovers there. Jenny, like Miranda, is proud of her ancestry, a mixture of most of the races of western Europe but absolutely no German; also like Miranda, Jenny has been "partly brought up by her grandmother and grandfather, her father's parents, for her mother had died young" (*SF*, 90).

In the relationship between Jenny and David all the familiar themes appear, but in a new combination. Their position with respect to the rejection theme and the alpha-beta distinction may be viewed in several ways. As individuals they occupy a middle position between alpha and beta. Theirs is a destructively oppressive union, but they are not so gross, so second-rate, as to strengthen the bond by marriage or resign themselves to its permanence. Each is determined to leave the other eventually. As *Ship of Fools* provides the classic illustration of scorn for men in Mrs. Treadwell's assault on Denny, so it presents the prototype of the destructive union in Jenny's dream-memory of a fight to the death between an Indian man and woman which she had seen in a Mexican village years before.

They swayed and staggered together in a strange embrace, as if they supported each other; but in the man's raised hand was a long knife, and the woman's breast and stomach were pierced. The blood ran down her body and over her thighs, her skirts were sticking to her legs with her own blood. She was beating him on the head with a jagged stone, and his features were veiled in rivulets of blood. They were silent, and their faces had taken on a saint-like patience in suffering, abstract, purified of rage and hatred in their one holy dedicated purpose to kill each other. Their flesh swayed together and clung, their life arms were wound about each other's bodies as if in love. Their weapons were raised again, but their heads lowered little by little, until the woman's head rested upon his breast and his head was on her shoulder, and holding thus, they both struck again. (*SF*, 144)

This scene, heavy with irony, sex, and death, is the perfect picture of marriage, that closest and most destructive of unions, as seen by the alpha heroine; and, to repeat, by every other character in Miss Porter's fiction insofar as he resembles this heroine. Jenny partially resembles her. She dreams repeatedly of the scene, and sees the faces change slowly into David's and her own (*SF*, 145). Later she thinks, "We aren't going to kill each other because I mean to get away before that happens. But we'll leave dents in each other. When I get through with David, he'll know the difference between me and the next woman." And she adds, in a horrible travesty on the procreative purpose of marriage, "I'll be carrying David like a petrified fetus for the rest of my life" (*SF*, 169). As a composite, Jenny and David symbolize the inner conflict of the alpha protagonist.

Although Jenny resembles Miranda in numerous ways, there is a flaw in her which enslaves her to a destructive union. Fundamentally, in terms of the rejection theme, her fault is that she is spiritually and sexually dependent on a man—that she is not adequately self-sufficient. Superficially she would seem to be free, but she knows better. "They had agreed . . . not to marry because they must be free, marriage was a bond cramping and humiliating to civilized beings: yet what was this tie between them but marriage, and marriage of the worst sort, with all the restraints and jealousies and burdens, but with none of its dignity, none of its warmth and protection, no honest acknowledgment of faith and intention" (*SF*, 145). Jenny's status is accurately gauged by the author's treatment of her. She receives considerable respect and sympathy—the dramatic point of view is occupied at considerable length with her thoughts, which are characterized by rather clear insight into her own weaknesses and miseries—but, on the other hand, she is patently foolish and superficial at times and as such is criticized tellingly by other characters. Freytag evaluates her near the end of the story as "a little nobody not worth a man's attention, just a moody, shallow neurotic American girl pretending to herself she was an artist to give herself false importance" (*SF*, 483). There is a rather distinct rift between Jenny's superficial conduct and her deepest inclinations, for she cannot break completely with her native moral conservatism. David observes that she "blasphemed as harmlessly as a well-taught parrot," but was offended by what she "prudishly" called his "dirty mind" (*SF*, 55). He also notices that her figure and walk resemble those of a "prim little schoolteacher" (*SF*, 28) reminiscent of the pseudo-Bohemian wife in "That Tree."

In David, the isolationist tendencies of the alpha protagonist are shown in their least flattering form. Because of his terribly unhappy and anxiety-ridden childhood, he has become a frightened weakling, enslaved by a puritanical conscience much more cripplingly than Jenny, whose superior feminine emotional integrity enables her to adopt sexual freedom more easily. His greatest suffering is caused by the sexual desires which violate his perfect hermit-like detachment from passion, and vitiate "his whole life of resistance to life itself" (*SF*, 416). Jenny, to whom he is bound by these desires and by his periodic emotional weaknesses, sees clearly through his false front of cynicism and can torture him almost at will. Thus, while David's pattern of rejection is basically the same as Miranda's, he is shown to be neurotic and cowardly; while she is presented in almost completely favorable terms. A good illustration of the kinship between these two characters is the motif of vomiting which appears several times in the stories, always as a more or less explicit rejection symbol. In David's case, it is clearly connected with his abnormal childhood. When his father, whom he scorned and hated (a trace of Miranda in him), ran off, his mother hysterically cradled him (aged nine) in her lap in an unwholesome embrace "as if he were a little baby," and the experience "made him so sick he threw up his supper" (*SF*, 130). During the voyage of the *Vera*, while combing his hair and worrying excessively about his increasing baldness, a symbol of his corrupt heredity, he recalls this traumatic experience so strongly that he vomits suddenly into the washbasin, thus establishing the link between his past and present abnormalities and rejections. In "The Downward Path to Wisdom," Stephen becomes so upset over the quarreling of his parents that he vomits, but the fact does not show him in an unfavorable light; in "Pale Horse, Pale Rider," Miranda vomits the cherry-colored pills which Adam gives her, but this manifestation of life-rejection is perfectly explained by her sickness.

But to return to the original point: David's instinct of rejection, essentially identical with that of other alpha protagonists, supplies the degree of coldness which is lacking in Jenny to make her an ideal alpha heroine. Her basic weakness is emotional instability; hers is a "restless seeking outlaw nature trying so hard to attach itself at any or at all points to the human beings nearest her: no matter who" (*SF*, 416). The contrast between her and David in this regard is pointed out with monotonous regularity. Miranda-like, Jenny loves to dance; but David hates dancing, cynically identifying it with the dirty stories, necking, and peeping which so violently disgust him. Jenny's warm, spontaneous nature is symbolized by her love for bright colors in clothing and art, which David succeeds temporarily in restricting to the somber blacks which he prefers. Just as her knowledge of his weaknesses gives her weapons which she uses, almost against her will, to injure him, so David has, in his awareness of Jenny's tender heart and of her real weakness for him, similar weapons for use against her. He has enough of a superficial love for her to keep her close and vulnerable, but his deep insecurity leads him repeatedly to injure her and retreat. Jenny, with "vague maternal feelings of the kind she abhorred in herself," longs to make him happy, but finds herself giving in to "fury and hatred" against him "in self-defense" (*SF*, 94). For "she wanted David to be comfortable, she wished to be easy within herself, and though David seemed coldly to devour everything, yet it was as if he were alone, he would not take her into his confidence, he would give nothing back. . . . He disliked her friends, and made none of his own. . . . he lived like a willful prisoner within himself, he would not let the door be unlocked" (*SF*, 145). She thinks of how he drank and practiced other "dull excesses in a methodical, uncommunicative frenzy of cold yet sensual enjoyment; and when he made love, Jenny knew he forgot who she was" (*SF*, 147).

Neither Jenny nor David is strong enough to break free of the other. Still, Jenny is more closely related to the cold Mrs. Treadwell than even the author seems to realize, and the result is a split in her personality which amounts to a serious defect in her portrayal. At times she gives promise of being a pleasant, human girl with whom the reader might feel inclined to identify and sympathize; but coldness keeps asserting itself, negating her attractive qualities and leaving her unpleasant and unreal. So different from Mrs. Treadwell at times, she at other times thinks and speaks exactly like her. There is often a cold aestheticism in her approach to others not adequately justified by the fact that she is an artist. On one occasion she sketches Herr Glocken's "harmonious, interesting deformity," and wonders "rather idly" what it might be like to live in such a hideous shape, the mere thought filling her with "a flash of blind terror and suffocation," and recalling the childhood experience of being locked in her grandmother's closet "narrow as a coffin" (*SF,* 86-87).

Along with Mrs. Treadwell's sense of oppression, Jenny shares her desire for isolation. She has escaped from her family, and her supposed love for them seems to have little if any real meaning. She is completely convincing when she tells David, to irk him, that she was happiest when alone once in a Veracruz "washed clean" of its present impurities. "I was there by myself and I saw it in my own way with no one to spoil it for me. . . . I had come off a boat from New York. Nine lovely days when I didn't know a soul on board, and spoke only to my waiter and my stewardess" (*SF,* 42). There is a familiar icy ring in her "refusal to admit the existence" of Amparo, justified though it seems, when the latter tries to shame her into buying a ticket to the fiesta (*SF,* 352). She is frequently made to act in a friendly manner that contrasts with David's coldness, but it is she who expresses the hope never to receive even a postcard from anyone on the ship as long as she lives. Jenny admits to herself that she sees love as a trap and yet falls in and out of it like "falling off a cliff." She foresees that she may have an affair with Freytag because he is handsome. Her standards, like Miranda's, are aesthetic; all her earlier lovers (who never seem quite real) were, she says, "beautiful and vain as the devil" (*SF,* 166). Her kind of love is strangely impersonal, "always with utter strangers and as if I were going under water," and, as she admits, compatible with not even liking the person. The warmth and openness to love which sometimes seems to appear in Jenny is degraded by this admission to the level of animal passion and emotional instability. Like her prototype, she feels that she has had a bitter life, and she escapes through art. If David's true isolationism be added to her own strong tendencies toward it, Jenny qualifies as a quite satisfactory alpha heroine.

Her words to a fortune-teller who predicts a new love affair will serve as final evidence of this fact: "I don't want any other man, the very notion gives me the horrors. I'll stick by the trouble I know. There are going to be a lot of other things much more interesting in my life than this man, or any other man" (*SF*, 370).

As stated previously, David is an almost pure instance of the alpha protagonist, and his character coincides with Jenny's in numerous particulars. He is attracted to her by her looks as well as by his sexual desire. Like her, he will never marry or let himself become involved again if he can but escape from this destructive union into which both he and Jenny were deluded by their earlier romanticism. He, too, is idealistic in ways he would never admit. He is offended when Jenny tells him that her earlier affairs weren't really love—he feels they should have been love. Like his feminine counterparts, he had "adolescent dreams and imaginings" of an ideal lover who would not "weigh on his mind and hound his feelings day and night and interfere with his plans and side-track him into places he had never meant to be" (*SF*, 450). He once thought Jenny was that ideal girl but is now aware of his mistake. Like her, he now hates love. David's only important divergence from the alpha pattern as embodied in Miranda is that in him, as in a sort of scapegoat, the undeniably negative and unwholesome aspects of the prototype are revealed clearly and condemned with impunity.

Freytag, a character of less importance—that is, less resemblance to the alpha prototype—may be dismissed briefly. He has sufficient intelligence, attractiveness, and stature to make him available as a complication in Mrs. Treadwell's life and a competitor with David for Jenny's attentions; but he is in himself of secondary interest. He is a target for the ironically misguided persecution of the Germans on board, and in this respect he furnishes an instance of oppression. In his relationship with Mary he reflects the familiar motif of escape from family; and in the fading of his highly aesthetic, romantic, Germanically sentimental love for her he illustrates the oppressive union motif. He becomes gradually less aware of the attractiveness of his marriage and more aware of its burdens. After he and Jenny have been acquainted for some time and Freytag has lost some of his "rosy honeymoon illusions," she notices that he is "talking about his wife as people talk about their dead" (*SF,* 306).

The two remaining characters of importance, Dr. Schumann and La Condesa, furnish especially interesting variations on Miss Porter's thematic pattern. It is because they possess a complexity which partially conceals their conformity to it that many readers have found these two the most interesting and significant in *Ship of Fools.* Of the two characterizations, most easily considered together, Dr. Schumann's is the more complex. He violates at least three of the author's thematic conventions by being male, German, and a believer in traditional dogma, and yet being admirable. In this he illustrates the hierarchy of importance among the motifs of the rejection pattern. He is portrayed primarily as a victim of inner and outer evils and draws from this thematic power-source his deepest validity as a character. The appeal which he at first has for the reader is roughly proportionate to the extent to which he transcends the familiar pattern; as it slowly asserts itself he becomes progressively diminished, and he is fittingly included in Granville Hicks's final verdict on the characters—"we watch unconcerned as . . . they drift away from us."

Dr. Schumann first strikes one as a strong man of mellow wisdom and benevolence. The mere fact that he is a doctor goes far to establish this image. By his observation of and personal contrast with the overwhelming majority of fools on the ship, he is elevated above them. On him, the *mensur* scar which is so loathsome to Charles Upton appears only as a sign of courage and good breeding. He does not hold himself obviously isolated from others as Mrs. Treadwell does; in his medical duties he associates with even the poor of the steerage level. He is the only man with the courage to confront the dancers during their brutal ticket-selling campaign. This episode is paralleled by one of his first actions in the story. Seeing Ric and Rac trying to throw the ship's cat overboard, he pulls them back and, "holding them firmly but with practiced gentleness," examines their eyes for a moment "with dismay at their blind, unwinking malignance, their cold slyness—not beasts, though, but human souls. Oh yes, human, more's the pity" (*SF,* 112). This episode is one of the first in an important series for him, for even the mature, urbane Dr. Schumann is to learn much about evil during the voyage—especially about that most insidious evil which is in his own heart. It becomes evident early in the story that the "perfectly poised ironical intelligence" which, as Schorer observes, "is constant and in complete authority," imposes its dark vision of life on every character whose thoughts it records. It is for this reason, among others, that it can validly be said that every character in every Porter story, to the extent that he really lives, is Miranda in thin disguise. For example, in the incident recorded above, Dr. Schumann sees Ric and Rac as identical except for "the mysterious stigmata of sex"—a typical Miranda observation but certainly not one typical of wise old doctors.

Dr. Schumann has, by his own diagnosis, "a very ordinary kind of heart trouble and might drop dead at any moment" (*SF,* 112). He cannot understand why he risked his life by rushing to save a cat, and wonders, "Given a moment for reflection, would he have leaped so and risked the stopping of his heart to save—even his wife?" (*SF,* 112) Thus the reader learns that Dr. Schumann's marriage, in so far as it really exists, is typically unhappy. His wife is absent and seems unreal besides, and the doctor is in the normal state of isolation, only apparently violated by his altruistic profession. In a lengthy meditation he reveals himself as another in the long line of skeptics about love. "Love! said the Doctor, surprised that the word should have popped into his thoughts. He put it out at once, with a proper regard for its true meaning," for he had spent the best years of his life "patching up the deceived, the foolhardy, the willfully blinded, the lover of suffering; and the most deadly of them all, the one who knew what he was doing and what he was bringing upon himself, and yet could not for anything resist one more fling at his favorite hot thrill of the flesh—drink, drugs, sex, food—whatever his particular concupiscence might be, though it might be his own death" (*SF*, 113). Love, then, is classified among the concupiscences. Dr. Schumann longs deeply to live, to stay "safely within himself, a place he knew as home," but he feels he has made his peace and his compromise with death; for he is willing to cling to life on very exacting terms of care and medication, and as far as the next life is concerned, he "believed in God, the Father, the Son and the Holy Ghost, and the Blessed Virgin Mother of God finally, in a particularly forthright, Bavarian Catholic way" (*SF*, 113).

From the first he feels "an unwilling admiration" for the Condesa because she is "so unusually beautiful," and his professional duties bring him into close contact with her. A lover of order, he feels that he can classify her sexual eccentricities as signs of "some acute form of nervous disorder" (*SF*, 115); he thinks of madness as "the temporary triumph of Evil in the human soul." He feels that the mystery in the life of man, which transcends the knowledge of science, can be explained "in the light of divine revelation"; yet he is "oppressed in flesh and spirit" (*SF*, 116). At her request he visits La Condesa, who is a Spanish noblewoman in political exile from Cuba to Tenerife and therefore literally a prisoner on the ship. The air in her cabin-prison is oppressive "with Turkish cigarette smoke, a mixture of heavy scents, and ether" (*SF*, 117). Terribly agitated, she fears that she is about to die, though otherwise the doctor finds her "sensible" except for a frank sexual amorality which is embarrassing to his modesty. From the very start the insidious growth of his passion for her is indicated by the sexual overtones of his medical attentions to her. When he kneads her stomach in exploration she gives "a slight sigh" and tells him, "All these charming attentions are making me deliciously sleepy, dear Doctor" (*SF*, 118). He disapproves morally of her use of ether as a stimulant but in pity prepares to give her a sedative, telling her it will be the only one and insisting that she stop using ether. Then "he pinched up the flesh of her arm, and at the slight stab of the needle she shuddered and said, "Ah, how delicious. How I love drugs, any kind of drug, to wake me or to make me sleep, I adore them all" (*SF,* 120). She enjoys his attention, given "as if you cared what happened to me." "I adore you," she tells the doctor, "you are such a preposterous good moral dull ridiculous man, but charming, charming!" (*SF,* 121) She falls asleep and he leaves, "the dank air of the passageway" striking him like a fresh breeze "after the fetid sweetness and rot of the cabin"; but he is already captivated by this "abandoned lost creature," and "nettles, poisoned barbs, fishhooks, her words clawed at his mind with the terrible malignance of the devil-possessed, the soul estranged from its kind" (*SF,* 122).

At the time of the incestuous incident involving Ric and Rac, Dr. Schumann and La Condesa are sitting on deck chairs, and he is lecturing her rather pedantically on the condition of man. Already he seems to be doubting some of his old certainties. "One has no new weaknesses, no new strengths," he muses, and apparent changes in character are mere illusion. "As one grows older, one is more conscious of the shifting, unstable elements in one's temperament. . . . one is immortal certainly, but not in this flesh" (*SF,* 196). He speaks tolerantly of his scolding wife and of the futility of his intention to go to sea for a rest. "I am astonished at myself for thinking, now maybe I shall learn something new about myself or the people I live with; but no such thing. I have seen all this before, over and over, only never until now did I see it on a ship. These people I have seen them all before, only in other places, under different names. I know their diseases almost by looking at them, and if you know what sickness is in a man you very often can tell what form his vices and virtues have taken" (*SF,* 197). Suddenly, as if to refute him, a young officer appears dragging Ric and Rac, too embarrassed to tell what he has seen them doing. La Condesa encourages him by saying she is a mother and can guess the worst, adding, "and truly I must say I do not find it so bad. What do you think, Doctor?" He replies that they are little monsters "entirely outside any usual mode of discipline" (*SF*, 198). The Condesa does not take the matter in the least seriously, commenting only, *"Il faut passer la jeunesse."* When the doctor insists that the children are "devil-possessed" she says admiringly, "What an old-fashioned sort of man you are." The Doctor feels he has now come into contact with an evil more absolute than he has ever known, and the Condesa's confident nonchalance shakes his certainties a bit more. She tells him frankly that since earliest childhood she has pursued the pleasures of sex and every other available pleasure with hedonistic abandon. He states that his childhood was innocent; then, at her urging, looks more carefully and finds memories of childhood seductions, which he blames on Original Sin. She jars him out of his theological complications with her serene assurance that children are "only perfectly natural little animals." They both then laugh at the concept of childhood as a "time of the tender bud, the unfolding leaf." La Condesa takes the Doctor's hand: " 'I love you,' she said, gently and unexpectedly. 'Not so much you, perhaps, though you are very nice, but I love what you are. I like gravity and seriousness and strong principles in a man. There is nothing more repellent to me than a frivolous, timid, vacillating man, who does not know his own mind and his own heart. And why? Because then he cannot ever know the mind and heart of a woman' " (*SF*, 201). She completely ignores the real meaning of the Doctor's seriousness and strong principles, subtly reducing them to the status of aids to romance. She asks him if he was ever unfaithful to his wife, and after a "quite proper" shocked hesitation he truthfully answers in the negative. Then, "posssessed by a demon of frankness," he admits that his marriage has been dull. She asks if he loves her, but the Doctor, still clinging to his idealistic view of love, says he does not. Finally he reveals his insecurity in the face of her prodding by becoming indignant and preparing to leave; but she confronts him frantically and convinces him that she is in need of another sedative injection. When he accuses her of continuing to use ether, she gives another evidence of her utter amorality by asking with "contemptuous impatience, 'When will you learn not to trust me in anything?' "

(*SF*, 204) Amazed by his own bitterness, he decides that for the sake of his health and the avoidance of scandal he must end the relationship, though he could still "be merciful and consign her to a narcotic limbo, which was, after all, her notion of Paradise" (*SF*, 204). He goes to her room and gives her an injection, once again under strongly sexual imagery.

Dr. Schumann begins giving La Condesa a regular series of shots. On one occasion they discuss the lewd and irreverent behavior of the Cuban students toward her; she shows him that she is completely superior to them and tolerates their conduct simply for the excitement, completely indifferent to their opinions and those of the other passengers. There is indeed a great strength and fearlessness in this woman, and also a certain fascination. La Condesa is related, at least distantly, to such diverse literary creations as Chaucer's Wife of Bath, Shaw's Alfred Doolittle, and the rowdy fraternity of Steinbeck's *Tortilla Flat*. All of them, by a completely honest and liberating admission of their amorality, acquire a certain charm and demand, from the reader aware of the dishonesty that so often accompanies virtue, a degree of grudging admiration. La Condesa seems to be paying for her dissolute life by nervous suffering, yet the strength she reveals in her moral indifference seems attractive enough to the Doctor to loosen him from his ideological moorings. When her condition grows worse, he has her confined more closely to her room and forbids visitors. He has ordered the stewardess to be present during the injections, a factor which diminishes their sexual significance. Nevertheless he finally comes to a frank realization of his "sinful love" for the woman and of the inevitable mutation by which "his wish to ease her sufferings was changing slowly into a wish to cause her suffering, of another kind, in which she would be made to feel his hand and his will" (*PH*, 238). He feels that his baseness should not even be called love, and in his guilt he goes to confession to "the sterner, more trap-jawed" of the Mexican priests, whose advice is, needless to say, excessively severe and unworthy of respect.

Dr. Schumann is next seen at the captain's table, in dis-

cussion with the narrowly pedantic Herr Hutten. The Doctor's
new humility and uncertainty about the nature of evil are emphasized by contrast with Hutten's dogmatic idealism. The
latter denies the reality of good and evil and asks the Doctor,
just for the sake of the argument, for his opinion.

"It is not for me a question of philosophy," said Dr. Schumann,
"and even if it were, I am not a philosopher. I rely on the teachings
of the Church and I am sorry I cannot argue the matter. I am a
poor sinner," he said, good-temperedly and dryly, "who needs divine
help every day. I agree with the Captain, it takes a strong character
to be really evil. Most of us are too slack, halfhearted, or cowardly
—luckily, I suppose. Our collusion with evil is only negative, consent by default, you might say. I suppose in our hearts our sympathies are with the criminal because he really commits the deeds we
only dream of doing! Imagine if the human race were really divided
into embattled angels and invading devils—no, it is bad enough as
it is," he said, crossing his knife and fork, "with nine-tenths of us
half asleep and refusing to be waked up."

(SF, 294)

Dr. Schumann's words carry weight, for Miss Porter has clearly
created him to be the novel's wise man. (His words echo her
own statement that *Ship of Fools* is "the story of the criminal
collusion of good people—people who are harmless—with
evil.") One can see in this speech the sobering effect of the
doctor's new contacts with evil and his admiration for La Condesa. She, with her Miranda-like honesty and independence, is
herself his most puzzling moral paradox as well as his personal
moral problem.

Dr. Schumann goes on to new and terrifying encounters with
"the evil he was discovering in his own nature" (*SF*, 316). La
Condesa's condition does not improve. Once, during a moment
of alarm for the safety of the ship, she says to the Doctor,
"Imagine, if the ship should sink, we should go down together
embraced, gently, gently to the bottom of the sea, quiet dark
love in the cool sleepy water. . . ." (*SF*, 316) In her the desire
to escape from oppression can only be a wish for death, as is
already evident in her drug addiction; for she has no illusions
about life—and she has the courage to recognize her desire

for what it is. The Doctor, chilled by her words, has "a savage impulse to strike her from him, this diabolical possession, this incubus fastened upon him like a bat, this evil spirit come out of her hell to accuse him falsely, to seduce his mind, to charge him with fraudulent obligations to her, to burden his life to the end of his days, to bring him to despair" (*SF*, 316). At the sight of the "resentful servility" of the stewardess who has neglected La Condesa, his sense of oppression spreads. He feels "the oppression of the increasing millions of subhuman beings, the mindless grave-stuff not even fit to be good servants, yet whose mere mass and weight of negative evil threatened to rule the world" (*SF*, 317). These are sad words to hear from the benevolent wise man of *Ship of Fools*.

Dr. Schumann witnesses the death of Echegaray, the poor Basque woodcarver whose suicidal attempt to save the Hutten's dog was prompted by the loss of his knife in the Captain's general confiscation of weapons. At the thought of it he experiences "a wave of weariness and hopelessness" (*SF*, 320). When the dancers post their insulting messages about various passengers, including a reference to La Condesa and her "devoted doctor," he angrily confronts them and sees in their eyes "some species of fierce beast peering out of a cave or ready to leap in a jungle, prowling and sniffing for blood; the same expression, only older, more intensely aware and ready, that had dismayed him in the eyes of Ric and Rac" (*SF*, 348). As he leaves them he thinks about the moral paradox that "the gauzy glittering surface of gaiety," which appeals to him strongly, lies "lightly over the foulest pools of evil" (*SF*, 349). In further self-condemnation, he feels that he loves La Condesa because she is "perverted, strayed, a taker of drugs, . . . outside religion, outside law, outside morality, . . . beautiful, willful, and . . . no doubt, a born liar" (*SF*, 350). He tells himself that he has not aided her with medicine or sympathy but has subdued her "by using against her the vice that harmed her most—drugs." At this thought "Dr. Schumann faced an aspect of his character he had not suspected until that hour" (*SF*, 350). He is overcome by the vision of the evil in himself. In spite of his reasonings "he was not consoled or reassured, and knew that he could never be by any means he was able to imagine now. She was a burden on his conscience he was condemned to carry to his death" (*SF,* 350).

When the time comes for La Condesa to leave the ship, Dr. Schumann feels weak, tired, and ill; but still he tries to convince himself that he has done "not right perhaps—who could be certain of that, ever?—but the only thing possible" (*SF,* 367). He tries to assure her she will be well treated on the island, but she only demands, "Oh, my friend, have you gone mad with virtue and piety, have you lost your human feelings, how can you have forgotten what suffering is?" (*SF,* 367) He admits that the night before, he kissed her as she thought she dreamed, and they embrace. Suddenly she says, "Oh, do you know what it is, coming so late, so strangely, no wonder I couldn't understand it. It is that innocent romantic love I should have had in my girlhood! But no one loved me innocently, and oh, how I should have laughed at him if he had! . . . Well, here we are. Innocent love is the most painful kind of all, isn't it?" (*SF,* 369) He replies that he has loved her guiltily, done her a great wrong, and ruined his life. As they part he is oppressed by the thought of death and fears his heart will burst. "Why of course, death," she says, "but not yet!" (*SF,* 369)

The Doctor's suffering and guilt feelings continue, drawing him slowly into a moral confusion so deep that "the whole great structure built upon the twin pillars of justice and love" seems to crumble around him (*SF,* 373). Suddenly, as in a lightning stroke, his emotional fog clears and with immense pain he sees his descent to "criminal sentimental cruelty" as "merely the symptom of his moral collapse" (*SF,* 373). He has wronged La Condesa, his patient; has "taken advantage of her situation as prisoner, . . . tormented her with his guilty love and yet . . . refused her—and himself—any human joy in it." And finally, he has "let her go in hopelessness without even the faintest promise of future help or deliverance. What a coward, what a swine" (*SF,* 373). He sends her an urgent message by which he hopes to maintain contact. Gradually, human grief for La

Condesa replaces his "perverse infatuation," and the decision to provide for her through "blameless charity" and "at a distance" brings him "hope, and relief of conscience" (*SF,* 374). His comfort is destroyed, however, when he learns that she has sent no answer to his message. From this time on he is despondent. On the fiesta night he is called upon to stitch up Herr Rieber's wounded head, and he is later roused from sleep to care for Denny, whose face is "a lumpy, discolored mass of ugly-looking little cuts and bruises, full of dried blood and already swelling" (*SF,* 468). Oppressed by his own despair and the events of the evening, he finishes his duties, "fearing he might collapse before he could reach the porthole in his cabin for a breath of air while he took his crystal drops." Then he makes his final comment on life:

In that moment, when he truly expected death, he looked upon all these intruders as his enemies. Without exception, he rejected them all, every one of them, all human kinship with them, all professional duty except the barest tokens. He did not in the least care what became of any one of them. Let them live their dirty lives and die their dirty deaths in their own way and their own time, so much carrion to fill graves. He crossed himself and folded his arms and lay still breathing carefully, turning his head slowly from side to side, denying his own bitter thoughts even as they rose and flowed again painfully all through him as though his blood were full of briers.
(*SF,* 469)

Dr. Schumann, then, finishes the voyage deeply embittered by the evil he has found within and around him. If he does not abandon his faith willfully, he seems nevertheless to have lost its support. This man who represents the highest wisdom in the world of the *Vera* not only proves a poor exponent of traditional beliefs but also comes precariously near to abandoning completely his faith in human nature. The one person who showed promise of bringing some positive value to this narrow fictional world turns out to be virtually just another alpha protagonist, isolated, bitter, hopeless in the shadow of death; and neither *Ship of Fools* nor the body of Miss Porter's work as a whole suggests any alternative for him. La Condesa, the chief instrument of his disillusion, comes to exactly the same end, though her superior truthfulness gives her a greater strength to bear oppression. Beneath the moral paradox she embodies, she is an especially strong, self-sufficient alpha heroine. In the clear, simple light of her independence, she has shown a grand contempt for men, even for her devoted doctor, from whom she escapes at last. Her final superiority to him (in terms of the acceptance of "reality" and of the ability to act) is an assertion of the rejection theme even in opposition to all social and moral standards. La Condesa has brought a new and piquant clarity to the alpha heroine, and almost—but not quite—a sense of humor.[28]

Much of the strength which makes Dr. Schumann and La Condesa by far the most interesting characters in the novel derives from the fact that they represent the only encounter in all Miss Porter's fiction of two strong and admirable alpha protagonists. There has always been a fundamental barrenness about Miranda and her counterparts, for they were always really isolated—never really entered into human relations. But in the case of these two characters, it is as if Miranda has met her match, or nearly so. For at least a brief time she is helplessly drawn into an oppressive union, forced to bring all her powers to a confrontation with a real human being. (A comparison of Dr. Schumann and Adam will reveal, this time by contrast, how unreal the latter was.)[29] As usual, the woman

28. In the above-mentioned Janeway interview (p. 5) Miss Porter reveals that La Condesa is based on a real woman whom she observed "in glimpses and snatches for a couple of weeks" on the voyage that inspired the novel. It seems probable that the at least partial individuality of Dr. Schumann may have a similar explanation.

29. This matter of Miranda-characters can be clearly illustrated in the following manner: Consider the characters whom the author portrays with relative fullness and with genuine respect as regards their basic stature as human beings—María Concepción, the heroine of "Theft," Granny Weatherall, Laura, Miranda, the Grandmother, Mr. Thompson (partially), Mrs. Thompson (perhaps), Aunt Eliza, Old Nannie, Stephen, Charles Upton, Mrs. Treadwell, Dr. Schumann, La Condesa. There is little uncertainty about the inclusion of any of these characters, and there is certainly no other important character who belongs in the list. An attempt has been made to show that all of these are alpha characters, basically identifiable with Miranda. Their defining common quality is an instinct of rejection accompanied by an openness to truth (the tragedy of the Thompsons being that, in an ambiguous manner, they lie). It is only in the case of Dr. Schumann and La Condesa

is superior in the all-important quality of truthfulness (even though "a born liar"), although the man is greatly purified in this respect in the course of the novel. Superficially, Dr. Schumann and La Condesa represent some of the most profound moral paradoxes that man faces. Their meeting is a clash between traditional Christianity and its almost complete negation; yet their value in terms of a serious examination of these problems is radically vitiated by their deeply determined conformity to the pattern of the rejection theme. They are drawn by romantic-aesthetic attractions into a brief union which is highly oppressive to them both; each inflicts terrible pain upon the other; then, by an inevitable repulsion, they are forced apart and left with only the sense of loss.

The other characters in the novel compose a rather wide spectrum of racial and psychological types, but all remain bound to the rejection pattern as it applies to beta characters. The members of the dancing troupe shade off into absolute evil, but there is no one who approaches absolute good. "Goodness," like "love," is a word which all the most significant characters would dismiss with scorn. This is not to say that the characters are morally condemned, for the author has said that she is not out to judge them morally, that she is on everyone's side. For even the lowest of them, Ric and Rac, Denny, and the lot, she provides a simple case history which does much to explain their vices. Characteristically, most have come from unhappy homes, oppressive marriages. Hardly ever was there normal love between the parents or between parent and child. Even Captain Thiele, the god of this little world, was warped by a brutal father; and as for his mother, he "had not liked her much" (*SF*, 430). Johann's viciousness is pretty thoroughly explained by his situation, and the sadistic manner in which Ric and Rac are punished indicates how they have been debased, like their parents before them. The pathetic Elsa and little Hans have been given poor starts in life, which can in turn be explained by the eccentricities and fears of their elders.

There are in the novel numerous minor thematic motifs, most

that two of these characters of highest stature enter into a close relationship. Inevitably, it is a conflict.

of which can be easily reduced to manifestations of the rejection theme. Germany is the oppressor on a world scale, the Jews the oppressed. Religion, like most other traditional beliefs, is rather generally rejected, as can be seen in the disillusion of Dr. Schumann, the brutality of the men who attack the skeptics immediately after hearing Mass, the inhumanity of the Mexican priests, Herr Graf's loathsome piety, and so on. Sex is consistently shown as a degrading and burdensome "stigma," brief in its pleasures. After Johann's longed-for rendezvous with Concha, he emerges "almost blind with the bitter rapture of lust that struck him like a blow from an unknown source, with a violence not of pleasure but like a mortal sickness or other disaster he had not dreamed of, and no one had warned him" (*SF*, 485). The strongest impression left by the book is one of a general lovelessness in which communion is destructive and isolation miserable. Freytag in imagination tells his wife, "People on a boat, Mary, can't seem to find any middle ground between stiffness, distrust, total rejection, or a kind of invasive, gnawing curiosity. Sometimes it's a friendly enough curiosity, sometimes sly and malicious, but you feel as if you were being eaten alive by fishes" (*SF*, 133). The gradual growth of awareness of the evil in the human heart and in fate is a theme illustrated by Dr. Schumann but also evident in others. The knowledge gradually penetrates even the German idealism and sentimentality of the Huttens. The only form in which evil functions, however, is that of oppression.

The three epigraphs are clearly related to the rejection theme. Part I begins with Baudelaire's question, *Quand partons-nous vers le bonheur?* which echoes the desire for escape that animates the travelers as they embark, and comments ironically on the elusive happiness many of them are seeking. It is the futile cry that was on Miranda's lips until she learned that there is no happiness. *Kein Haus, Keine Heimat* describes the condition of the travelers, both physically and spiritually; the *Heimat* is just as illusory as *bonheur*. There is bitter irony in the application of Saint Paul's line, "For here we have no continuing city." He used the words to direct the thoughts of his hearers to heaven, but only the negative half of the statement applies to *Ship of Fools*. The voyage ends, and so does life, and that is all.

Ship of Fools is a climax in the work of Katherine Anne Porter in its physical magnitude and in its partial advance toward a genuine portrayal of human relations. Yet its reach has, in a sense, exceeded its grasp; for its large cast of characters, together with its stylistic clarity, serves primarily to reveal the limitations of its author's artistic comprehension of human nature. Miss Porter works with great power in certain limited veins, and within the broad field of *Ship of Fools* her consistent thematic lines have been free to extend themselves to new lengths. Her thematic power, however, retains in the novel its fundamental narrowness; and the forced extension of this power over a framework of such ambitious dimensions sharply illuminates its oppressive poverty. This poverty is graphically illustrated by the fact that the person in the novel who possesses the greatest self-awareness and underlying forcefulness—because she is pre-eminent in that essentially negative openness to truth which is the supreme desideratum of the rejection theme—is the corrupt, dope-addicted, amoral Condesa. The bizarre consequences of extending this observation to a generalization about life are obvious; but it is just as obvious that this novel does not really generalize about life. Miss Porter's artistic vision, both for better and for worse, is strictly personal. It is, in the last analysis, this extreme subjectivity, combined with the author's peculiar thematic limitations as illustrated by the rejection theme, which renders *Ship of Fools* basically unsatisfactory as a commentary on human existence. Certainly man is surrounded and sometimes overwhelmed by evil. But, as inductive reasoning in the sciences must begin with an adequate grasp of a multiple reality, so the artistic apprehension of evil, to be universally meaningful, must arise from a reasonably comprehensive grounding in the variety and complexity of life. One cannot, for example, speak with authority of the paradoxical sufferings involved in human love if he denies love from the start. It is a deficiency in the primary vision of reality that vitiates much of Miss Porter's art; the very existence of that art is proof that her deficiency is not one of honesty or of courage.

6

The Art of Rejection

The principle of rejection which is the central impulse in the thematic structure of the works of Katherine Anne Porter may be seen in a general way in her artistic practice and in more specific ways in the formal characteristics of her fiction. This pervasiveness of the rejection principle is both a further evidence and a natural consequence of the fact that her art is a particularly full and profound expression of her nature. Even her numerous essays and published statements, which she is at great pains to separate sharply from her art, clearly reflect her attitudes and preoccupations, thus helping in many ways to round out the portrait which has been sketched in such strong lines by her fiction.[1]

1. Two excellent short studies of Miss Porter's criticism, both treating the essays collected in *The Days Before* (New York: Harcourt, Brace and Company, 1952), are the following: Lodwick Hartley, "The Lady and the Temple: the Critical Theories of Katherine Anne Porter," *College English,* XIV (April, 1953), 381-91; and Edward Schwartz, "The Way of Dissent: Katherine Anne Porter's Critical Position," *Western Humanities Review,* VIII (1954), 119-30. As their titles suggest, they emphasize Miss Porter's supreme regard for art and the element of dissent in her thought.

Two of the most striking and frequently noted facts about Miss Porter's literary career are the consistently high formal quality of her work and the smallness of her output. Both these characteristics are related to rejection processes in her approach to writing. Certainly one obstacle to steady production has been the need for ideal writing conditions, which her life has seldom provided. In an effort to preserve the highly personal and autonomous nature of her artistry as much as possible, she has developed instincts and habits which quite often take the form of rejection. Wescott records one instance of this from a letter she wrote to him, in which she spoke of those parasitic persons who attach themselves to writers. " 'They are as rapacious and hard to fight off as the bluejays,' but, she boasted, 'I have developed a great severity of rejection that I did not know I was capable of. We are all brought up on the Christian and noble idea that we have no right to deny our lives and substance to anyone who seems to need either or both. Never was a fonder delusion.' "[2] (The reader will note here the rejection of childhood teachings so persistent in her stories.) Mention might also be made of another kind of interference against which she has carefully guarded her art—the literary influence of other writers, editors, and critics. Her long apprenticeship was spent in isolation from literary society; this, as she has said, admittedly prolonged it but also protected her from the dangers of imitation and discipleship. In her introduction to *The Days Before* (p. vii), she refers to her practice with regard to editors. "My stories had to be accepted and published exactly as they were written: that rule has never once been broken." She has also shown a strongly defensive attitude toward the critics of her work. One example of this occurs at the beginning of her essay on "Noon Wine."

There was a time when critics of literature seemed quite happy to try digging out the author's meanings without help; or, failing to find any,

2. Glenway Wescott, *Images of Truth: Remembrances and Criticism* (New York: Harper & Row, 1962), p. 28. The intention here is not to deny that authors are plagued by admirers or to suggest that they are not justified in protecting themselves; it is simply to point out the vigor of this author's reaction and her characteristic way of expressing it.

to invent meanings of their own, often just as satisfactory to everybody—except perhaps to the author, whose feelings or opinion traditionally do not count much, anyway.

The private reader too has always been welcome to his own notions of what he is reading, free to remark upon it to his heart's content, with no cramping obligation to be "right" in his conclusions, such as weighs upon the professional or paid critic; it is enough for him to be moved and stimulated to speak his thoughts freely; the author will not mind even harshness, if only he can be sure he is being read![3]

All of these manifestations are in harmony with the deeply personal manner of Miss Porter's writing, according to which even she herself seems to play less the part of deliberate maker than of sensitive instrument, recording the inner truth. They are directed toward safeguarding the purity and vitality of her art. Another of her practices, on the contrary, tends to diminish quantity, though it favors quality. This is her habit of extremely rigorous selectivity, which permits only a very small proportion of her work to be "finished" and made public. There is ample evidence of this in her recollections of traveling about weighted down by trunkloads of manuscript and of destroying numerous unfinished works, including more than one novel. Meanwhile, the product of her half-century of devotion to her craft has been three small books of stories and one large novel. This critical selectivity is no doubt intimately related to a much more profound and less deliberate selectivity which has probably been the most important factor in limiting her work and at the same time maintaining its high quality.

There is clear evidence of the principle of rejection in Miss Porter's very choice of material for her fiction. She has stated frequently that much in her creative process is, so to say, beyond her control. She has spoken of the manner in which scenes from memory lie deep within her, often for many years, undergoing a slow transmutation until they come together in the proper pattern and she can write the story quickly and inevitably, often at one sitting. In all vital fiction there is the work of the imagination upon memory and the selection and ordering of elements,

3. "'Noon Wine': The Sources," *Yale Review*, XLVI (September, 1956), 22.

and all selection implies extensive rejection. But in Miss Porter's case there seems to be a minimum of free and arbitrary imaginative play and a maximum of what might be called inner determination—the "profound, inward, hidden way of working" which Wescott attributes to her, observing that she proceeds "not just thoughtfully, methodically, as perhaps prose writers ought to be able to work, as indeed in her case the finished product suggests that she may have done." He continues, quoting Miss Porter: " 'I spend my life thinking about technique, method, style,' she once told me. 'The only time I do not think of them at all is when I am writing.' "[4] In other words, almost all the rejection in this author's creative process is performed inwardly, instinctively. Her beautiful essay on the development of "Noon Wine" illustrates perfectly how at least the conscious part of this process takes place.

Turning next to the stories themselves to see precisely what has been rejected, one finds that the answer seems to be almost everything which is not a vivid part of the author's own memory-hoard. In reviewing the first edition of *Flowering Judas* in 1930, Allen Tate observed that Miss Porter

neither overworks a brilliant style capable of every virtuosity nor forces the background of her material into those sensational effects that are the besetting sin of American prose fiction. . . . While American prose fiction as a whole is chiefly occupied with the discovery and then the definition of its materials, . . . Miss Porter already has a scene which is her instinctive, automatic, unconscious possession; a background that she does not need to think out, nor approach intellectually; a given medium which at once liberates the creative impulse from the painful necessity to acquire its material and sets it about the true presentation of it.[5]

This comment, reflecting as it does the critic's preoccupation with the "new provincialism," points out once again Miss Porter's integrity in rejecting whatever is spurious for her. More important, it again calls attention to that inner way of working which restricts her not only to a familiar geographical, social, and ideological background (evident not in all, but in the

4. Wescott, *Images of Truth,* p. 28.
5. "A New Star," *Nation,* CXXXI (October, 1930), 352-53.

greater part of her most characteristic work), but especially to her personal spiritual "background." Ray B. West has investigated this matter of imaginative dependence on memory, and makes the following statement: "The important thing to notice is that in all cases, Katherine Anne Porter's characters possess qualities which have some point of similarity with her own experience. If they are Irish or Mexican, they are also Roman Catholic—or they are political liberals. They are usually Southerners. I don't mean to suggest this as a serious limitation, but it may help to account for the relatively small amount that Miss Porter has written. At the same time, it may also account for the consistently high level which her work represents, a level probably unsurpassed by any writer of her time."[6] This study has been partially an attempt to illustrate and amplify the statement that all of Miss Porter's characters "possess qualities which have some point of similarity with her own experience." She herself has stated, in words that might have been spoken by Miranda, "My one aim is to tell a straight story and to give true testimony."[7] It would seem that even the creation of independent, alien characters would have taken Miss Porter outside the bounds of what is artistically true for her.

James W. Johnson has summarized well the various types of rejection which have narrowed the author's work:

Had Miss Porter left those trunksfull of manuscripts unburned, the objection based on volume could have been met. Yet this very act of selectivity is an indication of the guiding principle which has made her unique. Her critical judgment, as accurate and impartial as a carpenter's level, has limited her artistry in several ways. It has not permitted her to universalize but has confined her to being a "witness to life." Consequently, her fiction has been closely tied to what she herself has experienced firsthand. The fact that Miss Porter's essays parallel her stories in theme—love, marriage, alien cultures—is significant in this light. Her artistic preoccupation with "truth" has prevented the fictional generalizations often thought of as scope.

6. "Katherine Anne Porter and 'Historic Memory,'" *South: Modern Southern Literature in Its Cultural Setting,* ed. Louis D. Rubin and Robert D. Jacobs (Garden City, New York: Doubleday & Company, Inc., Dolphin Books, 1961), p. 304.

7. Quoted in Lodwick Hartley, "Katherine Anne Porter," *Sewanee Review,* XLVIII (April, 1940), 206.

Moreover, Miss Porter's "truth" is the truth of feeling and behavior rather than that of ideas. . . . Because she narrows her attention to specific individuals, . . . her stories give the impression of constriction. In addition, her people are in no way exceptional, . . .

Finally, Miss Porter's self-criticism has prevented her from publishing, or even preserving, anything less than perfect by her own severe standards.[8]

The close agreement of Johnson's observations with the rejection theme will be noted. Both the completeness with which the stories are confined to the "truth of feeling and behavior" and the peculiarly uniform narrowness of that feeling and behavior help to explain the sense of constriction.

The tendency in modern American writing toward simplicity and compression, referred most frequently to Hemingway, obscures somewhat the fact that Katherine Anne Porter developed her oft-praised concise, transparent style largely on her own. Certainly she felt the influences, both literary and non-literary, which led other writers toward the simple style. She is widely read in modern as well as traditional literature and is intensely aware of the world in which she lives. Still, critics are virtually unanimous in assigning to Miss Porter a unique and pre-eminent position as a stylist, and her works as well as her autobiographical statements make it clear that she has not been an imitator. The key to her stylistic power would seem to have been, once again, her instinct of rejection; for it happens that this instinct tends to produce many of the qualities which characterize clear, powerful prose. In the creation of Miss Porter's style, the instinct of rejection has been delicately regulated by her fine sensitiveness to the nature and resources of her language. Her verbal fastidiousness, while it led at times to a bareness which some have criticized, never led her to the eccentricity which trapped Gertrude Stein or even to the stylized understatement of Hemingway, to whose work hers bears some close resemblances. Hers is a strong, flexible style which seldom calls attention to itself. One aspect of it which does sometimes

8. "Another Look at Katherine Anne Porter," *Virginia Quarterly Review,* XXXVI (Autumn, 1960), 612-13.

attract attention, though only rarely in an unfavorable way, is its punctuation. The tendency to reject every nonessential in the interests of smoothness and intensity shows up clearly in Miss Porter's habit of reducing punctuation to the lowest possible minimum. Periods and semicolons are reduced to commas, and commas are skipped whenever possible. The practice seems to have developed gradually. It begins to appear in the two stories in *Flowering Judas*—"The Jilting" and the title story —which utilize the fluid language of the mind in its dreams and wanderings. It occurs most frequently in dialogue and interior monologue, as in Miranda's meditations at the end of "Old Mortality." It is increasingly frequent in the later works, including *Ship of Fools,* where its use is more habitual and less carefully regulated than in the stories. A good example of its deliberate use, and also of stark simplicity and the avoidance of every unnecessary word, is the passage describing Mrs. Thompson's collapse after the murder in "Noon Wine": "Mrs. Thompson sat down slowly against the side of the house and began to slide forward on her face; she felt as if she were drowning, she couldn't rise to the top somehow, and her only thought was she was glad the boys were not there, they were out, fishing at Halifax, oh, God, she was glad the boys were not there" (*PH,* 154).

Like her style, Miss Porter's structures, except in *Ship of Fools,* are remarkably compressed. The short stories contain hardly an excess word, and "Old Mortality" and "Noon Wine" are marvels of richness in a small space. Numerous examples have been given of brief passages which function in a multiplicity of ways, or which compress long periods of time into a sentence. One aid to this economy both of style and of structure is the author's insistence, reminiscent of Poe's, on the necessity of knowing the end of the story before writing toward it. "The important thing to know when you start to write a short story . . . is precisely how it will end. . . . I had tried to write about forty stories before I discovered what was wrong. . . . Then I wrote the end of a story first and spent the greater part of seventeen days and nights writing and polishing. The result was my first published story, which I sold to *Century* when I was twenty-eight. . . . I wrote the last four pages of my novel, 'No Safe Harbor,' ten years ago and I am just finishing it now."[9]

The structural aspects of Miss Porter's stories have been capably discussed by Lodwick Hartley,[10] and several of his observations are of particular interest in the light of the rejection theme. He quotes the author's statement of her intention to "tell a straight story and give true testimony," but applies it differently than she seems to by taking "straight story" to mean a dramatically well-ordered one. In keeping with his formal criteria, he assigns superiority to such stories as "He," "María Concepción," "The Jilting," "Hacienda," "The Cracked Looking-Glass," "Noon Wine," "Magic," "Rope," and "The Grave"; and he finds fault with "Theft," "Flowering Judas," "Old Mortality," and "Pale Horse, Pale Rider." It will be observed that what he has done here is to divide the stories almost perfectly into the alpha and beta groups. He singles out for criticism exactly the four stories which center around the mature Miranda—the true alpha stories which comprise Miss Porter's most characteristic work. His objections to these stories may be summed up under the heading of subjectivity. "When Miss Porter identifies herself subjectively with her heroines, she at times loses strength and directness."[11] He criticizes the endings of "Old Mortality," "Theft," and "Flowering Judas" as follows: "Old Mortality"

is told with great richness and beauty of detail, but its purpose is not entirely certain and its climax lacks the authority of complete inevitability. The development of Miranda throughout the story hardly justifies laying the "turn" of the story on her shoulders, especially since her revolt in the final analysis involves much more than the theme of the story demands for satisfactory completion.[12]

9. Quoted by Charles Boutell in "Authors Are Like People," *New York Post,* September 21, 1944. It is interesting to note the author's statement, almost twenty years before the appearance of *Ship of Fools,* that the novel was nearly finished. Elsewhere, too, Miss Porter has spoken of knowing how certain episodes of the novel would end but having to wait to find out the means. Perhaps this manner of writing is related to her tendency toward uniform character portrayal rather than free and spontaneous development of character.

10. "Katherine Anne Porter," *Sewanee Rev.*

11. *Ibid.,* p. 211.

12. *Ibid.,* p. 210.

Incorporated in a dream comes Laura's final self-accusation of murder and cannibalism, the ultimate sentimentality of which becomes fully apparent when one compares it with the conclusion of "Theft," . . . In "Theft" Miss Porter uses a simple incident, the theft of the heroine's purse by a janitress, to reveal a fundamental failure in the heroine's character and to explain her tragedy. Between the thief and the owner of the purse she develops a psychological situation of power. From it, however, we are led to a passage of wistful cerebration that might better have been a part of "To the Lighthouse" or "The Years."[13]

These objections are valid, and an awareness of the rejection theme helps to explain why Miss Porter, usually so expert, should err in this direction. All the passages in question record crucial rejections and consequently carry a thematic force so strong that it distorts the dramatic structure of the individual story. In each case there is indeed, as Hartley says of "Old Mortality," the "indulgence of an emotional bias."[14] Awareness of the rejection theme and of the consequent close relationship between the stories adds a new level of complexity to their understanding and evaluation; furthermore, awareness of the numerous and sometimes concealed hints of rejection in each story should lead the critic to find the climactic rejection scenes less incongruent than at first appears. Considered within the framework of the rejection theme, these passages contain not the self-pity of egocentric females, but choric comment on the downfall of a heroine. That they nevertheless strike the reader as sentimental is one indication of the deficiency of the theme itself. Hence it is clear that the principle of rejection is responsible not only for much of the excellence in the stories but also for some of their deepest defects; as always, rejection proves itself ambivalent.[15]

13. *Ibid.*, p. 213.
14. *Ibid.*, pp. 213-14.
15. In the light of the rejection principle, it is interesting to note how often criticism of Miss Porter's work has taken an essentially negative form. This applies to both favorable and unfavorable judgments. The Schwartz bibliography, cited above, makes possible a quick survey of early Porter criticism. The following selection of excerpts contains almost every stylistic criticism listed: Margaret Marshall (1940): Miss Porter's prose "has extraordinary purity and concentration; . . . all the dross has been distilled out.

Katherine Anne Porter introduces *The Days Before,* the collection of her essays published in 1952, with the following statement:

It is my hope that the reader will find in this collection of papers written throughout my thirty years as published writer, the shape, direction, and connective tissue of a continuous, central interest and preoccupation of a lifetime.

They represent the exact opposite of my fiction, in that they were written nearly all by request, with limitations of space, a date fixed for finishing, on a chosen subject or theme, as well as with the certainty that they would be published. I wrote as well as I could at any given moment under a variety of pressures, and said what I meant as nearly as I could come to it: so as they stand, the pieces are really parts of a journal of my thinking and feeling. Then too, they served to get me a living, such as it was, so that I might be able to

---

What is more important, it never gives the effect of irrelevant or insipid prettiness, never therefore becomes a 'style' because it never once, for its own sake, becomes separated from the story she has to tell." Louise Bogan (1930): In the writing of *Flowering Judas,* "nothing is fortuitous." Eleanor Clark (1935): *Flowering Judas* is "written with subdued and exceptional brilliance." William Troy (1935): "Throughout these stories it is the . . . strict adherence to the fact for what the fact can produce that saves Miss Porter both from the rhetorical emphasis of Mrs. Woolf and her followers and from the equally rhetorical understatement of the Hemingway school." Edith Walton (1935): "To a style as subtle and beautiful as Kay Boyle's she adds greater vitality and a freedom from rarefied mannerisms. . . . Clearly one of the best and most fastidious of modern short story writers." Ben Belitt (1937): In "Noon Wine" "Miss Porter's simplicities . . . are strategems, and the story's impact, for all its incidental rewards, is muted by its rigors." Clifton Fadiman (1939): In "Pale Horse, Pale Rider," Miss Porter shares with Hemingway "and a mere scattering of other American authors, both the will and the ability to create by suggestion. She makes us sense more than she tells. The apparent content of her stories has less dimension than her real subject matter. . . . Yet she never stoops to the easy devices of symbolism but writes always with purity and directness." Lewis Gannett (1939): "Miss Porter writes little, and the subtlety of her art conceals its real strength." Ralph Thompson (1939): Miss Porter "has nothing like a 'manner' and no stylistic preciosity. . . . Her work is . . . simple in pattern." Glenway Wescott (1939): In *Pale Horse, Pale Rider* Miss Porter's style is "in every technical aspect . . . rather a bare art. It is not corporeal or sensual: the colors in it are primary; the odors evocative only in a general way . . . the shapes of things not geometrical or richly similitudinous; the faces not fussed over. . . . As Miss Porter works, it is simply the story that is laid bare." Joseph W. Beach (1945): In *The Leaning Tower* "she is refreshingly free from self-consciousness. . . . She is more a truth-teller than a realist. To Steinbeck she is the perfect antidote." Glenway Wescott (1944): "Miss Porter's style is, so to speak, perfection. . . . There is no vanity of trying to be original, no playfulness with vocabulary, no self-indulgence."

write my stories in their own time and way. My stories had to be accepted and published exactly as they were written: that rule has never once been broken. There was no one, whose advice I respected, whose help I would not have been glad to get, and many times did get, on almost any of these articles. I have written, re-written, and revised them. My stories, on the other hand, are written in one draft, and if short enough, at one sitting. In fact, this book would seem to represent the other half of a double life: but not in truth. It is all one thing. The two ways of working helped and supported each other: I needed both.[16]

It is profoundly true that Miss Porter's essays and other non-fictional statements reflect, in a manner both distinct from and complementary to that of her fiction, a unified, lifelong preoccupation with certain beliefs and attitudes. While not as deeply and uniformly governed by their author's central thematic orientation as is the fiction, they are nevertheless highly personal and remarkably consistent. In a recent interview she herself comments, "It's astonishing how little I've changed: nothing in my point of view or my way of feeling. I'm going back now to finish some of the great many short stories that I have begun and not been able to finish for one reason or another. I've found one that I think I can finish. . . . I started it in 1923, and it's based on an episode in my life that took place when I was twenty. Now here I am, seventy, and it's astonishing how much it's like me now."[17]

Robert Penn Warren, in his introduction to the Schwartz bibliography (p. 216), calls attention to the personal quality of Miss Porter's nonfiction. He identifies her with the type of writer whose work is "a mere extension, in a direct and fairly innocent way, of his being," and adds, "For such a writer, the

16. P. vii. The most important of Miss Porter's essays up to 1952 are in *The Days Before*. A reading of this volume, together with the interview by Barbara Thompson recently published in the *Paris Review*, XXIX (Winter-Spring, 1963), 87-114, and the essay, "Noon Wine': The Sources," is adequate to give a relatively full knowledge of her non-fictional statement. Her numerous early essays and interviews are mostly brief and repetitious, dealing largely with her methods of writing and the sources of such stories as "Flowering Judas."

17. Thompson, "Katherine Anne Porter: An Interview," *Paris Review*, p. 112.

little odds and ends of writing, the letter, the quick review, the incidental essay may carry some of the finest bits and flashes, and some of the wisest remarks." Miss Porter's essays are indeed, considerably more than most essays, an extension of their author's being. In them as in the stories, the search for truth does not proceed far along the path of abstraction and generalization but stays close to the immediate and the personal. Miss Porter's mind is not speculative and her attempts at generalization are often erratic. Her judgments frequently tend to be impulsive, and her tone is predominantly ironic, her irony mostly humorless. The majority of the essays are strongly tendentious, and one can often detect defensiveness beneath their aggressive exterior. Only a few of them—the author's musings over her search for a home, her genial reminiscences about the Old South, her light and sentimental ramblings on "the flower of flowers" and on John James Audubon, her sketches of the native life and the "charmed life" in Mexico—only these are pensive and relaxed.

Ray B. West, in a recent introductory study of Miss Porter, observes acutely, "It is true, perhaps, that what Katherine Anne Porter liked best in others were qualities nearest to her own."[18] This is without doubt the dominant fact about her critical essays, which constitute the majority of those she has written. One is even inclined to say they are more valuable as revelations of their author than as commentary on their subjects. Her truest insights into the work of others usually apply with equal or greater relevance to her own work. Consequently, even the essays on other writers furnish a wealth of self-description. Her fundamental critical criteria are integrity and painstaking crafts-manship—precisely her own most valued possessions. It is by this standard that she exalts James, Cather, Mansfield, Pound, and Forster, and bitterly condemns Gertrude Stein. Combined, or confused, with her artistic ideals is her commitment to skepticism and dissent. All of these sympathies are evident when she says approvingly of Henry James that, though maimed for life in an accident, "he of them all never broke, never gave way, sought

18. *Katherine Anne Porter* (Minneapolis: University of Minnesota Press, 1963), p. 45.

for truth not in philosophy nor in religion, but in art, and found his own" (*DB,* 13). Like Miranda, James got his education "in his own time and his own way, . . . by listening, by gazing, dawdling, gaping, wondering, and soaking in impressions and sensations at every pore, through every hair" (*DB,* 14). Like hers, the knowledge he gained was "knowledge at the price of finally, utterly 'seeing through' everything—even the fortunate, happy childhood" (*DB,* 19). The art of Henry James, like Miss Porter's own, is an art of memory, to judge from a passage of his which she records: "I foresee moreover how little I shall be able to resist, throughout these notes, the force of persuasion expressed in the individual *vivid* image of the past wherever encountered, these images having always such terms of their own, such subtle secrets and insidious arts for keeping us in relation with them, for bribing us by the beauty, the authority, the wonder of their saved intensity" (*DB,* 21). She describes James as "rummaging through his precious scrapbags of bright fragments, patching them into the patterns before his mind's eyes" (*DB,* 21).

The pattern is followed as closely in other essays. Miss Porter admires Katherine Mansfield's craftsmanship and devotion to art, and finds also in this fellow artist qualities similar to her own. "She was magnificent in her objective view of things, her real sensitiveness to climate, mental or physical, her genuinely first-rate equipment in the matter of the five senses, and my guess, based on the evidence of her stories, is that she by no means accepted everything, either abstractly or in detail, and that whatever her vague love of something called Life may have been, there was as much to hate as to love in her individual living" (*DB,* 85-86).

There is yet a further kinship: "I judge her work to have been to a great degree a matter of intelligent use of her faculties, a conscious practice of hard-won craftsmanship, a triumph of discipline over the unruly circumstances and confusions of her personal life and over certain destructive elements in her own nature" (*DB,* 85). Miss Porter's attraction to José Lizardi is certainly owing primarily to the fact that she sees in him a kindred spirit—a writer of integrity and a suffering member of the great fellowship of dissent. Her description of his childhood and background recalls, almost word-for-word, her description of her own. "The child, who seems to have been precocious, willful, and somewhat unteachable, spent his childhood and early youth in an immensely Catholic, reactionary, socially timid, tight-minded atmosphere of genteel poverty and desperately contriving middle-class ambitions."[19] In "La Conquistadora" she admires, if not an artist, at least a strong, self-sufficient woman who created a sort of bizarre world of her own. Scornful of traditional religion, she can find nothing good to say of T. S. Eliot after his conversion; and she ranges herself, against him and the Bishop of Wakefield, on the side of Thomas Hardy, in whom she sees sincerity and free inquiry as opposed to hypocrisy, self-righteousness, and "theological hatred," that "most savage of all emotions generated in the snake-pit of human nature" (*DB,* 23). One instance of Miss Porter's tendency toward emotional bias and intellectual superficiality is her irritation at Eliot's use of the word "edifying" in relation to art; another is this passage, the warmth of which makes it clear that she is speaking not just for Thomas Hardy:

His mind, not the greatest, certainly not the most flexible, but a good, candid, strong mind, asked simply the oldest, most terrifying questions, and the traditional, orthodox answers of the church did not satisfy it. It is easy to see how this, from the churchly point of view, is diabolic. But the yawning abyss between question and answer remains the same, and until this abyss is closed, the dissent will remain, persistent, obdurate, a kind of church itself, with its leaders, teachers, saints, martyrs, heroes; a thorn in the flesh of orthodoxy, but I think not necessarily of the Devil on that account, unless the intellect and all its questions are really from the Devil, as the Eden myth states explicitly, as the church seems to teach, and Mr. Eliot tends to confirm.

(*DB,* 26-27)

These lines are governed not by thought, but by feeling. The closing lines of Miss Porter's essay on Hardy furnish a perfect de-

19. *The Days Before,* p. 205. Miss Porter has described her own childhood character as "precocious, nervous, rebellious, unteachable" (*Current Biography,* 1940).

scription of her own art of rejection: "By his own testimony, he limited his territory by choice, set boundaries to his material, focused his point of view like a burning glass down on a definite aspect of things. He practiced a stringent discipline, severely excised and eliminated all that seemed to him not useful or appropriate to his plan. In the end his work was the sum of his experience, he arrived at his particular true testimony; along the way, sometimes, many times, he wrote sublimely" (*DB*, 35).

The essays also, of course, tell us much about Miss Porter directly. She speaks often of her own life and art, emphasizing most frequently her long and independent effort to master the discipline of writing, the inner determinism that seems to characterize her artistic life as well as her creative process, and her method of working exclusively from memory. In relation to the role of memory in her work, one of the services performed by the essays is that of revealing much of the autobiographical background of the stories. "Portrait: Old South" is simply a documentation of some of the *Leaning Tower* sketches. Except for their diminished intensity and polish, such passages as these about Miss Porter's grandmother might have been taken from "The Source":

Her hands were long since ruined, but she was proud of her narrow feet with their high insteps, and liked to dress them in smooth black kid boots with small spool-shaped heels. When she went "abroad"—that is, shopping, calling, or to church—she wore her original mourning gowns, of stiff, dull, corded silks, made over and refurbished from time to time, and a sweeping crape veil that fell from a peaked cap over her face and to the hem of her skirt in the back.

(*DB*, 160)

She could not endure to see a horse with its head strung up in a checkrein, and used to walk down a line of conveyances drawn up around the church, saying amiably to the dozing Negro drivers, "Good morning, Jerry; good morning, Uncle Squire," reaching up deftly and loosing the checkrein. The horses hung their heads and so did the drivers, and the reins stayed unfastened for that time, at any rate.

(*DB*, 161)

"Why I Write About Mexico" reveals, among numerous auto-biographical details, that Miss Porter's own father spent a pleasant time in Mexico, as did Miranda's in "Old Mortality." In the *Paris Review* interview she gives once again, and in new detail, the background of "Flowering Judas." The essay on "Noon Wine," in addition to revealing historical counterparts for most of the characters and events of that story, contains the original Uncle Jimbilly—even to the name; and the geologist of "The Charmed Life" is obviously the geologist of Miss Porter's first published story.

The author's references to her dependence on memory are numerous. The "Noon Wine" essay has this as its specific theme, and her most recent published statement reaffirms the point: "The truth is, I have never written a story in my life that didn't have a very firm foundation in actual human experience— somebody else's experience quite often, but an experience that became my own by hearing the story, by witnessing the thing, by hearing just a word perhaps."[20] When the interviewer asks whether some ordeal similar to that of Miranda in "Pale Horse, Pale Rider" played an important part in her writing career, Miss Porter makes what is easily her most significant revelation about the personal experience behind her work:

Yes, that was the plague of influenza, at the end of the first World War, in which I almost died. It just simply divided my life, cut across it like that. So that everything before that was just getting ready, and after that I was in some strange way altered, ready. It took me a long time to go out and live in the world again. I was really 'alienated', in the pure sense. It was, I think, the fact that I really had participated in death, that I knew what death was, and had almost experienced it. I had what the Christians call the "beatific vision", and the Greeks called the "happy day", the happy vision just before death. Now if you have had that, and survived it, come back from it, you are no longer like other people, and there's no use deceiving yourself that you are. But you see, I did: I made the mistake of thinking I was quite like anybody else, of trying to live like other people. It took me a long time to realize that that simply wasn't true, that I had my own needs and that I had to live like me.[21]

20. Thompson, "Katherine Anne Porter: An Interview," *Paris Review,* p. 103.
21. *Ibid.,* pp. 96-97.

The extreme importance of this statement is obvious, dealing as it does with the event which has already been seen to be crucial in Miss Porter's art as well as in her life. It confirms what the stories themselves suggest: that there is an intimate relationship between her writing career and the instinct of rejection, which finds its clearest embodiment and its strongest personal justification in these visions of death and paradise. The illness occurred several years before Miss Porter began publishing her stories, and the sense of alienation and the strong awareness of unique individuality (aspects of the same central impulse) which seem to stem from it have impressed themselves strongly on all her work.

Katherine Anne Porter's essays, like her stories, fall into the characteristic pattern of rejection. On the philosophical-religious level this involves a denial of every kind of dogma and a strong advocacy of the "great tradition of dissent." Paralleling this on the social level is a general rejection of human contact which appears in many guises, as in the fiction. Oppression and escape in their various forms permeate the essays. These motifs fill the very language of many of Miss Porter's statements, and she seeks out the words of other writers which strike similar chords. She says of herself, in the introduction to the Modern Library *Flowering Judas,* "all the conscious and recollected years of my life have been lived to this day under the heavy threat of world catastrophe," and she speaks of the "shape and weight of present misfortune." Of her life in Mexico she remarks, "Well, I know it was good for me. I would have been completely smothered—completely disgusted and revolted—by the goings on in Europe."[22] Other examples are plentiful. Here are a few: "Henry James the younger had great good of it [the family wealth], yet it did create the very atmosphere which later on he found so hard to breathe that he deserted it altogether for years, for life" (*DB,* 5). "Henry the first . . . also wrote in his fragment of autobiography, 'I should think indeed that our domestic intercourse had been on the whole most in-

22. *Ibid.,* p. 99.

nocent as well as happy, were it not for a certain lack of oxygen which is indeed incidental to the family atmosphere and which I may characterize as the lack of any ideal of action except that of self-preservation' " (*DB*, 5-6). A particularly interesting example is the following comment on childhood and family life which Miss Porter has taken from "Miss Cather's superb little essay on Katherine Mansfield" (the ellipses being Miss Porter's own):

I doubt whether any contemporary writer has made one feel more keenly the many kinds of personal relations which exist in an every-day "happy family" who are merely going on with their daily lives, with no crises or shocks or bewildering complications. . . . Yet every individual in that household (even the children) is clinging passionately to his individual soul, is in terror of losing it in the general family flavor . . . the mere struggle to have anything of one's own, to be oneself at all, creates an element of strain which keeps everybody almost at breaking point.

. . . Even in harmonious families there is this double life . . . the one we can observe in our neighbor's household, and, underneath, another—secret and passionate and intense—which is the real life that stamps the faces and gives character to the voices of our friends. Always in his mind each member is escaping, running away, trying to break the net which circumstances and his own affections have woven about him. One realizes that human relationships are the tragic necessity of human life; that they can never be wholly satisfactory, that every ego is half the time greedily seeking them, and half the time pulling away from them.

(*DB*, 64)

Not surprisingly, Miss Porter comments, "This is masterly and water-clear and autobiography enough for me: my mind goes with tenderness to the big lonely slow-moving girl who happened to be an artist . . . sitting by the fireplace to talk down an assertive brood of brothers and sisters, practicing her art on them, refusing to be lost among them—the longest-winged one who would fly free at last."[23] Oppressiveness is often, in Miss Porter's thought, related to chaos. She says of herself, "I had

23. *The Days Before*, pp. 64-65. This community of feeling about the oppressiveness of family life suggests, of course, interesting possibilities for investigation; the point here, however, is simply the attraction that such expressions seem to have for Miss Porter.

had time to grow up, to consider, to look again, to begin finding my way a little through the inordinate clutter and noise of my immediate day, in which very literally everything in the world was being pulled apart, torn up, turned wrong side out and upside down; almost no frontiers left unattacked, governments and currencies falling; even the very sexes seemed to be changing back and forth and multiplying weird, unclassifiable genders" (*DB*, 66). Or again: "When I say, then, that the evening Mr. Forster spoke in Paris was dusty and crowded, it was literally true: but it also is a way of saying that Communists in numbers running a show anywhere always gave me this sense of suffocation; and heaven knows they were there, with their usual solidarity of effrontery, efficiency and dullness, all over the place making muddlement, as ubiquitous and inescapable as a plague of June bugs in Texas." (*DB*, 116-17).

The common denominator of all these passages, one begins to see, is violation of the rights and the integrity of the individual, either by deliberate agents or by life in general. Mr. Forster, we are told, "pokes fun at things in themselves fatally without humor, things oppressive and fatal to human happiness: megalomania, solemn-godliness, pretentiousness, self-love, the meddlesome impulse which leads to the invasion and destruction of human rights" (*DB*, 118). The theme can be found even in "The Flower of Flowers." The rose "was, and is, thorny by nature, for it detests the proximity of any other kind of plant, and serious botanists have deduced seriously that the rose was given its thorns as a weapon against other crowding vegetation. With such a perfume as it has, it needs more than thorns for its protection" (*DB*, 138).

The appearance of the same motif in "A House of My Own" suggests, perhaps, one of the causes behind Miss Porter's restless wandering. "I remember a remark of Mr. E. M. Forster on taking possession of his woods: the first thing he noticed was that his land made him feel heavy. I had become almost overnight a ton weight of moral, social, and financial responsibility, subject to state and county tax, school tax, and an astonishing variety of insurance" (*DB*, 175). In "The Charmed Life" she says, "My own life was full of foolish and unnecessary complications, and I envied him his wholeness" (*DB*, 270). Such "wholeness" has indeed not been hers: "And I suppose that's why it has taken me twenty years to write this novel: it's been interrupted by just anyone who could jimmy his way into my life."[24] The recent interview carries on the theme, returning to memories of earlier years. "I remember that I felt a little suffocated and frightened. I felt a little trapped. . . . And I was at the age of rebellion then, and it really scared me."[25] For Miss Porter, as for Miranda, oppression leads inevitably to escape. "But, you know, I was always restless, always a roving spirit. When I was a little child I was always running away."[26] "At sixteen I ran away from New Orleans and got married. And at twenty-one I bolted again, went to Chicago, got a newspaper job, and went into the movies."[27] Then, "I just got up and bolted. I went running off on that wild escapade to Mexico, where I attended, you might say, and assisted at, in my own modest way, a revolution."[28] "It was a time of revolution, and I was running with almost pure revolutionaries."[29] (Note the enthusiasm for large-scale political rejection.) In the 1962 Janeway interview cited earlier, Miss Porter speaks of a distaste for "competition" among writers and adds that she can't bear to hear children quarrel. "I never quarreled as a child. I just went somewhere else."

An interesting manifestation of a negative tendency in *The Days Before* is Miss Porter's habit of mentioning, usually with obvious complacency and often in the opening sentence of an essay, what she has *not* read or done. She begins her discussion of Gertrude Stein as follows: "All I know about Gertrude Stein is what I find in her first two books, *Three Lives* and *The Making of Americans*. . . . I can go only by what I find in these pages" (*DB*, 36). "Reflections on Willa Cather"

24. Thompson, "Katherine Anne Porter: An Interview," *Paris Review*, p. 109.
25. *Ibid.*, p. 93.
26. *Ibid.*
27. *Ibid.*, p. 94.
28. *Ibid.*, p. 97.
29. *Ibid.*, p. 99.

opens, "I never knew her at all, nor anyone who did know her; do not to this day. . . . I had never felt that my condition of beginning authorship gave me a natural claim on the attention of writers I admired, such as Henry James and W. B. Yeats. Some proper instinct told me that all of any importance they had to say to me was in their printed pages, mine to use as I could" (*DB,* 61). Later in the same essay she states, "I am not much given to reading about authors, or not until I have read what they have to say for themselves" (*DB,* 65). And near the end: "Mr. Maxwell Geismar wrote a book about her and some others, called *The Last of the Provincials.* Not having read it I do not know his argument" (*DB,* 72). Early in "The Art of Katherine Mansfield" she recalls, "It must be a round dozen years since I have read any of her stories" (*DB,* 82). Of Eudora Welty she says approvingly, "She considers her personal history as hardly worth mentioning" (*DB,* 101). (She has said much the same of herself.) Of Miss Welty she adds, with obvious satisfaction, "She has never studied the writing craft in any college" (*DB,* 103).

In "Virginia Woolf" Miss Porter speaks of the independent development of her own taste, "Reading as I did almost no contemporary criticism, talking to no one, . . ." (*DB,* 113). In "A House of My Own," she tells of the long effort to satisfy her inflexible requirements, then of finally deciding on a house without even consenting to look inside. But the most interesting example of this negative habit is the opening sentence of "Marriage Is Belonging." It begins, "Having never written a word about marriage, so far as I remember . . ." (*DB,* 185). This essay, however, immediately follows one on marriage written three years before, as Miss Porter admits in a good-natured footnote: "See preceding. So much for memory." In "The Future Is Now" she boasts, "I never read other peoples' descriptions of great cities, more particularly if it is a great city I know" (*DB,* 198). Ten years later the habit remains. In the *Paris Review* she states, "I never did make a profession of understanding people, man or woman or child, and the only thing I know about people is exactly what I have learned from the people right next to me."[30] Later, speaking of the voyage which inspired *Ship of Fools,* she recalls, "I don't think I spoke a half-dozen words to anybody. I just sat there and watched— not deliberately though."[31] Admittedly this evidence of negativism, taken alone, is not of great significance; yet the frequency of Miss Porter's use of the negative, particularly in the transition from the inner thought-stream to formal discussion, must say something about her habitual mental climate.

A life of rejection leads to a life of emptiness, and Miss Porter seems to share Miranda's vague sense of deprivation. She begins her essay on E. M. Forster in this way: "Dates memorable to me escape my mind, so I write them down on bits of paper. Bits of paper escape me too; they love to hide themselves at the bottom of large baskets of other papers marked 'Miscellany' " (*DB,* 116). The usual manifestation in the essays of the sense of loss is, however, more general and more profound. A passage on James bears a striking resemblance to the story of Miranda.

For although no writer ever "grew up" more completely than Henry James, and "saw through" his own illusions with more sobriety and pure intelligence, still there lay in the depths of his being the memory of a lost paradise; it was in the long run the standard by which he measured the world he learned so thoroughly, accepted in certain ways—the ways of a civilized man with his own work to do—after such infinite pains: or pangs, as he would have called them, that delight in deep experience which at a certain point is excruciating, and by the uninstructed might be taken for pain itself.

(*DB,* 20)

The fruitless search for an aesthetic ideal of happiness is the real subject of "A House of My Own" and the real source of its poignance: "There was never, of course, much money, never quite enough; there was never time, either; there was never permanency of any sort, except the permanency of hope" (*DB,* 173). Having, in a sense, come within ten miles of her dream, she nevertheless concludes wistfully, "It seems a very long ten miles, perhaps the longest I shall ever travel. I am saving the

30. *Ibid.,* p. 109.
31. *Ibid.,* p. 112.

pheasant feathers to burn, for luck, on the first fire I light in the fine old fireplace with its bake oven and the graceful mantelpiece. It will be high time for fires again, no doubt, when I get there" (*DB,* 178). The successive challenges of the second World War and the atomic bomb provoked Miss Porter to statements which reflect her attitudes toward life in general. In "American Statement: 4 July 1942," she alludes once again to the intolerable reality and the bright possibility. "But we are not going to lose this war, and the people of this country are going to have the enormous privilege of another chance to make of their Republic what those men who won and founded it for us meant for it to be" (*DB,* 195). One cannot be so easily confident in the face of the universal bomb scare, but the least—and perhaps the most—we can do is face the fact: "It is such a relief to be told the truth, or even just the facts, so pleasant not to be coddled with unreasonable hopes" (*DB,* 196). But even in this dire situation Miss Porter turns again to hope, that last vague and desperate recourse when the present has failed. "And yet it may be that what we have is a world not on the verge of flying apart, but an uncreated one—still in shapeless fragments waiting to be put together properly. I imagine that when we want something better, we may have it: at perhaps no greater price than we have already paid for the worse" (*DB,* 202). There is a more personal wistfulness in the author's admiration for the free, simple, beautiful existence of the old man who is the subject of the final essay, "The Charmed Life." Twenty years later, the sense of deprivation has been generalized into a fragmentary philosophy of life. "I have a very firm belief that the life of no man can be explained in terms of his experiences, of what has happened to him, because in spite of all the poetry, all the philosophy to the contrary, we are not really masters of our fate. We don't really direct our lives unaided and unobstructed. Our being is subject to all the chances of life. There are so many things we are capable of, that we could be or do. The potentialities are so great that we never, any of us, are more than one-fourth fulfilled."[32]

32. *Ibid.,* p. 96.

The thread of bitterness running through the two essays on marriage is largely an acute sense of discrepancy between the ideal and the real in that institution. "The trouble with me is—always was—that if you say 'marriage' to me, instantly the word translates itself into 'love,' for only in such terms can I grasp the idea at all, or make any sense of it. The two are hopelessly associated, or rather identified, in my mind; that is to say, love is the only excuse for marriage, if any excuse is necessary. I often feel one should be offered" (*DB,* 185). With an idea of love based on her lost vision of paradise, Miss Porter has not, of course, found the experienced reality even remotely satisfactory. As always, deprivation strengthens desire.

It is hardly possible to exaggerate the need of a human being, not a madman, or a saint, or a beast, or a self-alienated genius who is all of these in one, and therefore the scapegoat for all the rest, to live at peace—and by peace I mean in reconciliation, not easy contentment—with another human being, and with that one in a group or society where he feels he belongs. The best, the very best, of all these relationships is that one in marriage between a man and a woman who are good lovers, good friends, and good parents; who belong to each other, and to their children, and whose children belong to them: that is the meaning of the blood tie that binds them, and may bind them sometimes to the bone.

(*DB,* 189)

Since marriage is a state of most intimate contact between individuals, and since Katherine Anne Porter's instinct of rejection is directly opposed to such contact while at the same time powerfully attracted toward an ideal vision of it, one is not surprised to find the greatest personal disgust, the largest proportion of irrationality, in her essays on that subject. Marriage as seen in real life is to her a mutually destructive union—"all too often the art, or perhaps only the strategy, and a risky one, of surrendering gracefully with an air of pure disinterestedness as much of your living self as you can spare without incurring total extinction" (*DB,* 185)—a union acceptable, perhaps, for beta characters, but certainly not for the elect: "If this all sounds a little monotonous, and gregarious, well, sometimes it is, and most people like that sort of thing" (*DB,* 189). The current pseudo-scientific approach is a fit vehicle for the scorn Miss Porter heaps on the institution of marriage and all it involves.

> Let us recall a few generalities about marriage in its practical aspects which are common knowledge, such as: it is one of the most prevalent conditions of the human adult, heading the list of vital statistics, I believe. It has been made very easy to assume, and fairly easy in the legal sense, at least, to abandon; and it is famous for its random assortment of surprises of every kind—leaf-covered booby traps, spiders lurking in cups, pots of gold under rainbows, triplets, poltergeists in the stair closet, and flights of cupids lolling on the breakfast table—anything can happen.
>
> *(DB,* 186-87)

Note the choice of imagery: pots of gold and cupids are imaginary; booby traps, spiders, and triplets are real. The treatise on marriage continues, introducing scorn for men, which is only less pervasive of *The Days Before* than of the Miranda stories themselves.

> In its present form it is comparatively modern. As an idea, it must have begun fairly soon after the human male discovered his highly important role in the bringing forth of young. For countless aeons, we are told by those who pretend to know, it was believed that the powers of generation were vested in women alone, people having never been very bright about sex, right from the start. When men at last discovered, who knows how? that they were fathers, their pride in their discovery must have been equaled only by their indignation at having worshiped women as vessels of the Great Mystery when all along they should have been worshiping themselves. . . .

Then there come the children. Gladly, willingly (if you do not think so, I refer you to the birth records of this country for the past ten years. There haven't been so many young wives having so many babies so fast for at least four generations!) these pairs proceed to populate their houses, or flats—often very small flats, and mother with a job she means to keep, too—with perfect strangers, often hostile, whose habits even to the most adoring gaze are often messy and unattractive. They lie flat on their noses at first in what appears to be a drunken slumber, then flat on their backs kicking and screaming, demanding impossibilities in a foreign language. They are human nature in essence, without conscience, without pity, without love, without a trace of consideration for others, just one seething cauldron of primitive appetites and needs; and what do they really need? We are back where we started. They need love, first; without it everything worth saving is lost or damaged in them; and they have to be taught love, pity, conscience, courage—everything. And what becomes of them? If they are lucky, among all the million possibilities of their fates, . . . they will learn the nature of love, and they will marry and have children.

(DB, 187-89)

Furthermore,

All this is to be accomplished in a physical situation of the direst intimacy, in which all claims to the most ordinary privacy may be disregarded by either, or both. I shall not attempt to catalogue the daily accounting for acts, words, states of feeling and even thoughts, the perpetual balance and check between individual wills and points of view, the unbelievable amount of tact, intelligence, flexibility, generosity, and God knows what, it requires for two people to go on growing together and in the same directions instead of cracking up and falling apart.

(DB, 188)

"The direst intimacy": no expression could be more characteristic of the alpha heroine. Nor could there be a much clearer echo than the above of the Miranda of "The Fig Tree"—"Back into the house she went on tiptoe hoping not to be seen, for Grandmother always asked: 'Where are you going, child? What are you doing? What is that you're carrying? Where did you get it? Who gave you permission?' and after Miranda had explained all that, even if there turned out not to be anything wrong in it, nothing ever seemed so nice any more. Besides it took forever to get away"[33]—and of "Pale Horse, Pale Rider"—"Daylight will strike a sudden blow on the roof startling them all up to their feet; faces will beam asking, Where are you going, What are you doing, What are you thinking, How do you feel, Why do you say such things, What do you mean? No more sleep. Where are my boots and what horse shall I ride?" (*PH*, 179) Resentment at the violation of individual integrity, a motif usually present with that of oppressiveness in general, is most acute in relation to marriage. In discussing this point Miss Porter

33. "The Fig Tree," *Harper's Magazine*, CCXX (June, 1960), 56.

shows her strongest feeling. "And if I say faithfulness consists of a great many things beside the physical, never let it be dreamed that I hold with the shabby nonsense that physical infidelity is a mere peccadillo beneath the notice of enlightened minds. Physical infidelity is the signal, the notice given, that all the fidelities are undermined. It is complete betrayal of the very principle on which love and marriage are based, and besides, a vulgar handing over of one's partner to public shame. It is exactly as stupid as that, to say nothing more" (*DB*, 188). Our concern here is not with the truth or falsity of the ideas expressed but with the over-all pattern of thought and feeling. Although Miss Porter concludes "Marriage Is Belonging" on the positive note that successful marriages are quite common in every generation, like every statement that runs counter to the rejection pattern, this one is swallowed up by the surrounding darkness. Even the hint of comedy that occasionally graces the marriage essays cannot hide their prevailing bitterness. Finally, it is eminently fitting that the single example mentioned of a happy marriage is that doubly rare phenomenon, a union of two artists—the Robert Brownings (*DB*, 191).

As one proceeds through the essays, divergent lines gradually come together and the interrelation of familiar themes grows more evident. The unifying concept emerges as a duality of *chaos* and *order*. The present reality is, in Miss Porter's view, chaotic; order is the desired goal, the ideal, paradise. Chaos is, furthermore, double—both within man and outside him. The chaos outside oppresses the individual with its abrasive complexity, impinging on him most sharply in his closest contacts with others. The chaos within is even more painful and more deeply ambiguous. In personal relationships it appears as spontaneous hatred, "The Necessary Enemy," so much more easily learned than love. Though most acute in marriage, it is present in all human contacts, as shown in this description of a hypothetical young married woman:

She is dismayed, horrified, full of guilt and forebodings because she is finding out little by little that she is capable of hating her husband, whom she loves faithfully. She can hate him at times as fiercely and mysteriously, indeed in terribly much the same way, as often she hated her parents, her brothers and sisters, whom she loves, when she was a child. Even then it had seemed to her a kind of black treacherousness in her, her private wickedness that, just the same, gave her her only private life. That was one thing her parents never knew about her, never seemed to suspect. For it was never given a name. They did and said hateful things to her and to each other as if by right, as if in them it was a kind of virtue. But when they said to her, "Control your feelings," it was never when she was amiable and obedient, only in the black times of her hate. So it was her secret, a shameful one. When they punished her, sometimes for the strangest reasons, it was, they said, only because they loved her—it was for her own good. She did not believe this, but she thought herself guilty of something worse than ever they had punished her for. None of this really frightened her: the real fright came when she discovered that at times her father and mother hated each other; this was like standing on the doorsill of a familiar room and seeing in a lightning flash that the floor was gone, you were on the edge of a bottomless pit. Sometimes she felt that both of them hated her, but that passed, it was simply not a thing to be thought of, much less believed. She thought she had outgrown all this, but here it was again, an element in her own nature she could not control, or feared she could not. She would have to hide from her husband, if she could, the same spot in her feelings she had hidden from her parents, and for the same no doubt disreputable, selfish reason: she wants to keep his love.

(*DB,* 179-80)

This passage incorporates several Porter motifs. "Hatred" is here Miss Porter's term for what the reader has come to know as the principle of rejection. No one who has looked into himself is unaware of the distressing negative potency lurking there, but the crucial point in Miss Porter's case is that she seems to have given this element a special preponderance and even to have clung to it as the only safeguard of personal integrity. Prevented by this fundamental orientation from embracing other persons in that communion which is the individual's principal key to the meaning of external reality as a whole, in her quest for order she turned inward, only to be faced by the darkness that waits there. Frustration does not blunt desire but rather sharpens it;

the retreat from human contact, meanwhile, gives an excessively subjective coloring to the entire quest. The result can only be a restless search for "my truth—what is true for me." And with no stable reference to external reality, such a quest can lead only to a constantly deepening sense of deprivation, as well as to a steadily growing impression of external chaos which in turn strengthens even more the instinct of rejection. The individual's search for order takes the form of a search for an ideal love, an impossible harmony with other persons, a perfect equilibrium of communion and solitude. Hence the desire, expressed at the end of the above passage, for a love both undeserved and unobtainable. It is the failure, in Miranda's eyes, of the older generation to come to terms with this mystery of evil and this insistent desire for order—its failure to "tell her the truth about anything"—that engenders the complete intellectual rejection that accompanies the social one. The essays are full of this spirit of rejection of all that has been taught or handed down from earlier generations, just as they are full of the desire for undeserved and unobtainable love. The latter motif appears near the end of *Ship of Fools,* it might be added, in the only passage in the novel emphasized by italics: "What they were saying to each other was only, *Love me, love me in spite of all! Whether or not I love you, whether I am fit to love, whether you are able to love, even if there is no such thing as love, love me!*" (*SF,* 480) A passage from the 1950 essay, "Orpheus in Purgatory," traces more clearly the implications of this motif:

It is hardly possible to exaggerate the lovelessness in which most people live, men or women: wanting love, unable to give it, or inspire it, unable to keep it if they get it, not knowing how to treat it, lacking the humility, or the very love itself that could teach them how to love: it is the painfullest thing in human life, and, since love is purely a creation of the human imagination, it is merely perhaps the most important of all the examples of how the imagination continually outruns the creature it inhabits. . . . Having imagined love, we are condemned to its perpetual disappointments; or so it seems.

(*DB,* 88)

The ideal love is here linked firmly to the dream of paradise that is the heart of "Pale Horse, Pale Rider"; with a despair like

Miranda's at the end of that story, Miss Porter faces the final emptiness. There is, needless to say, no escape from the vicious circle. To make matters worse, Western civilization has catered to this futile desire by creating and perpetuating the tradition of Romantic Love, which "crept into the marriage bed, very stealthily, by centuries, bringing its absurd notions about love as eternal springtime and marriage as a personal adventure meant to provide personal happiness. To a Western romantic such as I, though my views have been much modified by painful experience, it still seems to me a charming work of the human imagination . . ." (*DB,* 183). Romantic Love, she adds, "did not come by hazard, it is the very imperfect expression of the need of the human imagination to create beauty and harmony out of chaos, no matter how mistaken its notion of these things may be, nor how clumsy its methods" (*DB,* 184). There remains, it would seem, no doubt in Miss Porter's mind that, for the fugitive from chaos, the path of human relations and love is a dead-end street.

It has already been seen that Miss Porter often relates the two motifs of oppressiveness and chaos. She seems, in fact, quite strongly inclined to think of her life in these terms and to characterize various aspects of external reality as both oppressive and confused. In "Three Statements About Writing" she observed,

Political tendency since 1930 has been to the last degree a confused, struggling, drowning-man-and-straw sort of thing, stampede of panicked crowd, each man trying to save himself—one at a time trying to work out his horrible confusions. How do I feel about it? I suffer from it, and I try to work my way out to some firm ground of personal belief, as the others do. I have times of terror and doubt and indecision, I am confused in all the uproar of shouting maddened voices and the flourishing of death-giving weapons. . . . I should like to save myself, but I have no assurance that I can. . . .
(*DB,* 128)

She has left no doubt that she considers marriage chaotic and has "learned better than to have any theories about it" (*DB,* 185). The rejection of "theories" might, in fact, be adduced as a characteristic of her whole mental life. Over-simplification is evident in many of her statements, characterized as they often are by hasty generalizations and dogmatic pronouncements. This extreme subjectivism, which has been noted before, corresponds perfectly to that of her fiction. The characteristic may be seen in a recent statement about her life: "I started out with nothing in the world but a kind of passion, a driving desire. I don't know where it came from, and I do not know why—or why I have been so stubborn about it that nothing could deflect me."[34] Even at the age of seventy the sense of chaos and the natural agnosticism remain, though they have taken a more generalized, superficially philosophical form:

There seems to be a kind of order in the universe, in the movement of the stars and the turning of the earth and the changing of seasons, and even in the cycle of human life. But human life itself is almost pure chaos. Everyone takes his stance, asserts his own rights and feelings, mistaking the motives of others, and his own . . . Now nobody knows the end of the life he's living, and neither do I . . . We don't really know what is going to happen to us, and we don't know why. Quite often the best we can do is to keep our heads, and try to keep at least one line unbroken and unobstructed.[35]

There is certainly no doubt as to what Miss Porter thinks of as the single line which she has tried to keep "unbroken and unobstructed." An early statement is of particular value as indicating some of the personal characteristics which have helped to determine the partly instinctive, partly deliberate orientation of her life:

My personal life has been the jumbled and apparently irrelevant mass of experiences which can only happen, I think, to a woman who goes with her mind permanently absent from the place where she is. . . . I have very little time sense and almost no sense of distance. I have no sense of direction and have seen a great deal of the world by getting completely lost and simply taking in the scenery as I roamed about getting my bearings.[36]

Art has been the lifeline of Katherine Anne Porter's existence, and from the above self-description one could deduce some of

34. Thompson, "Katherine Anne Porter: An Interview," *Paris Review,* pp. 88-89.
35. *Ibid.,* p. 113.
36. Quoted in Hartley, "Katherine Anne Porter," *Sewanee Rev.,* p. 206.

the characteristics her art and her thought would likely manifest. She speaks of herself as one who goes through life with mind turned habitually inward, finding the outer world almost entirely disordered and meaningless except in the impressions it presents immediately to the senses. In such a person one would expect powerful imagination, acute sense perception, preoccupation with vivid memories of concrete experience, concern with the inner life, a sense of independence and isolation, a sense of oppression by a chaotic world. It is not surprising that in the effort to "get her bearings" she should have chosen the compass and quadrant of art.

The art of fiction has been, according to Miss Porter's testimony, by far her most serious concern. A statement to this effect appears in her recent interview: "But this thing between me and my writing is the strongest bond I have ever had— stronger than any bond or any engagement with any human being or with any other work I've ever done."[37] There is a decided note of inevitability about it; in 1940 she said,

I did not choose this vocation and if I had any say in the matter, I would not have chosen it. I made no attempt to publish anything until I was 30, but I have written and destroyed manuscripts quite literally by the trunkload. I spent fifteen years wandering about, weighted horribly with masses of paper and little else. Yet for this vocation I was and am willing to live and die and I consider very few other things of the slightest importance.[38]

That Miss Porter sees fiction as primarily a means of ordering experience, she has indicated many times. For example, in "The Future Is Now" she speaks of the "spirit which moves the artist to labor with his little handful of chaos, bringing it to coherency within a frame," since "on the visible evidence we must admit that in human nature the spirit of contradiction more than holds its own" (*DB,* 199-200). The quotation which she selected as epigraph for the title essay of *The Days Before* was no random choice: "Really, universally, relations stop

37. Thompson, "Katherine Anne Porter: An Interview," *Paris Review,* p. 89.

38. Quoted by Elizabeth Janeway, *The New York Times Book Review,* April 1, 1962, p. 5.

nowhere, and the exquisite problem of the artist is eternally but to draw, by a geometry of his own, the circle within which they shall happily *appear* to do so.—H.J.: Preface to *Roderick Hudson"* (*DB,* 3). One of Miss Porter's most formal and considered statements on her faith in art occurs in the introduction to the 1940 Modern Library edition of *Flowering Judas.*

In the face of such shape and weight of present misfortune, the voice of the individual artist may seem perhaps of no more consequence than the whirring of a cricket in the grass; but the arts do live continuously, and they live literally by faith; their names and their shapes and their uses and their basic meanings survive unchanged in all that matters through times of interruption, diminishment, neglect; they outlive governments and creeds and the societies, even the very civilizations that produced them. They cannot be destroyed altogether because they represent the substance of faith and the only reality. They are what we find again when the ruins are cleared away. And even the smallest and most incomplete offering at this time can be a proud act in defense of that faith.

As numerous readers have remarked, the terms in which she speaks of art are frankly religious. At various times she has linked saints and artists, spoken of the artist's "state of grace," called entrance into the life of art an "act of faith," and spoken of art as a way of "salvation." There is a particularly clear pronouncement on the parallel between art and religion in the last of "Three Statements About Writing": "I agree with Mr. E. M. Forster that there are only two possibilities for any real order: in art and in religion. All political history is a vile mess, varying only in degrees of vileness from one epoch to another, and only the work of saints and artists gives us any reason to believe that the human race is worth belonging to" (*DB,* 132). There is a certain nobility of dedication in this attitude toward art and a degree of validity in some of Miss Porter's statements exalting it—yet it is impossible to miss the strongly negative tone about the whole thing.

As has already been seen in its personification in Miranda, Katherine Anne Porter's life of art is ambivalent; it is both a quest and an escape. From his reading of *The Days Before,* Lodwick Hartley reasons acutely along these lines. He suggests that Miss Porter's "own peculiar experience has developed in her such a profound distrust of institutional religion and of human relationships that she has felt compelled to seek certainties elsewhere and that, consequently, her theory of art, beautiful and praiseworthy though it is, arises out of a peculiar personal necessity rather than out of a completely universal one."[39]

In the 1940 introduction to *Flowering Judas,* Miss Porter spoke of the "heavy threat of world catastrophe" and added, "Most of the energies of my mind and spirit have been spent in the effort to grasp the meaning of those threats, to trace them to their sources and to understand the logic of this majestic and terrible failure of the life of man in the western world." Some critics have viewed Miss Porter's fiction as a pursuit of this theme; Hartley comes much closer to the truth when he observes, "But these efforts to understand the failure of life in the Western world, however important they may be in her heart and mind, could hardly be said to be the major subject of her art. Indeed, her writing—imaginative and critical—seems more nearly an attempt to escape from the central problem. . . . her work . . . does not illuminate the supreme tragedy of which she speaks."[40] Whether viewed as quest or as escape, Miss Porter's art is characterized by a strong sense of personal necessity. In the closing lines of the essay on James she gives particularly clear expression to this feeling. After agreeing with certain philosophers that relations are never concluded, she goes on to say, "Maybe that is why art is so endlessly satisfactory: the artist can choose his relations, and 'draw, by a geometry of his own, the circle within which they shall happily *appear* to do so.' While accomplishing this, one has the illusion that destiny is not absolute, it can be arranged, temporized with, persuaded, a little here and there. And once the circle is truly drawn around its contents, it too becomes truth" (*DB,* 21-22). The intense desire for at least a personal "illusion" of order, combined with a certain vagueness about the nature and limitations

39. "The Lady and the Temple," *College English,* p. 387.
40. *Ibid.,* p. 391.

of artistic truth, continues to characterize Miss Porter, as her recent *Paris Review* interview shows. There she takes "meaningfulness" as a criterion in discussing the work of several other writers. After criticizing William Styron's "The McCabes" for lacking this quality, she goes on to insist,

But I tell you, nothing is pointless, and nothing is meaningless if the artist will face it. He hasn't got the right to sidestep it like that. Human life itself may be almost pure chaos, but the work of the artist—the only thing he's good for—is to take these handfuls of confusion and disparate things, things that seem to be irreconcilable, and put them together in a frame to give them some kind of shape and meaning. Even if it's only his view of a meaning. That's what he's for—to give his view of life.[41]

Miss Porter also includes Scott Fitzgerald among the artists who "simply will not face up to the final reckoning of things." Asked whether she means this in a philosophical sense, she replies, "I'm thinking of it now in just the artistic sense—in the sense of an artist facing up to his own end meanings."[42] Continuing, she defines her position more clearly, unmistakably identifying her search for truth with her highly personal, inward, artistic re-creation of memory.

Surely, we understand very little of what is happening to us at any given moment. But by remembering, comparing, waiting to know the consequences, we can sometimes see what an event really meant, what it was trying to teach us. . . . In that sense it has sometimes taken me ten years to understand even a little of some important event that had happened to me. . . .

If I didn't know the ending of a story, I wouldn't begin. I always write my last lines, my last paragraph, my last page first, and then I go back and work towards it. I know where I'm going. I know what my goal is.[43]

Certainly there can remain no doubt that for Katherine Anne Porter the search for truth and the process of artistic creation are one and the same. But is not this true for every artist? Mark Schorer has made explicit a fact that modern criticism

41. Thompson, "Katherine Anne Porter: An Interview," *Paris Review*, pp. 100-1.
42. *Ibid.*, p. 100.
43. *Ibid.*, p. 101.

well knows: technique in some way *is* discovery. With this realization one comes close to the heart of Miss Porter's strength, and of her weakness.

For the artist is not only a maker; he is also a seer. Through his act of creation he gives body to the vision of life which he holds both consciously and unconsciously; hence we may not separate the evaluation of his art from the evaluation of his vision. Eliseo Vivas has, in terms much like Miss Porter's own, described the artist's role: "Having freed us from our 'ideas,' he substitutes his own freshly organized experience, through which we are able to understand aesthetically, to grasp by immediate apprehension, those aspects of contemporary experience that without his aid would remain for us threatening and oppressive because they would remain chaotic."[44] Applied to Katherine Anne Porter these words indicate clearly the nature and the extent of her limitations. The austere beauty and truth of Miss Porter's art reflects in part, and can speak powerfully to, twentieth-century man. Yet so narrow is the range of her vision, so numerous and important are the realities that fall outside it, that her appeal cannot but be limited. Neither can this exquisite structure she has built support the weight of personal human need she seems to have placed upon it. Perhaps it is an uneasy sense of this inadequacy that has compelled Miss Porter to justify and defend, time after time, her art and the life and the theory behind it. Perhaps, too, this is the truest sense in which she has "needed both" the fiction and the essays.

44. *D. H. Lawrence: The Failure and the Triumph of Art* (Evanston: Northwestern University Press, 1960), p. x.

7

Conclusions

This study of the thematic vision of Katherine Anne Porter has been, like the rejection theme itself, ambivalent. While negative in many of its conclusions, it nevertheless strongly confirms two facts which have long been recognized: that Miss Porter possesses a remarkable literary talent and that she is an artist of perfect integrity. At the same time it has attempted to show with new clarity another fact of which critics have been increasingly aware—that of the strong organic unity which binds together all the author's superficially varied works and makes of them, both individually and collectively, a profoundly "true testimony" to the truth as she sees it. Vernon A. Young, one of Miss Porter's most capable critics, has stated that "there is no writing today which is more organically connected with its subject matter than hers,"[1] and he might have added that there is no subject matter more organically connected with its author. The strongly subjective orientation of Miss

1. "The Art of Katherine Anne Porter," *New Mexico Quarterly*, XV (Autumn, 1945), 327.

Porter's work is immediately evident; she has made little effort to conceal the almost completely autobiographical nature of her principal heroine and of several other characters who are very similar to that heroine. It has, however, taken a more careful reading to appreciate the full extent of the kinship among these characters, and between them and all the others.

The common quality which unites all Miss Porter's characters is their conformity to the life-pattern represented by the rejection theme. All those who are of sufficient stature to hold and act upon a conscious attitude toward life adhere deliberately to this pattern; in proportion as characters lack human dignity, they have this same pattern thrust upon them by their instincts or by external circumstance. The pattern is a completely negative one and the view of life which corresponds to it is one of unrelieved darkness. For all of them, life begins in bitterness and corruption, proceeds in pain and lovelessness through successively deeper disillusions, and ends in nothingness, the foreknowledge of which casts a gradually thickening pall of despair over all of life.[2]

2. James W. Johnson, in an essay already referred to which constitutes a major turning-point in Porter criticism, formulates the first systematic statement of the narrowness and negativism of the author's fictional view of reality (pp. 610-11). In this respect his findings are parallel to those of this study. He describes Miss Porter's "logos" as follows:

"The child is born into a world seemingly ordered and reasonable but it is in fact chaotic, ridiculous, and doubt-ridden ("The Old Order"). He learns at an early age that he is an atomistic creature, often unloved ("The Downward Path"), and that the delightful spectacle of life masks fear, hatred, and bitterness ("The Circus"). He discovers that life and love must end in death ("The Grave," "The Fig Tree"). He must inevitably reject his heritage as lies and his family as hostile aliens ("Old Mortality"); but when he tries to substitute something else in their place, he is driven back by his own weaknesses to what he has been conditioned to ("María Concepción," "Magic"). If he makes the break with the past and tries to replace the lost old love with a new, he is doomed to despair ("Pale Horse, Pale Rider"). If he tries to substitute another heritage for his own, he finds it full of evil ("The Leaning Tower"); or he discovers that he has lost his power to love through denying his own tradition ("Flowering Judas"). There is nothing for him to cling to but his desperate belief in his own courage and integrity ("Theft") and what little of love and certainty he has in life ("The Cracked Looking-Glass"). But life is senselessly cruel ("He"), full of frustration and contention ("Rope," "That Tree," "A Day's Work"); and it ends in annihilation and the extinction of all hope ("The Jilting of Granny Weatherall"). Such is Miss Porter's fictional philosophy."

I have found nothing in the author's unified thematic pattern which would

Miss Porter has said that her stories represent "what I was . . . able to achieve in the way of order and form and statement in a period of grotesque dislocations in a whole society when the world was heaving in the sickness of a millennial change." It has been seen that her statement of order is extremely limited, even radically flawed. As regards the cause of this, the evidence points overwhelmingly toward not the disturbed world situation but a limitation within the author's own nature which has prevented her from seeing large areas of ordinary human life as anything other than threatening and oppressive because chaotic. Her artistic competence has not extended beyond the concrete and immediately personal, and consequently her art has been only a statement of her own limited, personal, strongly negative truth.[3] Robert Penn Warren's early essay on Miss Porter's fundamentally ironic method proposes that her irony has a center, that her evasion of commitment denotes a valid emphasis on the

---

tend in any important way to refute this dark view. The rejection theme tends, on the contrary, to reinforce, order, and unify it. It will be noted that Johnson bases most of the important stages in this composite life-story on alpha works and that consequently, with only minor changes, it represents the life of the alpha protagonist. The two elements provided by beta stories— the driving back to oppressive union by one's own weakness, and the falling back upon "what little of love and certainty" the protagonist has in a union with another—have been seen to apply only to beta characters, consisting as they do of stagnation in oppressive unions. The rejection theme further emphasizes the lovelessness of this life; there is no real evidence in it of even the least early reception of love or power to love on the part of the alpha heroine. "Love" appears in the pattern only as a lost ideal of the alpha protagonist, a concomitant of beta degradation, or, in rare instances, as a transcendence of the beta pattern. The most important contribution the rejection theme can make to Johnson's formulation is to show that the characteristic life-pattern is not fragmented among the stories so completely as the summary suggests, but permeates all the stories in its fullness or in great part. For example, the motif of reliance upon one's own courage and integrity appears not only in "Theft" but also in every other story listed, with the possible exception of the beta stories "Magic," "He," and "A Day's Work." Similar extensions could be made for each motif. Finally, Johnson's formulation could certainly be summed up as one of oppression and rejection.

3. It may be well to mention here that, although attention has been directed predominantly to negative and limiting aspects of the author's work, there is no intention of applying to Miss Porter the "myth of the sick artist," to use the words of Lionel Trilling, who has strongly refuted that theory in the essay entitled "Art and Neurosis" in *The Liberal Imagination* (Garden City, 1950), pp. 155-75. No matter how deep a wound there may be, or how closely related it may be to the author's work, it remains distinct from the bow of her art.

truly human act of discrimination. Skepticism is valued highly in our modern world, but perhaps it was valued more highly in the third and fourth decades of this century than it is today— and it is to those decades that Miss Porter's fiction, including *Ship of Fools,* belongs. Most of the early critics, after praising her style, went on to praise her penetrating skepticism; it is only recently that readers have begun to question her values in a systematic way.

Since, on the level of her central thematic meaning, Miss Porter can tell us little more than "how immensely difficult, for all but the stupid and the cruel, is the task of sheer day-by-day living in our time,"[4] perhaps her most significant contribution may be said to lie precisely in her role of product and sensitive recorder of the present age. Her life, like those of Miranda and the Grandmother before her, has been organically related to its historical setting and has been formed by it, perhaps decisively. She has shown abundant awareness of this. Our time has been called a time of the "locked-in ego"; it, too, has to a great extent rejected traditional certainties, and placed its emphasis on the scientific, skeptical, inquiring mind. Ironically, this has resulted, for the modern world as for Katherine Anne Porter the artist, in subjection to the unconscious mind. On a world scale the consequences have been tragic, as Miss Porter well knows. The isolationism which has grown in recent years under the specious disguise of rationality has indeed brought with it much that is negativistic—adding to the degenerative tendency which is inseparable from human nature at any time. Freud and Camus, among others, have formulated the awareness of a death wish within man which has already made its presence strongly felt both individually and socially. Schopenhauer's words, "Life is a business that doesn't cover its costs,"[5] are quite similar to the plaint of the dying man in "Pale Horse, Pale Rider" that "the crime of which he was accused did not merit the punishment he was about to receive." Miranda has had a

4. Young, "The Art of Katherine Anne Porter," *New Mexico Qtly.,* p. 341.
5. Quoted in Martin Heidegger, *An Introduction to Metaphysics* (Garden City, New York: Doubleday & Company, Inc., Anchor Books, 1961), p. 149.

stark experience of a truth formulated by Heidegger: "To the opinionated life is only life; death is death and only death. But life's being is also death. Everything that enters into life also begins to die, to go toward its death, and death is at the same time life."[6]

Miranda's story fails to rise to the level of tragedy, though in the context of her world it would seem to. In proportion as Miss Porter's characters receive her sympathy they become not tragic but sentimental. The irony which permeates her fiction is not cosmic, tragic irony; for its cosmos is no larger than the locked-in ego. Even Miranda's descent through her purgatorio to her paradiso and back to her inferno is basically narcissistic and sentimental, as the end of her story shows. The real irony of her life is the small, sad irony of the individual whose supposed quest for truth is in reality a blind, instinctive flight from it.

The general impression that Miss Porter's work makes on the reader is one of frustration and coldness, of the absence of human warmth and human aspiration. Two critics who pointed this out a number of years ago were Christopher Isherwood and Edward Weeks. Their verdicts would no doubt be even harsher after *Ship of Fools*. In 1939 Isherwood observed,

The work of so important an artist as Miss Porter must be judged by the lowest as well as the highest standards—and, curiously enough, it is by the lowest standards that she fails. She is grave, she is delicate, she is just—but she lacks altogether, for me personally, the vulgar appeal. I cannot imagine that she would ever make me cry, or laugh aloud. No doubt she would reply that she doesn't want to. But she should want to. I wish she would give herself a little more freely to the reader. I wish she would paint with bolder, broader strokes. I wish she wouldn't be so cautious.[7]

On the appearance of *The Leaning Tower and Other Stories,* Edward Weeks commented, "Nothing much happens in these stories. The people do little to excite your curiosity or deepen your sympathy. One must respect the sheer virtuosity of Miss

6. *Ibid.,* p. 111.
7. From a criticism of *Pale Horse, Pale Rider: Three Short Novels* in the *New Republic,* XCVIII (April 19, 1939), 312.

Porter's prose, which is supple and ever so carefully selected. But style without warmth . . . can be a tedious affair."[8]

The dominance of the principle of rejection in the art of Katherine Anne Porter has resulted in a unique body of work. Operating upon her generous literary talent, it helped, first of all, to form a prose style of strength, clarity, and a range which extends from primitive simplicity to poetic beauty. It led to the creation of a small but relatively perfect body of short stories and novelettes characterized by concentration, intensity, suggestiveness, and extreme power. At the same time, however, it restricted severely the area within which this power was able to flow. It led on the one hand to the creation of several stories of stylistic and structural perfection but narrow and degraded humanity, and on the other to a body of interrelated work, centered around a heroine of undeniable dignity, which presents with great power certain limited and painful insights into life— but a body of work formally distorted and warped toward sentimentality by excessive subjectivity. Finally, Miss Porter's artistic principle of rejection seems to have imposed crippling and almost totally destructive difficulties on a work which went counter to so many of its tendencies—the writing of a long novel, *Ship of Fools*. Only in a few brilliant instances, particularly "The Grave" and "Noon Wine," did the author's devotion to truth triumph over her inner limitations to produce masterpieces of that combined beauty and truth which constitutes great art.

The principle of rejection which impelled Katherine Anne Porter into art, while it severely restricted that art both in quantity and in scope, nevertheless enabled her to give form to a limited area of human experience in such a way that she has provided for her contemporaries a penetrating insight into the dark reality that faces them. Miss Porter's technical ability deserves the ample praise it has received. Her pursuit of truth, while severely limited in its success, yet contains elements of honesty and courage which demand respect. The fact of her life and work—of this proud but flawed achievement so intricate-

8. "The Atlantic Bookshelf," *Atlantic Monthly,* CLXXIV (November, 1944), 131.

ly wrought out of blended courage and fear, vision and blindness—stands as a compelling reminder of the mystery that lies at the center of man, of woman, and of art. If her works seem to express grave doubts about the possibility of human achievement, those very works constitute an achievement that contradicts that doubt.

Bibliography

Boutell, Charles. "Authors Are Like People," *New York Post,* September 21, 1944.

Burnett, Whit, ed. *This Is My Best.* New York: The Dial Press, 1942.

Girson, Rochelle. "The Author," *Saturday Review,* XLV (March 31, 1962), 15-16.

Hartley, Lodwick. "Katherine Anne Porter," *Sewanee Review,* XLVIII (April, 1940), 206-16.

————. "The Lady and the Temple: The Critical Theories of Katherine Anne Porter," *College English,* XIV (April, 1953), 386-91.

Heidegger, Martin. *An Introduction to Metaphysics.* Garden City, New York: Doubleday and Company, Inc., Anchor Books, 1961.

Hicks, Granville. Review of *Ship of Fools, Saturday Review,* XLV (March 31, 1962), 15-16.

Isherwood, Christopher. " 'Pale Horse, Pale Rider,' " *New Republic,* XCVIII (April 19, 1939), 312-13.

Janeway, Elizabeth. Interview with Katherine Anne Porter, *The New York Times Book Review,* April 1, 1962, pp. 4-5.

Johnson, James William. "Another Look at Katherine Anne Porter," The *Virginia Quarterly Review,* XXXVI (Autumn, 1960), 598-613.

Mooney, Harry John, Jr. *The Fiction and Criticism of Katherine Anne Porter*. Pittsburgh: University of Pittsburgh Press, 1957. Revised edition, 1962.

Porter, Katherine Anne. *The Days Before*. New York: Harcourt, Brace and Company, 1952.

———. "The Fig Tree," *Harper's Magazine*, CCXX (June, 1960), 55-59.

———. *Flowering Judas and Other Stories*. New York: Random House, The Modern Library, 1940.

———. *The Leaning Tower and Other Stories*. New York: Dell Publishing Co., Inc., Delta Books, 1962.

———. " 'Noon Wine': The Sources," *Yale Review*, XLVI (September, 1956), 22-39.

———. *Pale Horse, Pale Rider: Three Short Novels*. New York: Random House, The Modern Library, n.d.

———. *Ship of Fools*. Boston: Little, Brown and Company, 1962.

Prager, Leonard. "Getting and Spending: Porter's 'Theft,' " *Perspective*, XI (1960), 230-34.

Rubin, Louis D., Jr., and Robert D. Jacobs, eds. *South: Modern Southern Literature in Its Cultural Setting*. Garden City, New York: Doubleday & Company, Inc., Dolphin Books, 1961.

Schorer, Mark. Review of *Ship of Fools*, *The New York Times Book Review*, April 1, 1962, pp. 1, 5.

Schwartz, Edward. "Katherine Anne Porter: A Critical Bibliography," *Bulletin of the New York Public Library*, LVII (May, 1953), 211-47.

———. "The Way of Dissent: Katherine Anne Porter's Critical Position," *Western Humanities Review*, VIII (1954), 119-30.

Tate, Allen. "A New Star," *Nation*, CXXXI (October, 1930), 352-53.

Thompson, Barbara. "Katherine Anne Porter: An Interview," *Paris Review*, XXIX (Winter-Spring, 1963), 87-114.

Trilling, Lionel. *The Liberal Imagination: Essays on Literature and Society*. Garden City: Doubleday & Company, Inc., Anchor Books, 1957.

Van Gelder, Robert. *Writers and Writing*. New York: Charles Scribner's Sons, 1946.

Vivas, Eliseo. *D. H. Lawrence: The Failure and the Triumph of Art*. Evanston: Northwestern University Press, 1960.

Warren, Robert Penn. "Katherine Anne Porter (Irony with a Center)," *Kenyon Review*, IV (Winter, 1942), 29-42.

Weeks, Edward. "The Atlantic Bookshelf," *Atlantic Monthly*, CLXXIV (November, 1944), 131.

Wescott, Glenway. *Images of Truth: Remembrances and Criticism.* New York: Harper & Row, 1962.

West, Ray B. "Katherine Anne Porter and 'Historic Memory,'" *South: Modern Southern Literature in Its Cultural Setting.* Ed. Louis D. Rubin and Robert D. Jacobs. Garden City, New York: Doubleday & Company, Inc., Dolphin Books, 1961.

————. *Katherine Anne Porter.* Minneapolis: University of Minnesota Press, 1963. Pamphlets on American Writers, Number 28.

Wilson, Edmund. "Katherine Anne Porter," *The New Yorker,* XX (September 30, 1944), 64-66.

Young, Vernon A. "The Art of Katherine Anne Porter," *New Mexico Quarterly,* XV (Autumn, 1945), 326-41.

Index